Alison Peirse is ̲ ̲ ̲ ̲ ̲ ̲ ̲ ̲ ̲ ̲ ̲ Lecturer in Film and Television Studies at the University of Northumbria. She has published widely on horror film and television and is co-editor of *Korean Horror Cinema* (EUP, 2013).

AFTER DRACULA

The 1930s HORROR FILM

ALISON PEIRSE

I.B.TAURIS

LONDON · NEW YORK

Published in 2013 by I.B.Tauris & Co Ltd
6 Salem Road, London W2 4BU
175 Fifth Avenue, New York NY 10010
www.ibtauris.com

Distributed in the United States and Canada exclusively by Palgrave Macmillan
175 Fifth Avenue, New York NY 10010

ISBN: 978 1 84885 531 1

A full CIP record for this book is available from the British Library
A full CIP record is available from the Library of Congress

Library of Congress Catalog Card Number: available

Typeset by Newgen Publishers, Chennai
Printed and bound in Great Britain by Page Bros, Norwich

MIX
Paper from
responsible sources
FSC   FSC® C023114
www.fsc.org

To Paul and Kitty,
with much love

CONTENTS

LIST OF ILLUSTRATIONS

ACKNOWLEDGEMENTS

There are many people and a number of institutions that have made it possible for me to write this book. The AHRC funded an early stage of my research and Northumbria University funded a semester-long sabbatical that enabled me to write a number of chapter first drafts. Philippa Brewster, my editor at I.B. Tauris, deserves a mention for her support of this project, as does my excellent copyeditor Frances Follin. A special thank you goes to Annette Kuhn for reading early versions of some of the chapters and her continual support of my academic career. Faye Woods and Robert Spadoni: your assistance with my archival research has made an immeasurable difference to this book. Jonny Davies at BFI Special Collections and Maimie Balfour at Northumbria University (possibly the best subject librarian ever) deserve singling out for their friendly, professional and speedy responses to my numerous queries. I am similarly grateful to Peter Howden for agreeing to speak to me about his experience of screening *Vampyr* at the Electric Cinema in London.

I really do need a separate thank you section for the people who have had to put up with me during the writing of *After Dracula*. It turns out that relocating 100 miles from your family, having a baby and then attempting to write your first monograph immediately after returning from maternity leave isn't a very good idea. So the entire film team at Northumbria deserve a medal for looking after me during this rather taxing period. Three people in particular made the whole process much more endurable. Russ Hunter read chapters, put up with my queries about historical reception studies, made excellent coffee and was generally just lovely. Jamie Sexton was extremely patient, encouraging and pragmatic; his unstinting support got me through the final stages of the book. Peter Hutchings read draft versions of nearly everything I wrote and his perceptive and generous feedback transformed the way I write and think about film studies. My family have played an equally big part in making this book happen: my parents Helen and John Peirse and my parents-in-law Sheila and Peter Fairclough have provided abundant amounts of childcare, endured lengthy journeys up and down the A1, made endless cups of tea and have got really good at doing sympathetic faces. Also, Chris Peirse, Lynn Dart and Kristyn Gorton have always known how to make me smile when things got a bit too much.

I have dedicated the book to my husband Paul Fairclough and our daughter Kitty because it is impossible to articulate how important they are to me in the acknowledgements alone. Paul, you are my world and I wouldn't be who I am without you. You have lived this book for the past year and I think my greatest gift to you is that I have finished it.

Much earlier versions of Chapters 4 and 5 have been previously published as follows: 'The impossibility of vision: Vampirism, formlessness and horror in *Vampyr*', *Studies in European Cinema* 5/3 (2009), pp.161-70; 'Bauhaus of horrors: Edgar G. Ulmer and 1930s film', in Gary D. Rhodes (ed.) *Edgar G. Ulmer: Detour on Poverty Row* (Lanham, MD: Lexington Press, 2008), pp.275-88. I would like to thank Intellect and Lexington Press respectively for permission to reprint.

WHEN THE COFFIN CREAKS

Silence has endured, but in a castle dungeon, a coffin now begins to creak. The coffin lid lifts and a bony white hand emerges, a rat scurries amongst the dust and decay. Then a figure stands in the centre of the image, calm and still, his face cast with a luminescent glow. Enticed by his bright white stare, the camera slips uneasily forwards, but a wolf howls and the mesmeric spell is broken. He climbs the stone steps out of the dungeon, and our first encounter with the vampire is complete. We are, of course, watching *Dracula* (1931) and meeting Bela Lugosi's vampire for the first time. *Dracula* was released in February 1931, followed nine months later by James Whale's *Frankenstein* and then in December, Rouben Mamoulian's *Dr Jekyll and Mr Hyde*.[1] This trio of nineteenth-century gothic literature adaptations marks the beginning of the horror film genre as we understand it today while also inaugurating the 1930s cycle of 'talkie' horror films. This book has been written because of the easy recognition of not just the film moment described above, but rather the three films in general. There has already been more than sufficient scholarship about these films, *Dracula* in particular, and I do not wish to add to the corpus. I'm not denying the power of Lugosi's performance or the importance of the vampire as a cultural icon: they cast a long shadow (of sorts) over many of the films in this book. *After Dracula* isn't an attempt to destroy the canon; I simply want to put certain films to one side, as their unquestioned prominence is detrimental to the scholarship on other innovative and original 1930s horror films in Europe and America. Reading horror film histories today gives a sense that the decade is done with, there is nothing more to be said about this period of cinema. What *After Dracula* does is view the Transylvanian vampire as an absent host; his omnipresent gaze may always be with us but we will choose to take an alternative path through 1930s horror cinema.

In his exemplary work on film genre, Steve Neale has pointed out that 'it is not possible to write about genres without being selective, and that many of the deficiencies of a good deal of writing on genre stem from defining and selecting on the basis of pre-established and unquestioned canons of films'.[2] The first sound horror cycle is commonly understood to span *Dracula* to *Dracula's Daughter* (1936) and as much as I feel I shouldn't simply accept this – following Neale in attempting to question canons – I do broadly agree with the demarcation. My only contention with this is that one of the films I discuss, the British horror film *The Man Who Changed His Mind* (1936), was released several months after *Dracula's Daughter*, in September 1936 in London and then in December in New York; but this, I think, says much about the time lag of British horror film cycles, which is discussed further in Chapter 6.[3]

Horror films were generally on the wane from 1936 for a number of reasons, including the ousting of Universal Studios' Carl Laemmle and the end of its commitment to A-budget horror films.[4] Film censorship in both the UK and USA is also a major factor in the decline of horror films during the decade. In July 1934, the Production Code Administration (PCA) was established within the Motion Picture Producers and Distributors of America (MPPDA). Run by Joseph Breen, its purpose was to enforce the Production Code, established in 1930, which related to moral obligations and censure: essentially what was considered appropriate, proper and decent for audiences to watch at the cinema.[5] Until Breen's appointment the Production Code was self-regulatory, which allowed studios, writers and producers to incorporate all manner of horrors into their productions. When *Island of Lost Souls* was made in 1932, the Studio Relations Committee advised Paramount that the concept of 'crossing animals with humans' was very risky and the film 'should be abandoned, for I am sure you will never be allowed to suggest that sort of thing on screen'.[6] Paramount knew that the protests would come to nothing and forged ahead regardless, creating one of the nastiest and most unsettling horror films of the decade, a film so hideous that it was banned internationally and not screened in the UK until 1967. Hence the enforcement of the Production Code in

1934 was particularly significant, especially as producers became expected to consult with censorship bodies at the initial scenario and draft script stages: macabre and grotesque occurrences were removed before the director could shout 'Action'. The newly empowered PCA was certainly not that keen on horror films: in 1936 Breen counselled the studio producers of *Dracula's Daughter* that 'the making of a horror picture at this time is a very hazardous undertaking from the standpoint of political censorship generally'; similarly in the UK, the reaction of Colonel J.C. Hanna, Vice President of the British Board of Film Censors (BBFC) to the film's scenario was equally discouraging: *Dracula's Daughter* 'would require the resources of half a dozen more languages to adequately express its beastliness. I consider it absolutely unfit for exhibition as a film'.[7]

Hanna's response to *Dracula's Daughter* is symptomatic of the BBFC's concern with American horror films. In the UK the market for horror films was significantly reduced from the mid 1930s. Using the recently introduced 'H' (Horrific) advisory certificate, the BBFC passed only five horror films in 1934, two in 1936 and one in 1937.[8] This censorship wasn't restricted to American productions either; it included the British films *The Ghoul* (1933) and *The Tell-Tale Heart* (1934), as well as European art-horror film *Vampyr* (1932).[9] Indeed, British horror films encountered as much reticence from the BBFC as their American counterparts; when reviewing the initial synopsis for *The Man Who Changed His Mind*, one BBFC reader commented 'this story comes under the criticisms of "horror" films made by the President at Cardiff. I consider the methods used to destroy the bodies revolting – in my opinion this story could never be suitable for production as a film'.[10] This is the reason why the majority of the films to be discussed in this book are those produced in the first half of the decade: as Rhona J. Berenstein explains, the majority of the genre's most acclaimed films emerged before 1934, evading the 'post-1934 domestic and foreign censorship boards, which were far more ruthless than their predecessors'.[11]

I want to discuss how this body of films, born after *Dracula* and dying out in 1936, can be understood as a specific cycle of production rather than simply as part of the horror film genre. The distinction between cycle and genre is an important one. As Peter Hutchings has explained, while 'genre' definitions can be rather generalised and thus obscure localised specifics, film sequels and cycles 'usually have a historical specificity to them. They exist in relation to particular times and particular places and they offer an intermediate stage between the uniqueness of individual films and the formulaic nature of generic production'.[12] Amanda Ann Klein provides an instructive definition of film cycles for this purpose:

> Like film genres, film cycles are a series of films associated with each other through shared images, characters, settings, plots or themes. However, while film genres are primarily defined by the repetition of key images (their semantics) and themes (their syntax), film cycles are primarily defined by how they are used (their pragmatics).[13]

It is Klein's emphasis on the use value of film cycles that is particularly helpful, as much of my analysis questions the meaning and purposes of the films and locates them within their historical and production context: what type of film is the studio trying to make? How does this relate to or depart from earlier or contemporary horror film releases? How is this communicated in the promotional material? How are these ideas received in the press? One idea of Klein's that I do want to complicate slightly is her later point about the 'originary film'; that is, the financially or critically successful film 'that establishes the image, plot, formulas, and themes for the entire cycle'.[14] While this makes sense in the context of the examples she provides, in the case of 1930s horror film the cycle is rather more diverse. *Dracula* is undoubtedly the originating text of this film cycle and Universal's *The Mummy*, made the following year, is a clear reworking of *Dracula*. Even the poverty-row production *White Zombie* (1932) has its Lugosi-as-vampire elements. Nonetheless, many of the films that appeared over the next few years diverged quite significantly from the mechanics of Universal's gothic vampire story. The Gaumont-British film *The Clairvoyant* (1933) is grounded in spiritualism and British popular culture; *Murders in the Zoo* (1933) is a story of lip-sewing sadism and murder set amongst real-life big cats and snakes; while *The Black Cat* (1935) is an occult shrine to modernist architecture and design. Indeed, many of the films discussed in this book are doing something quite different to the be-cob-webbed, gothic past presented in *Dracula*. Bearing this in mind, I want to emphasise the diversity of horror film production during the 1930s. My chosen films were made not only in America but also in Europe, by independent and poverty-row producers as well as the mainstream studios. They encompass literary adaptations, folktales and original screenplays, and their settings move from London music halls and Yorkshire coal mines to South Sea islands, via Hungarian modernist houses of horror, ancient Egypt and a deserted flour mill on the outskirts of contemporary Paris. What they have in common is their intention to unsettle the audience: in various locally and culturally specific ways they are employed as texts of horror. Hence, *After Dracula* focuses on the films some-what marginalised in horror film studies, exploring the intriguing, unusual, really quite horrible and frequently critically neglected.

GENRES, CYCLES – HORROR SEMANTICS

Let's get our definition of the 'horror film' out of the way early on. By pinpointing *Dracula* as the progenitor of the horror talkie, I'm not suggesting that horror films did not exist before this period. German films *The Cabinet of Dr Caligari* (1920), *Genuine* (1920) and *Nosferatu* (1922) are commonly listed as important silent examples, but there was also a significant amount of horror-centred produc-tion going on elsewhere: in Hungary, Károly Lajthay's *Drakula halála* (1921) was the first cinematic adaptation of *Dracula*, while in France Jean Epstein's avant-garde *La chute de la maison Usher* (1928) provides an earlier aesthetic example of how to represent the 'undead'.[15] *When Soul Meets Soul* (1912) and *The Avenging Hand* (1915) are American and British examples of the mummy film; the British film *The Beetle* (1919), an adaptation of Richard Marsh's novel, in which the High Priestess of Isis is reincarnated as a loathsome beetle, has a similar Egyptian bent.[16] It is, however, probably the gruesome physical performances of Lon Chaney in American silent films such as *The Hunchback of Notre-Dame* (1923) and *The Unknown* (1927) that provide much of the groundwork for American audiences and film critics' acceptance of horror films in the 1930s. Throughout the 1920s the reviews of Chaney's films discussed the 'horror' of his performances; the *Daily Boston Globe* talked of showing *London After Midnight*'s vampires (1927) 'in all their disgusting horror', the *Atlanta Constitution* described 'chills of creeping horror with moments of the tensest drama' in the same film, while the *New York Times* argued that *The Unknown* 'has enough horror to appeal to them both' (Chaney and his director Browning).[17] These critics may not have been talking about horror as a film genre, often classifying Chaney's films as 'weird', 'eerie' or 'tense melodrama', but what they clearly address is the effect of these films on the audience's sensibilities. The reception of Chaney's films paved the way for film critics in the early years of the horror talkie to discuss such productions in terms of the 'weird', 'uncanny', 'horrific' and 'gruesome'; something discussed in Chapter 1 in the critical reception of *The Mummy*, which constantly refers back to actors and themes of horrors past.

As this discussion suggests, before the 1930s, films were not produced or consumed as horror films as we understand the term today, and their classification as such is retrospective.[18] In light of this it is wise to heed Lincoln Geraghty and Mark Jancovich's warning about the creation of generic canons, that one 'needs to be careful not to transfer one's own understandings of genre terms and their meanings back onto previous periods in which the terms and their meanings might have been very different'.[19] Indeed, as Jancovich's instructive work on 1940s horror cinema has revealed, many films commonly understood today as part of film noir or the 'paranoid woman' cycle were in fact understood at the time as horror films.[20] I don't think the 1930s horror film is quite this complicated, though. Certainly in the early 1930s, horror was not consistently or systematically acknowledged as a cycle or genre by studios, censorship bodies, newspapers or trade journals, but as a term it did circulate via film discourses. *Dracula* was primarily categorised by the newspaper and trade paper film critics as a 'mystery picture', and as Robert Spadoni has argued, labelling the film as a mystery performs a useful function, as it 'supplied the film's makers, marketers, critics and general audiences with a means to categorise, describe and evaluate *Dracula* until such time as a more appropriate context for these discursive activities emerged'.[21] This wouldn't take too long, as many of *Dracula*'s critics repeatedly used the words 'horror', 'eerie' and 'blood-curdling' in their reviews.[22] Similarly, in her exemplary research on 1930s cinema, Angela Marie Smith has revealed that, in 1931, Colonel Jason S. Joy, an administrator of the Production Code, wrote to Paramount to discuss the forthcoming *Dr Jekyll and Mr Hyde* in terms of 'horror pictures'. A few days later he wrote to Will Hays, president of the MPPDA. He grouped together *Dracula*, *Frankenstein*, *Dr Jekyll and Mr Hyde* with other forthcoming films including *Island of Lost Souls*, and asked of Hays, 'is this the beginning of a cycle that ought to be retarded or killed? I am anxious to receive your advice'.[23]

While Joy may have seen the nascent beginnings of the 1930s horror film cycle, this was not something universally accepted at the time, so films *were* described as 'horror' but intermittently so; there is no sense of generic stability during or just after *Dracula*. The term began to creep in with increasing regularity throughout early 1932. In April of that year *White Zombie* was defined by the *Chicago Daily Tribune* as belonging 'to the cycle of horror films. Not as terrifying as *Frankenstein* and more bloodcurdling than *Dracula*', and two days later the trade paper *Film Daily* published as its front page headline 'Schedules Show Cycle of "Horror" Pictures Continuing', referring to forthcoming productions of *Island of Lost Souls* and *King Kong*.[24] But again, the move towards a single genre definition was not consistent; when *Island of Lost Souls* was at pre-production stage in mid 1932, it was variously described as part of the 'exploration and adventure' trend, which included *The Most Dangerous Game* (1932), and as 'fantasy', grouped alongside *The Invisible Man* (1933).[25] By December 1932, film critics tended to conflate horror with melodramas, chillers, shiver pictures or the aforementioned mysteries. As Mollie Merrick of the *Los Angeles Times* noted that month, regarding *Island of Lost Souls*' Hollywood preview, 'mysteries with the horror angle are still the most popular form of Hollywood picture'; other critics reviewed the film in terms of horror, shudder, chills, and shocker.[26] Yet in February 1933, just two months later, the idea of horror as a genre appeared to be solidifying: *Variety* revealed that Universal was combining several Edgar Allan Poe stories 'to form the basis for another horror picture', and described *The Black Cat* as 'Universal's Next Horror Pic'.[27]

As this rather tangled web of examples reveals, there is no single moment in the 1930s at which horror becomes acknowledged either as a specific cycle, or a stable generic category. At varying points from 1931 to 1933 the word 'horror' changes from referring to the effect it has on the audience to attaching to a 'type' of film. This transition occurs at different times depending on the country in which the word is used, and whether in a newspaper, trade journal, magazine, etc. When and where this takes place and by whom seems to depend on personal preference and (I assume for critics) editorial control. Some American critics, especially the most enthusiastic advocates of 'shocking' cinema, used the term regularly and with gusto from late 1931, while others, most disdainful of the thrills provided, used it only as a term of denigration from around 1933 onwards. Some studios, such as Universal, pushed the horror angle early; others, such as MGM, were later adopters of the genre. Censorship bodies are a different matter again: in the UK, thanks to Annette Kuhn's important work on the history of British censorship, we can trace back the use of 'horror film' to a Home Office circular *Children and 'A' Films*, distributed in March 1933.[28]

In America, we have seen how the MPPDA was made aware of the 'horror picture' angle in 1931, but significant inroads into the censorship of horror film production did not occur until 1934 when the Production Code was enforced. And as Chapter 7 on *Werewolf of London* (1935) reveals, the amendments and deletions demanded by the PCA could be circumnavigated by a smooth-talking, silver-tongued (and probably highly paid) producer. So while there may be many meanings tied up in the word 'horror' through the 1920s and 1930s, I have chosen to use it in relation to a specific cycle of 1930s films that do remarkable, despicable, often supernatural and frequently murderous things on screen. I do not attempt to define 'essential' features of this period for the simple reason that there are none. No single tradition emerges from this body of work: in my survey of a multiplicity of spine-chilling, blood-curdling terrors, some draw on the gothic literary canon and some are brand-new stories, some are nationally specific, some are seemingly universal, a few have had a major influence on later generations of horror filmmaking but many have already critically crumbled to dust, until this moment forgotten and unloved.

AFTER DRACULA

In 2007, Jancovich published a review-essay of recent horror-film books for the journal *Screen*. His essay is extremely useful, not only in demonstrating the growing importance of horror film in the academy, but also as a symptom of the popularity of certain methodologies and approaches. Jancovich laments that much of the current writing on horror film lacks an engagement with the study of genre itself. He suggests that the work of Neale and James Naremore destroys the idea that 'there *is* something called the horror film that exists as a stable and consistent body of work'.[29] Rick Worland's *The Horror Film* is a case in point: for Jancovich, Worland's research questions assume: 'that there is something called the horror film, rather than numerous historically contingent definitions of horror that are not necessarily commensurate, and it is precisely this kind of assumption that has been questioned by contemporary genre theory'.[30] Jancovich's prominent positioning of genre theory – simultaneously turning away from psychoanalysis – can be usefully contextualised historically by considering Christine Gledhill's work, where she explains that genre 'is particularly useful now for its potential to fill a gap left by the fragmenting of grand theory, which once promised to grasp films as part of a totalising "social formation" or "historical conjuncture"'.[31] She posits that 'genre provides the conceptual space where – issues of text and aesthetics – the traditional concerns of film theory – intersect with those of industry and institution, history and society, culture and audiences'.[32] These kinds of discussion are symptomatic of recent shifts in approaches to horror film studies, in which a more diverse, empirically grounded set of methodologies can be found. The work of such people as Jamie Sexton, Tim Snelson, Kate Egan, Daniel Martin and

Russ Hunter emphasises culturally specific readings, censorship debates, critical reception studies and the unpicking of the 'taken-for-granted-ness' not only of 'Theory' but also of horror as a stable genre.[33]

But where does this leave those of us who still have an eye for the uncanny? I'm keen not to build this book around 'top-down' theoretical approaches, yet equally I refuse to reject psychoanalysis as a useful mechanism for understanding *some* of the address of *some* of the films in this book. Some films are crying out to be psychoanalysed; *Vampyr* is just one of them. The basis for this book therefore comes from the way I look at individual films: what is interesting about them? What specific moments stand out? How are these moments made? To understand this, I variously turn to formal analysis, psychoanalytic theory, industrial discourses (how film studios attempt to make meaning through marketing and exploitation) and critical reception (the responses of film journalists and critics through previews, interviews and reviews). Despite the diverse range of approaches, my analysis is always underpinned by an engagement with the film text and the question of how 'horror' is created, in various different national, historical and industrial contexts. In essence, the methodology and meaning-making varies according to the perceived needs of the film analysis, the chapters attempt to valorise the pleasures and peculiarities of the individual films themselves.

So what precisely does *After Dracula* do? We begin with the idea that *Dracula* has been canonised to the detriment of other innovative and original 1930s films produced across Europe and America. Having established this, the three specific focuses of the book begin to take shape. First, *After Dracula* is concerned with the interplay between Continental, British and transatlantic film texts and contexts. Chapter 1 considers the cultural impact of *Dracula* on Universal's follow-up film *The Mummy*. It is argued that remembrance – the association of memory with death – is key to understanding the film's complex intertextual plays and, in remembering horror, *The Mummy* constantly looks to the past, not only to the films of 1931 but also to German silent cinema. Chapter 5's case study, *The Black Cat*, is primarily a study of the complex relationship between set design and horror, following

Tim Bergfelder *et al.*'s position that sets aid 'in identifying characters, fleshing out and concretising their psychology; and … help in creating a sense of place in terms of "mood" or "atmosphere…"' and are 'crucial in defining a film's genre'.[34] Yet exploring the film through its architecture, highlights how European modernism and a burgeoning émigré culture in Hollywood engender a distinctly Continental sensibility in the spaces of American horror film. Similarly, while Chapter 3 locates *White Zombie* within its poverty-row contexts – belonging as it does to a small and select group of independent 1930s films, including Frank R. Strayer's *The Vampire Bat* (1933) and *Condemned to Live* (1935) – of equal importance are the film's aesthetic connections with French silent cinema, particularly *La chute de la maison Usher*.

The second aim of this book is to consider the horror genre's transatlantic evolution; many of the European horror films of this period have had (to be generous) only the most cursory scholarship and some (particularly some of the British films) have had none at all. Chapter 6 offers a wide-ranging and ambitious survey of British horror cinema in the 1930s, a topic that may come as somewhat of a surprise to many film historians who have suggested for years that the genre simply did not exist in Britain at this time. Drawing on *The Ghoul*, *The Clairvoyant* and *The Man Who Changed His Mind*, the chapter illuminates a unique moment in film history: the British film industry's attempt to internationalise its outputs at the same time as the emergence of the horror genre in sound film. Chapter 4 explores *Vampyr* and contextualises it simultaneously as both European art cinema and horror film. The last major concern of the book sees a return to American cinema. *After Dracula* attempts to question and complicate histories of horror film and within this the usual choices of 'origin' films and film moments. This relates directly to my decision to consider this body of films in terms of a film cycle, rather than as a snapshot of a broader genre. As Klein explains:

> More often that not, a genre ends up being defined by a few central, or 'classic' texts, or those texts that conform to one critic's definition of a particular genre. This traditional approach to genre is fundamentally ahistorical, marginalising texts that could enrich, rather than

detract from, our understanding of a genre, its context, its function, and even its aesthetics.[35]

White Zombie is a case in point. George Romero's films, first released in the 1960s, are often considered the 'true' beginnings of the zombie film genre yet a close analysis of *White Zombie* and its intertexts reveals a unique and historically specific form of zombie: the undead are represented (and interpreted in the media) as an exciting glimpse into Haitian voodoo practices quite distinct from America's own horror lineage. Similarly, in Chapter 7 I demand a rethinking of the werewolf genre. *The Wolf Man* (1942) is not where the werewolf film begins; we need to go back a further seven years to *Werewolf of London* to reveal the subgenre's genesis. In a similar vein, scholarly accounts of female monsters have often focused on the monstrous women that emerge in 1970s horror films such as *The Exorcist* (1973), *Carrie* (1976) and *The Brood* (1979). Even those who explore female monstrosity during the classical Hollywood studio era commonly turn to *Cat People* (1942), or at a push *Bride of Frankenstein* (1935).[36] Using Barbara Klinger's work on historical reception studies as a framework, Chapter 2 analyses *Island of Lost Souls'* pre-publicity campaign, interviews, film posters and publicity photographs, reviews, feature articles and industry practice, in order to explore the representation of the film's panther woman and to trace the origins of the female monster back to 1932.

My intention with *After Dracula* is to widen the scholarly debate and understanding of 1930s horror cinema, but it is certainly not the final word on the subject. *Mad Love*'s (1935) *grand guignol* pleasures and the fast-talking, wisecracking reporter films *Doctor X* (1932) and *Mystery of the Wax Museum* (1933) are just a few of the American examples I haven't been able to include. There are still lost films yet to come to light; George E. Turner has spun a fascinating story of the lost RKO horror talkie *The Monkey's Paw* (1933) and I am waiting for the day that someone discovers it in a rusty canister, abandoned and unlabelled in the depths of a studio basement.[37] In conjunction with Michael Price, Turner has also brought to light the cast, crew and plot details of a number of 'poverty row chillers', but there is still scholarly work to be done on Strayer's *The Monster Walks* (1932), *The Vampire Bat* (1933) and *Condemned to Live* (1935).[38] Beyond America, Gary D. Rhodes produced good work on the 1930s Mexican horror cycle but there is still much work to be done on German cinema of the early 1930s, and how films such as *Alraune* (1930), *Unheimliche Geschichten* (1932) and *Der Student Von Prag* (1935) work through ideas around horror.[39] In order to enrich our understanding of just *how* diverse the 1930s were as a decade of production, I want to highlight the increasing availability of East Asian horror cinema: *Ye Ban Ge Sheng/Song at Midnight* (1937) – a Chinese version of *Phantom of the Opera* – and the Japanese *bakeneko eiga* (ghost cat film) *Kaibyo nazo no shamisen/The Ghost Cat and the Mysterious Shamisen* (1938) are just a few of the East Asian films that potentially open up vibrant new areas of research in horror film history. While my choice of films is necessarily limited, I hope that my interdisciplinary approach will reveal something more of the wide disparities across horror filmmaking in the 1930s and bring to light a cycle of films of which many have been forgotten and unloved – until now.

1

REMEMBERING HORROR IN *THE MUMMY*

In contemporary Cairo, Imhotep the mummy (Boris Karloff) puts Helen Grosvenor (Zita Johann) into a trance and lures her to his apartment. They kneel together at the edge of a deep pool and he whispers 'you will not remember what I show you now, and yet I shall awaken memories of love and crime and death'. The swirling smoke dissipates to reveal a flashback of their past lives in ancient Egypt, Helen as Princess Anckesenamon and Imhotep her lover. The return to the past is a tragic melodrama: Anckesenamon dies and Imhotep attempts to raise her from the dead; he is caught by the royal guards and mummified alive as punishment. As this sequence suggests, *The Mummy* explores remembrance. What this chapter considers is how the act of remembering is attuned to the dead. Memory-making occurs in the film itself: the lengthy flashback sequence depicts torture and death, the film uses photography to reveal corpses and it resurrects famous scenes (and re-employs some of the same actors) to evoke the romantic chills of *Dracula*, released the year before. This chapter also reflects upon the ways in which remembrance occurs in multiple discursive contexts, including a consideration of the relationship between Freud's essay on 'The Uncanny' (1919) and the wider journalistic and industry use of the term in the 1920s and 1930s. Publicity material and newspaper reviews are examined to illuminate a relationship between Karloff and deceased silent film actor Lon Chaney and to argue that the uncanny emerges in Karloff's uneasy negotiation of the critical remembrance.

The Mummy was directed by *Dracula*'s cinematographer Karl Freund and is one of the first horror films to emerge following the recent successes of *Dracula* and *Frankenstein*. By examining the film through the idea of remembrance, I suggest that the film looks into the past for its inspirations, both in its flashback structure and through cultural history, stardom and silent cinema. Hence, it is a rather unusual and somewhat reflective entry in the 1930s horror genre, markedly different in tone and address to the other 'pre-Code' films that follow it.

MEETING THE MUMMY

> I must say, gentlemen, that I am as much surprised as I am mortified at your behaviour – what am I to think of your standing quietly by and seeing me thus unhandsomely used? What am I to suppose by your permitting Tom, Dick and Harry to strip me of my coffins, and my clothes, in this wretchedly cold climate?[1]
>
> Edgar Allan Poe, 'Some Words with a Mummy' (1845)

Mummy unrollings were a fashionable pastime for the educated English in the nineteenth century.[2] A literally spectacular form of entertainment, the body of the mummy became a cultural object of morbid fascination, a trend explored in Poe's satire in which the assembled men are forced to stop the unrolling as the indignant mummy returns to life. *The Times* recounted 'quite a season of mummy unrolling' in London between 1829 and 1834, and then in June 1850 reported that 'on Monday afternoon the interesting process of unrolling a mummy was exhibited at the residence of Lord Londesborough, Piccadilly, in the presence of about 60 of his Lordship's private friends, including many of scientific, literary and antiquarian eminence'.[3] Even 40 years after Londesborough's exploits, the mummy continued to unravel for popular consumption. In January 1890, the London evening newspaper the *Pall Mall Gazette* reported from the Botanical Theatre at London University College, where Dr Erichson unrolled a mummy to a packed auditorium, every seat taken and students lining the walls:

> In the centre of the room, on a long-legged deal table, the silent form of an Egyptian peasant, who lived twenty-six centuries ago, swathed in hundreds of yards of grave clothes, with a hieroglyphic-covered coffin lid (which by the way did not fit the poor mummy) behind it. Mr Rider Haggard, who sat in the front row among a bevy of ladies,

was the observed of all observers – I should not be in the least surprised if his next story turned round some mysteriously embalmed subject of one of the Pharaohs.[4]

This account demonstrates the popularity of such cultural practices, where the crowd filled the auditorium to gaze upon the embalmed corpse of a dead man. The artifice of the event was highlighted in the throwaway comment that the hieroglyphic lid did not fit the coffin, suggesting that it had been added by the organisers to enhance the visual spectacle. It also gives us a sense of what the average reader would expect a mummy to look like, swathed in 'hundreds of yards' of fabric. An air of morbidity is also apparent in the full article, the writer commenting that, as Erichson entered the room, his scarlet academic gowns led people to whisper he was the 'chief mourner'. The report also connects social history to literature: the mummy became a popular literary figure during the late Victorian and Edwardian period, and audience member H. Rider Haggard's 'Smith and the Pharaohs' was eventually published in 1913.[5]

Mummy unrollings were part of a broader and long-standing cultural fascination with Egypt that began in 1798 with Napoleon's invasion of the country, a passion reinvigorated by Howard Carter's excavation of Tutankhamen's tomb in the Valley of the Kings in November 1922.[6] Public interest reached fever pitch in March 1923, when Carter's sponsor and official excavator, Lord Carnarvon, died and rumours circulated that death was due to an ancient Egyptian curse visited upon those who opened the tomb.[7] Hence, by the 1930s, the mummy was long established as a cultural object of horror and fascination. This is played upon in Universal's *The Mummy*, released ten years after the Tutankhamen excavation. The connection was recognised at the time, the *Atlanta Constitution* noting in its review that the film was reminiscent 'of the mysterious fate that overtook Lord Carnarvon and Howard Carter, Egyptologists who unearthed the tomb of King Tut'.[8] This appeal to cultural memories of horror is also evident in the film's opening sequence, where in a fashion more than a little reminiscent of the mummy unrollings, Karloff's bandaged-covered monster is revealed to the audience almost immediately.

The film begins in Egypt in 1921 as Egyptologists Dr Muller and Sir Joseph Whemple discover a sealed casket and the remains of a mummy, Imhotep. They stand outside the dig's office and argue over whether to break the seal that promises a hideous curse: eternal death to those that open it. They leave Ralph Norton, an eager young Oxford student, alone inside the office with the mummy with strict instructions not to open the accompanying casket. Norton inevitably opens the casket, unwraps the scroll within, and begins to read out loud the ancient Egyptian text. The initially inert mummy begins to respond to Norton's incantation. One eye opens ever so slightly, glimmering in the low light. His arms begin to move. Norton remains unaware of the mummy's awakening and the camera roams freely around the room in manner reminiscent of *Dracula* when the vampire count is first introduced in his castle dungeon. The camera settles by the scroll on the table and the mummy's hand appears in the left hand side of the frame, grasping at the paper. The moment owes a certain debt to Arthur Conan Doyle's story 'Lot No. 249', published in 1892, in which he describes the mummy as a 'horrible, black, withered thing, like a charred head on a gnarled bush' with a 'claw-like hand and bony forearm resting upon the table'.[9]

The revelation of the mummy's hand is a taunt to the viewer: it appears at the edge of the frame and the whole body cannot yet be seen. The initial revelation of the mummy, followed by its withdrawal to the space beyond the frame, plays with the idea of 'blind space', as described by *Cahiers du cinéma* critic Pascal Bonitzer, who argues that film space can be divided between on-screen space, which he classes as 'specular', and off-screen space, which is 'blind space'. The blind space is 'everything that moves (or wiggles) outside or under the surface of things, like the shark in *Jaws*. If such films "work", it is because we are more or less held in the sway of these two spaces'.[10] In *Le champ aveugle: essais sur le cinéma*, Bonitzer similarly argues that 'the cinema simply wants what takes place off-screen to have as much dramatic importance – and sometimes even more – as what takes place inside the frame'.[11] To adopt Bonitzer's coinage, the mummy 'wiggles' outside the surface of the frame, briefly becoming visible as his hand grasps the scroll. Norton turns around to face the mummy but the monster remains off-screen, the camera pans left and attempts to capture it, but it is too late. Two loose strips of bandage trail through the doorway as the mummy leaves the building. The scene ends as Norton laughs hysterically, his mind suddenly and irrevocably lost.

The awakening of the mummy is one of the central scenes of horror in the film. This was noted at the time by film critics in both the American and British trade press and newspapers; in *Variety*'s write-up of the 'weird' film, 'the transformation of Karloff's Imhotep from a clay-like figure in a coffin to a living thing is the highlight', while the revelation of the hand was described as 'ghastly' by the *Manchester Guardian*, 'presented by signs more horrible than a blunt statement'.[12] Audiences at the time also admitted to a certain amount of fear. In *An Everyday Magic: Cinema and Cultural Memory*, Annette Kuhn examined oral testimonies of British cinemagoers in the 1930s, including those who watched *The Mummy*. The awakening sequence is repeatedly identified as a particularly terrifying moment in the memories of her interviewees, many of whom were children at the time.[13] This sequence is then a demonstration of the way that horror emerges through the cinematic animation of the mummy, finally freed from the shackles of the lecture-theatre unrollings and the constraints of the printed word. This is not to say that this is the first mummy film; the monster had already appeared in the British films *The Haunted Curiosity Shop* (1901), *The Avenging Hand* (1915) and the American one-reeler *When Soul Meets Soul* (1913).[14] Nonetheless, this is the first mummy film after *Dracula* and thus has a certain cultural cache; it represents a turning point in the history of the horror genre as the studio reacts to the success of its films in 1931.

The film explicitly invokes the spectacle of *Dracula* in the following scenes, when the mummy reappears in order to find the reincarnation of Princess Anckesenamon. In writing *The Mummy*, John Balderston transplants the main story, characters and themes of *Dracula* onto 1930s Egypt, deviating from the typical narratives of *fin de siècle* literary fiction, which feature male protagonists falling in love with female mummies. As Bradley Deane remarks 'the men in these stories are less inclined to flee from a mummy than to marry her, to see in her a chance to be kissed rather than cursed'.[15] Ten years have elapsed since Norton's unfortunate meeting with the mummy. Joseph's Whemple's son Frank (David Manners) returns to Egypt with his colleague Professor Pearson to coordinate another dig. The mummy, now masquerading as a local Egyptian man Ardath Bey, appears at the excavation and informs Frank of the whereabouts of the tomb of Princess Anckesenamon. With Bey's assistance, Frank and Pearson coax Joseph Whemple out of retirement, locate the tomb and donate the contents to Cairo museum. Once the findings are on display in the museum, Bey secretly performs a ritual to resurrect Anckesenamon but the resurrection is unsuccessful; instead a young woman named Helen Grosvenor is hypnotically drawn to the museum where Frank finds her unconscious on the museum steps. His curiosity aroused, he takes her back to his apartment and when she wakes up he sits at the side of her *chaise-longue* and leans forward, asserting his attraction to her. Joseph Whemple and Helen's guardian Dr Muller (Edward Van Sloan) enter the room; at the same time Frank kisses Helen. The two elder men look upon the couple in horror, Whemple muttering 'the curse has struck her, and now through her, it will strike my son'. Less than a minute after Frank's daring kiss, Bey walks into the room. Frank looks searchingly at Helen but she does not return his look; she only has eyes for Bey, the other three men in the room forgotten (Figure 1.1).

This scene will have been familiar to 1930s audiences, having been enacted the year before when Count Dracula visited Dr Seward. Before his arrival, Seward's daughter Mina and her fiancé John Harker (also played by David Manners) sit together on the sofa holding hands. As they talk, Dr Van Helsing and Dr Seward enter the room and then Dr Seward has an unexpected visitor: Count Dracula. The vampire, still (for the moment) under the guise of an eccentric European aristocrat, is admitted into the room. He immediately turns his attentions to Mina, who gazes adoringly up at him, even as she holds her hand to her neck where a chiffon scarf disguises the wounds he has inflicted upon her. As the vampire and Mina chat, Van Helsing looks into the mirror of

Figure 1.1 Helen Grosvenor (Zita Johann) is mesmerised by Ardath Bey's (Boris Karloff) stare in *The Mummy* (1932, Karl Freund).

an open jewellery box and discovers that the count lacks a reflection; he sends Mina away and repels the vampire with a cross.

Fittingly for a film so bound up in the past, *The Mummy* invokes remembrance to expel the monster while simultaneously demarcating Muller as the Van Helsing character (a fairly simple deduction as actor Edward Van Sloan plays both parts). Muller instructs Frank to take Helen back to her hotel. Alone with the monster, Muller says, 'I have something else to show you, a photograph'. He reveals a picture of the mummy in his casket, taken ten years earlier at the time of the awakening and the original dig (Figure 1.2). Bey looks at the photograph and in a moment of shock he sees his own corpse; the moment resonating with Roland Barthes's suggestion of the '... rather terrible thing which is there in every photograph: the return of the dead'.[16] The photograph captures a specific moment in time and crystallises it, a corpse viewed by a man reliving his own, horrible death. The mummy may have managed to escape the roving camera in the awakening scene, but the photograph temporarily freezes his progress; it also functions as a demonstration

Figure 1.2 A point of view shot: Ardath Bey (Boris Karloff) stares at a photograph of his mummified corpse in *The Mummy* (1932, Karl Freund).

of Muller's own knowledge and power. The moment echoes Susan Sontag's perceptive comment that 'all photographs are *memento mori*. To take a photograph is to participate in another person's (or thing's) mortality, vulnerability, mutability'.[17] Muller brandishes the photograph as if it were a weapon; his temporary triumph over the monster is a reminder of the inevitability of the mummy's demise.

MONSTERS PAST AND PRESENT

After viewing the photograph, Bey returns to his apartment. He curses Joseph Whemple, killing him, and telepathically calls Helen to the apartment. Together they sit by the pool and a lengthy flashback unfolds, depicting their past lives as doomed lovers in ancient Egypt.[18] The photograph may capture a single moment of the past, but the flashback enables the audience to entirely relive it. This section then explores how the flashback uses memory to make moments of horror, mediated by the tragic romance of the two characters. In *The Mummy*, it is not only the monster that returns to his past life. From the 'present' of the 1930s, Helen watches herself die in ancient Egypt, mirroring the moment where the mummy sees himself as a dead body in the photograph. Towards the end of the film, when Anckesenamon possesses Helen, she is forced by the mummy to view 'her' death mask in the museum. Shocked, she says 'the figure of myself – it is my coffin made by my father against my death'. Death and resurrection circulate throughout the film, and with its constant play on the past and present, the flashback is the ideal mechanism for exploring this narrative conceit.

The flashback breaks down into seven separate sequential scenes, with six accompanied by Bey's voiceover; notably, the only sequence not narrated is Imhotep's death. Flashbacks were not commonly used in 1930s horror film, and did not gain prominence as narrative devices until the film noirs and melodramas of the 1940s. The flashback is also accompanied by a sustained voice-over by Bey, an equally rare occurrence as in 1932 synchronous sound had only recently emerged, a point affirmed by Mary Ann Doane's discussion of cinematic sound: she comments, 'the use of voice-off or voice-over must be a late acquisition, attempted only after a certain "breaking-in" period during which the novelty of the sound film was allowed to wear itself out'.[19] The continuing and extended use of the voice-over throughout the entire flashback deviates from the practice standardised in later films, where the voice-over is often simply an initial bridge from the present to past.

The first scene is set inside Anckesenamon's chamber, Imhotep watching as she dies. The location of ancient Egypt is made explicit in the costumes of the actors, particularly their headdresses: Imhotep wears a tight-fitting white skullcap while Anckesenamon is attired in a delicate, regal crown; behind them Egyptian paintings hang on the wall. In voiceover, Bey intones 'I knelt by the bed of death'. Imhotep looks to the royal guards pleadingly, but they slowly shake their heads, and the scene dissolves, its punctuation representing Anckesenamon's demise. The following scenes then briskly depict the events leading to Imhotep's death. They include Anckesenamon's funeral, Imhotep's theft of the Scroll of Thoth from the statue of Isis, and then his sacrilegious

attempt to bring her back from the dead, stymied by his discovery
by the royal guards. They conclude with Anckesenamon's father
condemning him to death.

While the flashbacks are set in ancient Egypt, their stylisation
reflects the émigré director's past work in German silent cinema,
a chapter of cinema history that profoundly influenced 1930s
American horror film. The sequences do not contain dialogue,
background music or sound effects, Bey's brief comments replace
intertitles and the acting is gestural and excessive. Yet possibly
the most important element is that every image is set within the
oval edges of the pool, so the audience is aware that the sequence
functions as a story-being-told, 'framed' by the mummy's account.
This framing recalls some of the films Freund worked on during his
time in Weimar Germany. Freund, who was born in Koenigshof in
the Austro-Hungarian Empire (now part of the Czech Republic)
worked as director of photography in a number of notable films,
including *Der Golem* (1920), *The Last Laugh* (1924) and *Metropolis*
(1927). It is *Der Golem* that *The Mummy*'s flashback echoes the
most, particularly its Rose festival sequence when a decorative
mask is used to create an almost symmetrical 'sunburst' across
all four sides of the frame. So while *The Mummy* may return to
ancient Egypt, in its evocation of European silent cinema it also
repeats a more recent past, personal to the film's director.

In the following scene the royal guards execute Imhotep. This is
one of the two moments (the other being Norton's laughter at the
beginning) singled out by the *New York Times* as being genuinely
horrifying.[20] It is certainly one of the most unsettling moments
in the film. Imhotep is bound, the bandages cover his mouth, and
the voiceover ends: as the mummy relives his death, he is silenced.
His body dominates the image, filling the tight medium shot.
His mouth opens, gasping for air, his pupils dilate and he des-
perately looks around for a means of escape. But then, for a brief
moment, he gazes into the camera, returning the audience's look
(Figure 1.3).[21] The returned gaze of the monster occurs regularly in
1930s horror films: it can be seen in Karloff's undead Egyptologist
in *The Ghoul* as he chases his niece and nephew around the old
dark house; similarly in *Island of Lost Souls* the frenzied beast men
attack the lens before dismembering Dr Moreau in the House of

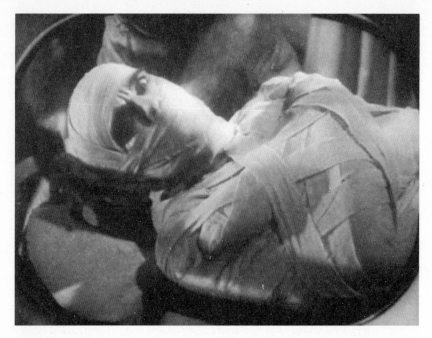

Figure 1.3   Imhotep (Boris Karloff) gazes despairingly into the camera as he is mummified alive in *The Mummy* (1932, Karl Freund).

Pain. In *Murders in the Rue Morgue*, Dr Mirakle looks into the camera as he insists to his assembled audience that he will prove man's kinship with apes, while in *Vampyr* the female vampire Marguerite Chopin looks into the camera as the audience is positioned from the point of view of protagonist David Gray – at that moment sealed within his own coffin. In *White Zombie,* Murder Legendre kills the heroine Madeline and walks into the camera creating a moment of all-encompassing blackness, and in *Werewolf of London* Dr Glendon kills the person that he loves the most, and in a big close up, howls his werewolf shame and anguish to the audience. The fact that only monstrous characters possess the power to return the gaze, and that this occurs only at moments of explicit horror, says much about the shock effect of a returned look. It is an attack on the viewer; it creates disquiet. Imhotep's anguished stare is cut off as bandages are wrapped across the remainder of his face. His wriggling, bound body is placed inside a sarcophagus, a death mask placed on top. He is now imprisoned by a series of constraints: the body is controlled by bandages then sealed within a sarcophagus; at the same time the scene is relived within a flashback. He is mummified and buried alive, the final moments of the flashback depicting his desert entombment. As the mummy calls Helen out of her trance, she likens her unconscious experience to being in a dream. Yet given the content, perhaps a nightmare would be a more appropriate analogy.

Remembering, binding and horror do not end here. During the second horror cycle of the 1940s, Universal produced a series of mummy sequels: *The Mummy's Hand* (1940), *The Mummy's Tomb* (1942), *The Mummy's Ghost* (1944) and *The Mummy's Curse* (1944). In the first few scenes of *The Mummy's Hand* the elderly high priest of Karnac meets his younger disciple at a hidden temple in the desert and together they look into his pool of memories. The High Priest provides the voiceover, the smoke dissipates and extensive footage from the 1932 film is revealed. The voiceover explains that 'Princess Ananka' has died, and Kharis (a name not unlike Karloff) is introduced as prince of the royal house, the man who loved Ananka and could not accept her passing. Like Imhotep, Kharis (Tom Tyler) is caught stealing, and the sentence decreed by the emperor remains the same: mummification alive. Intriguingly, the close-up binding of Kharis' face appears to be a very carefully wrought replica of the staging and framing of Karloff's struggle. Notably, there is no look into the camera, no plea to the audience: this monster does not engender sympathy. *The Mummy's Hand* combines new footage with moments from *The Mummy* as well as re-enacting certain scenes, including the enforced binding. While there is a certain pecuniary consideration when reusing footage and sets, there is also a great deal of effort required to replicate certain moments and edit together the different footage into one coherent flashback. A notable difference between the films is the contrasting sympathies for the monsters. This is indicated in the critical reception of *The Mummy's Hand*, in which the *Observer* critic felt compelled to provide a rhyming couplet as review:

So the mummy / isn't chummy / If it had been Bela Lugosi / It might have been less cosy / If it had been Peter Lorre / We might have felt sorry / If it had been Boris Karloff / We'd have run a mile off / But since it's only Tom Tyler / Trying to look viler / We can relax and smile-r.[22]

Kharis is an entirely stolid prince; his stony face barely flickers as his beloved dies. Yet the flashback in *The Mummy* creates sympathy for the monster, it delves into Imhotep's painful past to depict a man who broke the law because of his love for Anckesenamon. It is intriguing, then, that *The Mummy's Hand* chooses the flashback as the mechanism with which to recycle film footage, as if an ode to horrors past fits more comfortably into a story of remembrance. It is, in brief, a way of visualising memories: in *The Mummy* this encompasses not only the ancient Egypt depicted in the film, but references Egyptomania; in *The Mummy's Hand* it appeals to the cultural memory of the audience and the first cycle of horror films emerging in the previous decade, thereby branding Universal as the home of the monster movie.

'KARLOFF THE UNCANNY'

Following his success in *Frankenstein*, Karloff was billed on posters as 'Boris Karloff (Star of *Frankenstein*)' for his Columbia Pictures film *Behind the Mask* (1932) and as 'Boris Karloff (The *Frankenstein* Monster Himself)' in Universal's *Night World* (1932).[23] Yet for *The Mummy*, Universal made the intriguing decision to rebrand him 'Karloff the Uncanny'.[24] In the remainder of the chapter I will investigate the points of synergy between Freud's essay on the uncanny and the use of the term in 1930s industry, film culture and criticism. I will argue that the links between 'remembering horror' and the uncanny are evident not only in the film itself but also in its exhibition, exploitation, and reception, and its cultivation of Karloff's star status.

In his influential essay Freud claims that the uncanny 'undoubtedly relates to what is frightening – to what arouses dread and horror; equally certainly, too, the word – tends to coincide with what excites fear in general'.[25] He offers a number of suitably horrific examples, including 'dismembered limbs, a severed head, a hand cut off at the wrist – feet which dance by themselves – all these have something peculiarly uncanny about them, especially when, as in the last instance, they prove capable of independent activity in addition', before noting that 'many people experience the feeling in the highest degree in relation to death and dead bodies, to the return of the dead, and to spirits and ghosts'.[26] 1930s horror films have a certain conjunction with this idea. Just over a decade after Freud's essay was published, *Dracula* director Tod Browning (described at the time as 'the Edgar Allan Poe of Pictures') declared 'people are most easily frightened by the idea of a dead person not really being dead – the vampire, zombie or such undead creature. This is the foundation of all horror themes. Then comes the fright caused by the possibility of dead people being brought back to life'.[27]

In her analysis of *The Mummy,* Griselda Pollock suggests that the film is a play 'on the twin forces of the uncanny', owing to its focus on the return of that which was familiar and the resurgence of beliefs previously surmounted.[28] Freud links the uncanny to repression, arguing:

> …among instances of frightening things there must be one class in which the frightening element can be shown to be something repressed which recurs – for this uncanny is in reality nothing new or alien, but something which is familiar and old-established in the mind and which has become alienated from it only through the process of repression.[29]

For Freud, 'the uncanny is that class of the frightening which leads back to what is known of old and long familiar'; something buried in the unconscious that has now re-emerged in an unpleasant fashion.[30] This is crucial to Pollock's reading of *The Mummy* and its reincarnation narrative. Arguably, however, the uncanny is at its most prominent when the film works through remembrance: the appeal to cultural memory in the simulacrum of *Dracula*, something that reoccurs in *The Mummy's Hand* with its integration of footage from *The Mummy*, and in the return of the dead through the awakening sequence and the photograph of Imhotep. Memory binds the narrative, culminating in the flashback sequence of Anckesenamon's death, Imhotep's torture and murder. In her study of the cinematic flashback, Maureen Turim explains that it is a way of presenting 'images which are to be understood as memories. These films portray their own versions of how memories are stored, how they are repressed, how they return from the repressed'.[31] The uncanny and *The Mummy* pivot on the return of the repressed; the mummy returns from the 'undead', relives past traumas through photography and flashback and resurrects Anckesenamon's soul in Helen's body.

The narrative of *The Mummy* offers persuasive opportunities to read the film as uncanny in a manner not dissimilar to Freud's discussion of the subject. But I would argue that there is more to understanding this film than formal analysis alone can offer. As the studio branding of Karloff suggests, there is a great deal of contextual material surrounding the film which adds important material to this discussion. Universal promoted the film simultaneously as horror and romance, a tale of the undead and a reincarnation melodrama, a strategy evident in a poster published in *Variety* in December 1932. On the left hand side of the poster Karloff is dressed as the mummy in the awakening sequence. He is framed in side profile, one bandaged arm outstretched. He is lurching forward, his head droops towards the floor, a dead man walking. Running down the centre of the image is a column of promotional blurb:

> Karloff (the Uncanny) rises to new heights in the role of the MUMMY who comes to life and proves he is no dumb mummy by falling madly in love with the gorgeous girl as played by Zita Johann. The MUMMY sets a new pace for others to follow. The MUMMY is another proof of Universal's daring originality.[32]

Actress Zita Johann stands on the right hand side of the image. Her face is strangely blank and serious, as if the mummy has hypnotised her. She wears a short white slip, and appears to be pulling down one of the straps to reveal her bare shoulder, suggesting she is pliant, and read to do the monster's (potentially sexual) bidding. The monstrous elements then emerge from Karloff's appearance, star status and 'uncanny' branding, while the promotional material promises a story of undying love, sensuality emerging through Johann's pose.

In light of such strategies with multiple addresses, cinema managers then crafted a whole set of exploitation activities for its release, perhaps following *Variety*'s advice that 'any exhibitor who avails himself of a fraction of such opportunities in this direction should check *The Mummy* off in black'.[33] It went on limited Christmas release in America in 1932, before being generally released in January 1933, and premiering in the UK at the London Capitol Theatre in February 1933.[34] In New York it premiered at the RKO Mayfair Theatre on Broadway/47th Street, where the *Hollywood Reporter* revealed that 'there is a mummy case in the lobby, hitched up to a concealed loud speaker from which a sepulchral voice picks out certain people from the crowd and asks them to question the mummy', noting that 'crowds stand around the stunt all day long'.[35] The Mayfair's exterior displays were the most prominent attraction, *Universal Weekly* reported:

> The display reached from the sidewalk to the very top of the Mayfair Theatre building. The giant banner and solid wall display built over the top of the marquee were carried out in weird colours with yellows, greens and purples predominating. Two massive heads of Karloff were set in front of the wall display. The eyes were cut out and pasted over with glazed cloth. Dimmer light attachments were hooked up to these eyes and flashed them up and down with stunning effect.[36]

Karloff loomed over Times Square, appearing as two disembodied heads with flashing eyes and hinting at the mummy's mesmeric qualities. Upon entering the theatre, the cinemagoer had the opportunity to question his doppelganger, before settling down in front of the screen and being transported back in time to ancient Egypt. The intent was for Karloff to appear 'weird', achieved primarily through the outsize displays and clashing colours. In 1930s film journalism and film promotion, 'weird' is constantly used alongside and as a replacement for 'uncanny'. For example, reviewing *The Mask of Fu Manchu* (1932), MGM's horror film featuring Karloff released the month before *The Mummy*, the *Washington Post* described it as 'weird intrigues, sensations,

mysteries, thrills, uncanny torture chambers, the fantastic laboratory of the death ray – and various other uncanny details play
a part in the strange story'.[37] This was carried through into *The
Mummy's* reception in American newspapers. The *Washington Post*
described it as a 'strange and uncanny epic', while the *Atlanta
Constitution*'s preview on 4 March 1933 designated it as 'the weird-
est and most uncanny story yet put upon the screen'.[38] Even the
Daily Boston Globe's description of the film as 'sufficiently weird'
suggests the term.[39] The linking of the uncanny with that which
is weird, frightening or horrific goes back to 1920s film criticism,
if not earlier. Rex Ingram's *The Magician* (1926) was described as
'perhaps a trifle too uncanny to convey a strong popular appeal',
while Tod Browning's *London After Midnight* (1927), featuring actor
Lon Chaney, was 'uncanny, creepy and weirdly mysterious'.[40] It
would be foolish to claim that the studio, exhibitors and journalists were referring to Freud's definition, yet there are definite
moments of parity in their use of the term. It is also notable that
it is *The Mummy* for which Universal deployed this word as a promotional tool, to badge a film which – more than any other of the
studio's releases during this decade – follows many of the precepts
of the uncanny. Theoretical examinations of the uncanny rarely
consider promotional and reception material, likewise contextual
studies rarely explore the potential links with critical theory and
psychoanalysis. Bearing this in mind, the points of crossover suggest that it might be more useful to situate Freud's analysis and
ideas in terms of a far broader cultural discourse both before and
after his essay, than simply to use his ideas to explore the frightening dimensions of the film text itself.

   In the month that *The Mummy* was released, Rosalind Shaffer
reported for the *Chicago Daily Tribune* that 'weird pictures seem
to be the new rage. Never since Lon Chaney's hits has there been
such a furor [sic] over mystery pictures as lately'.[41] Chaney specialised in grotesque physical transformations that were often
connected to moments of film horror, the *New York Times* noting
in 1925 that: 'he made a speciality of appearing as a distorted or
crippled person. He was the wriggling cripple in *The Miracle Man*
and the hideous, hairy, wart-eyed hunchback in *The Hunchback
of Notre-Dame*'.[42] Chaney's roles had a significant impact on the

creation of the horror genre as we understand it today. In the Introduction I mentioned how his films were critically discussed as horror, but there are also various examples of his international notoriety. One such can be found in a legal report in *The Times* in January 1929, months before Chaney's death. Robert Williams, a 28-year-old carpenter, was indicted for murdering Julia Mangan, a housemaid, by slitting her throat with a razor while in London's Hyde Park. In his defence he claimed temporary insanity. The newspaper reported:

> The prisoner, in the witness box, said that while he was talking to the girl in the park noises came into his head and it seemed as if steam was coming out of the sides of his head, and as if a red-hot iron were being pushed into his eyes. He thought he saw Lon Chaney, a film actor, in a corner, shouting and making faces at him. He did not remember taking a razor from his pocket, or using the razor on the girl or himself.[43]

It is notable here that not only did the defendant 'see' Chaney but the actor, popularly billed as 'the man of a thousand faces', is also making faces. Chaney appeared at a moment of high stress and apparently precipitated acts of violence: it seems that the potentially 'harmful qualities' of the horror film became a legitimate form of defence even before the genre was properly established. What is of most interest here, though, is Mr Justice Humphrey's summing up of the case in court, counselling the jury. Talking of *London After Midnight*, the judge advised:

> If any members of the jury had seen [the film], or even the advertisements of Lon Chaney looked like when he was acting in that film, they might agree it was enough to terrify anybody – If the prisoner saw a film of this character the jury might not think it remarkable or as any way indicating insanity that he should, in a moment of emotional excitement, remember the horrifying, terrible aspect of an actor in a part in which he was purposely being terrible.[44]

Williams was found guilty and sentenced to death. As this material attests, throughout the 1920s, Chaney was understood to embody physically horrifying characters that were intended to scare and disturb the film audience. Like many silent film actors Chaney was reticent about the changeover to sound, and as late as 1929 Mollie Merrick reported from Hollywood that he refused to 'go talkie'.[45] Eventually, and in conjunction with Browning and Universal, Chaney planned to work on his first full speaking role as the Count in *Dracula*, but he died in August 1930 from complications arising from pneumonia.[46] Two months later, Lugosi signed the contract to make *Dracula* and the *Chicago Daily Tribune* suggested that Lugosi 'will get many of the horror and mystery stories of the sort Chaney used to do'.[47] Yet Chaney references dogged *The Mummy*'s critical reception. Writing in the *Atlanta Constitution,* Riley McKoy noted that Karloff was 'proclaimed by many as the successor of Lon Chaney', while the *Washington Post* exclaimed '*Frankenstein, The Old Dark House* – and now *The Mummy*! What a record for Karloff, the man Hollywood has curiously delegated to step into the shoes of the late Lon Chaney!'[48] Although Lugosi was initially set up as a possible successor, it was Karloff to whom the Chaney comparisons really adhered. Indeed, the year after *The Mummy* Karloff returned to Britain to film *The Ghoul* and the British film magazine *Picturegoer* continued the Chaney comparisons, suggesting Chaney's 'historic mantle has apparently descended on Mr Karloff' but cheerily pointing out that 'so far as I have heard, Hollywood has not yet learned to say, "don't step on it – it might be Boris Karloff".[49] At the time of *The Mummy*'s release, the horror genre was relatively nascent, so to conclude this discussion let us consider how critical discourses around *The Mummy* cohere around Chaney, a comparison that goes back to Karloff's performance in *Frankenstein* when the *New York Times* commented that this 'was the role which Lon Chaney all his life was anxious to play'.[50]

Chaney was notoriously publicity shy, *Photoplay* reporting in 1929: 'Lon Chaney won't be a good fellow. He won't give out interviews about his private life. He says – and believes – it is nobody's business'.[51] In the month after his death, the *Daily Boston Globe* ran a long eulogy with the headline: 'Who will take Lon Chaney's place in filmdom?' Chaney's agent Clarence Locan was interviewed, revealing that he never recovered his health after playing the armless man in *The Unknown*, and that in *The Road to Mandalay* (1926) the chemical drops that he used in his eyes permanently damaged his vision. It is Locan's discussion of *The Hunchback of Notre-Dame* that is most useful here:

> He hurt his spine with the harness he wore to stunt his body – he took the design from Victor Hugo's original drawings, made a sketch and propped it up in front of him. It took him three hours to put the hunchback make-up on. He was supposed to keep it on only three minutes at a time. Instead he would say 'O, I can stand it another half an hour until you get another shot'.[52]

While we cannot verify the extent to which Locan is telling the truth, what is useful is the emphasis on Chaney's physical transformation and his seemingly gruelling stints in the make-up chair. Similarly, Karloff's makeovers were dwelled upon in interviews with the actor, where he once declared that:

> …my worst makeup was in *The Mummy*. That took nine hours to get on. There were two makeups in that – one the mummy in the tomb, and the second, the mummy come to life. The nine-hour makeup was the first one. Clay was applied, allowed to dry, then covered in wrappings; then more clay and more wrappings. The second mummy makeup took four hours; it was uncomfortable in the extreme as the wrappings were put on wet and as they dried they tightened, and it was very difficult to speak my lines with my throat so constricted.[53]

References to Chaney in critical reception regularly occurred throughout the 1920s when emerging actors underwent 'characterisations' that were markedly different to their natural appearance; in 1930 actor Paul Muni complained bitterly that his ability to play a wide variety of markedly different people did not make him like Chaney, for his characters were not markedly grotesque: 'I take my characters from the street, real types everyone recognises. I've been playing these characters for nearly twenty years on the stage. I was Paul Muni in the theatre. Why can't I be Paul Muni in the studios?'[54]

By the 1930s and the advent of the horror film, press reception really focused its Chaney allusions on the new breed of monsters appearing on screen. This is the time when what I describe as the 'cult of the make-up chair' begins to appear in the popular press. Throughout the 1930s, whenever a (male) actor took a horror role requiring physical transformation, press and publicity reports dwelled on the length of the time that the makeover took, and the physical distress caused by inhabiting the role. The lengthier the time reported, the greater the discomfort, the better: Chaney was evoked with uncanny regularity in these discussions. Even by 1935 the comparisons had not let up. In response to *Werewolf of London*, *Variety* discussed Henry Hull's transformation into the werewolf and proclaimed 'Hollywood can certainly use another Lon Chaney, and here is one right in its lap'.[55]

But within this seam of criticism, there is something specific to Karloff that insistently binds him to the silent film star. It begins with *Frankenstein*, for which a reviewer described Karloff as 'affecting an augmented stature and a blood-curdling makeup that even a Lon Chaney would find it difficult to surpass in horrifying abnormality'.[56] While another newspaper article (or possibly studio publicity material masquerading as such) described in some detail Universal's 'Chamber of Horrors', otherwise known as make-up artist Jack P. Pierce's make-up room. According to the reporter, pictures of Chaney in *The Hunchback of Notre-Dame* and *The Phantom of the Opera* hang on the wall; alongside them a photo of Karloff in his Monster make-up is 'given the place of honour'.[57] Karloff discussed *Frankenstein* in a newspaper interview as production on *The Mummy* was coming to a close. He explained how he obtained the height and structure of the monster by 'mammoth boots weighing twenty pounds each, and by the heavy harness of fifteen more pounds. The whole make-up weighed nearly seventy-five pounds. At the end of a few hours I was exhausted'.[58] The interviewer then suggested that undertaking roles requiring extreme transformations was apposite timing following Chaney's recent demise. Karloff sharply rejected the idea: 'no...I don't want to be another Chaney. I would be extremely proud to follow in the footsteps of an artist like Chaney, but the things he did are his monument. No one has the right to go prowling around trying to steal it!'.[59] Karloff was evidently highly uncomfortable with such comparisons, not least because it undermined his uniqueness as a performer. Despite his own protests, though, the film's contextual material returns to a star of silent cinema and binds Karloff unwillingly to the deceased actor, haunting him. Freud suggests that one of the most prominent themes of the uncanny is the double, while Robin Wood has argued that 'the figure of the *doppelgänger*, alter ego, or double' is the privileged trope of all horror fictions, literary and filmic, created in the past century.[60] In a sense, Karloff became Chaney's unwilling double, compelled to repeat distressing make-up transformations in order to provide moments of horror for the audience: Karloff himself became uncanny.

The Mummy was released on 22 December 1932, and in selected cities was exhibited in competition with Paramount's *Island of Lost Souls*, discussed in the following chapter, which was also undertaking a limited Christmas release.[61] One of the cities featuring both films was Chicago, and the *Chicago Daily Tribune* printed publicity photos of the films side by side. *The Mummy*'s image is a staged shot taken of the pool of memories, where Karloff and Johann kneel side by side. Karloff, wearing the fez and long robes of mummy alter ego Bey, points towards the water while Johann, dressed in a heavy coat which hides her figure and a wide brimmed cloche hat that covers her hair, looks blankly ahead in a trance. *Island of Lost Souls'* publicity picture could not be more different. It depicts Lota the 'panther woman' clad in only a halterneck bra and skimpy flower sarong, her long dark curly hair tumbling down her back. She poses provocatively at the hero Edward Parker: her body is twisted towards him, accentuating the curve of her hip. She clings at jungle vines and pushes her chest out, she stares at him loftily with an insolent smile on her lips. With reciprocal interest, Parker stands close, his body turned to hers and their eyes interlocked. As the description suggests, the images offer a very different address to the audience. With its story of doomed love and chaste, buttoned-up remembrance, *The Mummy* errs far more on the side of the uncanny. It is weird and haunting, and offers only occasional moments of horror in the awakening and flashback sequences. It has none of the licentiousness of other pre-Code films such as *Island of Lost Souls,* which, as Chapter 2 will demonstrate, explicitly worked towards a consistently horrific framework designed to strike fear into the viewer. *The Mummy*'s genteel decision to err on the romantic side of 'weird pictures' was even noted at the time, the *Atlanta Constitution* pointing out 'contrary to what might be expected, this picture is not built on the "horror" theme – the picture is not one of creeps and horrified thrills, but is rather the story of a love which has endured through the ages'.[62] Whether it is horror or love that is explored through the ages, *The Mummy* is imbued with remembrance. It is organised through memory-making flashbacks and photography, it evokes cultural recollections of mummy unrolling and Egyptomania, and plays upon the expectations of an audience assumed to have seen *Dracula*. In its final turn to the past, it evokes silent cinema, both in its occasional reference to the aesthetics of Weimar productions and in the way that the reception of the film binds Karloff unwillingly to deceased actor Chaney, whose legacy haunts the monsters of 1930s horror cinema.

2

'STUBBORN BEAST FLESH': THE PANTHER WOMAN AND *ISLAND OF LOST SOULS*

It begins with a hunt for a girl. A very specific kind of girl. Age between 17 and 30, height between 5'4"and 5'8". She must be an unknown, with no screen credit to her name nor a cast credit in a professional stage production. She can be a blonde, brunette or redhead, so long as she is able to pass convincingly as a monster – a panther-woman to be precise, the creation of Doctor Moreau, arguably one of the nastiest of the many mad scientists to grace 1930s horror film.[1] In July 1932 Paramount initiated the nationwide hunt for the panther woman as part of the publicity drive for the studio's planned horror feature *Island of Lost Souls*, an adaptation of H. G. Wells' novel *The Island of Doctor Moreau* (1896). The winner would receive a five-week contract with Paramount at $200 a week, with expenses paid to travel to and stay in Hollywood.[2] The excitement was palpable: in Atlanta, for example, 180 girls submitted their photographs to E.E. Whitaker, manager of the Paramount Theatre, and in total over 50,000 girls across America auditioned for the role, generating nationwide interest in the film, particularly in cities that featured local young women in the final stages of the competition.[3] In late September, the *Chicago Daily Tribune* ran a photograph of 19-year-old local resident Kathleen Burke as one of the finalists in the national competition; Burke posed alongside the other three finalists, Gail Patrick, Lona Andre, and Verna Hillie. The following day, the same paper reported that Burke, who had previously worked as a copywriter and model, was the winner.[4]

For all the razzmatazz and ballyhoo of this sensational hunt for a new horror 'star', the panther woman herself retained a certain level of intrigue. She can be counted alongside the Bride in *Bride of Frankenstein*, Countess Marya Zaleska in *Dracula's Daughter* and Madeline Parker in *White Zombie* as one of the few female monsters in a decade of horror film inaugurated by and dominated by male monstrosity. Nonetheless, with her passion, agency and ferocity, she stands apart from even this select group. Zombie woman Madeline is merely a passive vehicle for male desire, Zaleska turns to psychiatry in an attempt to purge herself of her vampiric urges and the Bride is brought to life to mate with the monster, but can only express shrieking dismay and repulsion at her intended fate. The panther woman of *Island of Lost Souls* is beautiful, but also physically and mentally strong, she harbours intense emotions and falls in love with the male hero; she is brave and loyal and fights a beast man to the death to save her human friends, her heroic qualities further complicating her status as simply a 'monster'. Even in the history of the genre as a whole, she has a special place: in his classic essay, 'An Introduction to the American Horror Film', Robin Wood posits female sexuality as a central theme of horror and points to the panther woman and Irena in the 1940s horror film *Cat People* as the earliest examples.[5]

This chapter seeks to illuminate not only the importance of the panther woman as one of the few female monsters in this decade, but to consider how her representation in the film is at odds with its intertexts: what Barbara Klinger describes as the network of discourses, social institutions and historical conditions that surround the film.[6] The panther woman is certainly not a straightforward 1930s horror monster, the audition-led publicity campaign alone situates her as the hunted, not the hunter. Comparing Paramount's promotional strategies, the film's representation of gender and sexuality, and how these ideas were received in critical reception, allows us to unpick the conflicted narrative strategies that surround the panther woman. These include her contradictory depictions as a lustful sexual beast, a spirited gentle heroine, a dark-skinned creature from the South Seas, a pretty white girl from Chicago, central to the film narrative and yet also utterly expendable to the plot.

'THE ONLY WOMAN ON THE ENTIRE ISLAND'

The film begins as the hero Edward Parker is shipwrecked in the South Pacific on his way to Apia, Samoa and is forced to seek sanctuary on the island of mad scientist, Dr Moreau (Charles Laughton), a man forcibly ejected from English society after his crazed experiments upon animals. After dinner on the first evening, Moreau and his assistant Montgomery leave Parker alone and stride across the compound deep in discussion. Moreau comments 'I'm taking *her* to Parker', and muses 'how will she respond to Parker...? Will she be attracted...? Has she a woman's emotional impulses?' He then strides into the panther woman's room, utterly dominating the space with his rotund frame. The panther woman, now named Lota, stands motionless in the corner of the room with her back to the camera. She is naked but for the briefest swathes of fabric, one tied around her back, and one around her waist. Her head droops subserviently, obscured by the frothy cloud of black hair. She does not turn around and grunts only the briefest 'yes' in response to Moreau's revelation that she will meet a man from the sea (Figure 2.1). He takes her by the hand and leads her out of the room; her face and the front of her body remain obscured.

The initial sighting of the panther woman is only partial, playing upon prospective audience anticipation generated by the competition and Burke's casting. Suspense builds as the audience waits: what does she look like? Is she a monster or a woman? Can the panther woman really speak? Can Burke even act? Burke's appearance remained a source of fascination throughout the film's production, as the *Los Angeles Times* on-set visit in November 1932 revealed. Writer Philip K. Scheuer described her as having 'a thin face, large eyes that go feline at the corners, a sort of straggly Garbo bob, a most un-cat-like manner, and a keen mind', concluding 'she is undoubtedly one of the better creations in Dr. Moreau's human menagerie'.[7] Scheuer then interviewed Burke and reported back with tongue-in-cheek surprise that Burke did not consume blood but preferred malted milk drinks: 'fine goings on, I must say, for a Lady Leopard'.[8]

In the following scene Moreau leads Lota across the compound and she is finally, fully exposed as a slim, beautiful young woman with enormous almond-shaped eyes, whose tense body language is accompanied by darting glances of apprehension. Moreau takes her to Parker, who lounges unawares in the dining room. Moreau grins slyly, revealing to Parker that 'she's a pure Polynesian, the only woman on the entire island'. When Moreau

Figure 2.1 Doctor Moreau (Charles Laughton) explains to Lota the panther woman (Kathleen Burke) that she will meet a 'man from the sea' but that she must not discuss Moreau, the Law or the House of Pain in *Island of Lost Souls* (1932, Erle C. Kenton).

leaves Lota relaxes and begins to cautiously flirt with Parker. A medium close up brings them together in a single frame, Parker smoking thoughtfully and Lota gazing at him with wide, excited eyes. Hidden outside in the deep shadows of the night, Moreau spies on them through the barred window. A plume of smoke curls upwards from his cigarette, and a smile unfurls across his lips. His intention is clear: the panther woman is to mate with Parker.

As the film progresses, it becomes increasingly evident that Moreau (played in an outrageously camp fashion by Laughton) is attracted to Parker – insinuating dialogue, tactile gestures and body language leave the hero decidedly uncomfortable. Such predilections were not entirely unnoticed at the time of the film's release, the *Film Daily* describes Moreau as a 'queer scientist' and the *New York Times* uses 'queer Doctor Moreau'. While the newspapers were not necessarily using 'queer' to indicate homo-sexuality, Harry M. Benshoff has pointed out that both 'gay' and 'queer' were part of the 'homosexual lexicon' in the 1930s.[9] While *Island of Lost Souls* is without a doubt one of the most unpleas-ant of the 1930s horror films, its conventionality as a mad scien-tist film is made apparent through Moreau's initial gesture. In such (homoerotically inflected) narratives, men work together to create new life; they usurp women who remain objectified, lim-ited and controlled.[10] Despite being a monster, Lota becomes an object of exchange in male desire: as Rhona J. Berenstein has noted 'Moreau's choice of Parker for Lota is a form of displace-ment – Moreau exhibits what are conventionally assumed to be a heterosexual woman's emotional impulses (he flirts with Parker and deems him sexually desirable) while Lota performs the attrac-tion on Moreau's behalf'.[11] Moreau's passion for Parker is unrecip-rocated; in offering Lota to Parker, he is not only able to advance his research but use her as his substitute sexual agent. This is one of the first points where major tensions between the initial pub-licity campaign around the female monster and the docile panther woman character in the film become really apparent.

Wells' novel, as the literary source, provides some context for the panther woman character. *The Island of Doctor Moreau* is a satirical science fiction narrative that uses vivisection as a motif to explore humanity's need to make laws and violate them. Notably, in his book on Wells' cinematic adaptations, Keith Williams writes that Wells criticised *Island of Lost Souls* as 'a "mad scientist" travesty of his satire of Victorian anxieties about degeneration and the cul-tural forces keeping us precariously "human"'.[12] Despite this, there is much of the novel's atmosphere and affect captured in a care-ful and respectful fashion. To read narrator Edward Prendick's story is a gripping but entirely unsettling experience, the imagina-tive detail both of his witnessing of the vivisection sequences and their results have lost none of their disturbing power, as *The Times* book reviewer at the time noted when it was first published, 'the ghastly fancies are likely to haunt and cling…'.[13] Certainly, the ori-gins of the panther woman can be found in Wells' female puma, Moreau's most advanced pet project. In the novel Prendick is shocked to discover that the beast folk populating the island are animals vivisected by Moreau. They are sculpted into new human shapes and taught to speak and behave like humans. In explaining his research to Prendick, Moreau reveals three key points. First, he has been unable to maintain the beast's human shape: 'I have been doing better; but somehow the things drift back again, the stubborn beast flesh grows, day by day, back again. I mean to do better things still. I mean to conquer that. This puma...'.[14] He has also experienced immense difficulty with sculpting the hands, 'the human shape I can get now, almost with ease, but often there is trouble with the hands and claws – painful things that I dare not shape too freely'.[15] Finally, and most ominously, he remarks of his hopes for his puma, 'I have worked hard at her head and brain'.[16] After eight weeks of torture, the puma finally breaks free of Moreau's surgical room, known as the House of Pain, and comes face to face with Prendick:

> I heard a sharp cry behind me, a fall, and turning, saw an awful face rushing upon me, not human, not animal, but hellish, brown, seamed with red branching scars, red drops starting out upon it, and the lidless eyes ablaze. I flung up my arm to defend myself from the blow that flung me headlong with a broken forearm, and the great monster, swathed in lint and with red-stained bandages fluttering about it, leapt over me and passed.[17]

The puma is neither beast nor human; a bloodied and indeterminate mix. Sadistic Moreau has cut away her eyelids, and her last refuge from her torturer – the ability to look away from her ruination – is removed. There is something particularly dreadful about the lidless eyes, images of the sharp shining scalpel hovering over the trembling soft skin of the lid, readying to make the cut. The puma is then hunted down, shot and killed by Moreau, and her role in the novel ends.

The film publicity campaign emphasises the potential bestial horror of the character, akin to that of the puma, yet this is contradicted in the film itself, for its opening sequences feature pliant and beautiful Lota. A further contradiction is apparent in the following panther woman sequence: Parker whiles away the days on the island and Lota is encouraged to seduce him in order to find out if she can produce children. In doing this she becomes an amorous, sexual beast, and much of the horror of the scene emerges from the explanation that Moreau gives of his work in the novel: of the stubborn beast flesh growing back, the impossibility of perfect hands and the extensive work on the female puma. At the time this was seen as particularly gruesome scene, a point reaffirmed by the number of contemporary film critics that highlighted the seduction as a central moment of horror.[18] Parker sits alone by the pool, reading a book. In the top right hand corner of the frame, Lota's feet appear and quickly move left through the shot. She moves swiftly and silently with feline grace, dropping down daintily next to surprised Parker. She stretches her slim long legs, points her face into the sun and lets her hair cascade down her back, a spectacle of visual pleasure. Staring intently into Parker's eyes, she pushes herself against his body and gazes at his mouth (Figure 2.2). He finally succumbs and takes her into his arms, kissing her slowly and passionately, the pair encased in the gentle glow of soft, seductive lighting. Yet Parker suddenly

Figure 2.2 Lota the panther woman (Kathleen Burke) seduces Edward Parker (Richard Arlen) in *Island of Lost Souls* (1932, Erle C. Kenton).

stops kissing her and hangs his head. This is one of the most understated but intriguing moments of the whole film: why has he stopped? Arguably, it is because he feels guilt over his engagement to fiancée Ruth Thomas, but equally it could be that in her kiss Lota transmits something of the beast within, whether a sharp smell, a tiny, excited bite or a pointed tooth scoring the soft flesh of Parker's lips. Still overwhelmed by passion, Lota refuses to relinquish her gaze, pushing her face close to his. He grabs her hands and a moment of pure horror ensues: her fingernails are now garishly painted claws (Figure 2.3). The beast inside Lota has erupted as she experiences sexual pleasure, the panther breaks out of her carefully carved flesh. This is the female sexuality of which Wood spoke of in his essay, and while Wells' Moreau was only able to have 'hope' for the transformation of the puma, the horror film takes his idea to its logical conclusion: the vivisected panther woman, described as Moreau's 'most nearly-perfect creation', temporarily attains the hero Parker.

Figure 2.3 A close up of the panther woman's clawed fingernails, taken from Edward Parker's point of view, in *Island of Lost Souls* (1932, Erle C. Kenton).

The equation of female sexuality with horror is evident in some of the publicity photographs and posters of the film, although their meanings and address fluctuate at different periods of the film's production and distribution. The posters printed during the period of production, from October 1932 onwards, tend to promote the image of a woman who is striking-looking but wild owing to her 'native' origins in the South Seas. One specific image, reproduced in a number of newspapers at the time, shows Burke sitting on the floor, her legs stretched to one side out of shot. She leans backward with one hand clasping the back of her head. She wears a scrap of dark fabric around her waist and a tiny bandeau as a bra. Her long hair tumbles down her bare back and a long string of wooden beads winds around one breast.[19] During this period Burke also featured regularly in Paramount publicity photos printed in the *Chicago Daily Tribune*, in which she is conventionally made up, smiling and modelling the latest fashionable womenswear: one picture depicts her wearing 'a hostess gown of white crepe with large sleeved jacket of black crepe', another wearing 'tailored pajamas' in 'white crepe'.[20] There were two, related messages here: first, that she is the beautiful wild woman, the second that she is (again) beautiful, but this time a fashionable American girl.

Even here, the horror began to creep in, bit by bit. In a *Los Angeles Times* spread entitled 'Action Heroines' on 20 November, Burke features alongside Fay Wray in *The Most Dangerous Game* and Janet Chandler in the Western melodrama *The Golden West* (1932). Burke poses in a skimpy strapless dress and a long beaded necklace, but she eyeballs the camera directly and menacingly.[21] This increasingly aggressive and dramatic presentation of the panther woman came to a head in January 1933 in Paramount's full-page *Variety* publicity poster two weeks after the film's general release. It shows a drawing of a giant, angry panther woman, crashing down on top of Paramount's Broadway Theatre (screening, obviously, *Island of Lost Souls*), accompanied by the slogan 'something NEW hits blasé B'way!'[22] Accompanied by excerpts of effusive reviews, Lota stamps on the theatre roof as hundreds of (male) patrons queue underneath. By locating an oversized furious animal-monster in central New York, the scene is reminiscent of the more famous *King Kong* publicity posters in which the angry ape perches atop

New York's Empire State building – except that Lota's trashing of the Broadway theatre predates *King Kong*'s American release date by three months. Yet it is not only Lota's size and action that provokes an awestruck response. Even in this outsize mode, her body belongs to male fantasy. Her legs are long and gleaming, her waist tiny, her ample bosom entirely pert. But the horror emerges not only from her size and anger; in this image the stubborn beast flesh creeps out. While the body is to die for (literally), a closer look at the cartoon reveals hands clenched in anger with sharp claws curling inwards, and a distorted, pinched, mean face that owes little to Burke's actual appearance. This panther woman has black eyes and an open, shrill mouth: you may look at her body, revere her stature, but you will pay for desiring the female monster, as the hundreds of trilby-wearing men in suits and ties who walk below her en route to the cinema will soon find out.

The changing emphasis of the posters was symptomatic of the strong division of opinion between Paramount's home office and West Coast staff on the best way to sell the picture. *Variety* reported that 'one faction led to believe the horror angle should be the attack, while another contended it should be the "panther woman" idea'.[23] Sam Dembow, managing the Publix chain of theatres (part of Paramount) finally decided on the panther angle as Paramount had invested so much money and time on the initial campaign, and indeed, *Variety* reported in February that theatres that promoted the 'Panther Woman angle' had a stronger box office return.[24] This can also be seen as part of an industry-wide concern about the staying power of 'horror' pictures. Perusing *Variety* from late 1932 and early 1933 gives a definite sense that distributors and exhibitors were shying away from the horror angle. This in turn affected the studios, which became more cautious about making and promoting their movies as horror films, creating a (premature) feeling that the cycle was coming to a close. This feeling was particularly prevalent around the time of *Island of Lost Souls'* general release in January 1933. It opened at the Rialto in New York in competition with *The Vampire Bat* at the Winter Garden Theatre and *The Old Dark House* at Little Lennox.[25] It wasn't just the panther woman's film that was received with hesitancy by the film industry; when reviewing *The Vampire Bat*, *Variety* commented 'shiver picture, well enough done, but coming along too late in the cycle to figure in the money'.[26] Despite this reticence to commit wholeheartedly to horror, the seduction sequence and post-release film poster reveal that perhaps everyone eventually got their own way. The panther woman might remain the primary publicity tool, but the promotional turn away from 'all-American girl' to a cunning and sexualised bestial monster inspires as much dread and horror as lust.

'GO BACK TO THE SEA': WASHING AWAY RACE HORROR

After the failed seduction, a rescue mission for Parker arrives, and Captain Donohue and Ruth Thomas (Leila Hyams), Parker's fiancée, row ashore. It is worth pausing for a moment to discuss the story of Ruth and ape-man Ouran as it reveals much about the film's racial stereotyping of the panther woman. As Donohue and Ruth make their way through the jungle to Moreau's house, Ouran sees blonde-haired Ruth, then screeches and wrestles his fellow beast-man to the floor (Figure 2.4). Ouran is presented as the 'black buck' archetype, which Donald Bogle describes as 'always big, baaadddd niggers, over-sexed and savage, violent and frenzied as they lust for white flesh'.[27] This point is confirmed by Steven Jay Schneider in his work on race horror films, where he points out that the 'monsters' of *Island of Lost Souls*, along with *King Kong* and *Bride of Frankenstein* are coded as such 'primarily because of their savage (murderous, animalistic, lustful) and transgressive (specifically, cross-species) sexual desires'.[28] Although Bogle's argument is relatively superficial, the much deeper colouring of Ouran's flesh than that of the other beast men, his 'Negroid' facial contortions and his violent sexual actions racially stereotype his character. Notably, the actor playing Ouran, Heins Steinke, was a white German but in film posters Ouran is always depicted with black skin, echoing Benshoff's analysis of *Island of Lost Souls*' 'bestial link of animals and humans' as reflecting 'one of the era's most virulently racist tropes – the belief that black people were somehow less evolved than were whites, making them the "missing link" between white people and apes'.[29] While racism is prevalent

47

Figure 2.4 Race horror: the dark skin of ape-man Ouran (Heins Steinke) is contrasted with the white wardrobe and white lighting of Captain Donohue (Paul Hurst) and Ruth Thomas (Leila Hyams) in *Island of Lost Souls* (1932, Erle C. Kenton).

throughout 1930s horror film, we can also point to the film's literary source for much of this material. Wells repeatedly describes the beast folk in relation to black and brown skin, wearing turbans, their appearances arousing disgust and repulsion, and committing barbaric acts. When Prendick is first rescued and brought aboard the schooner, he sees a strange-looking man, 'in some indefinable way the black face thus flashed upon me shocked me profoundly – the huge half-open mouth showed as big white teeth as I had ever seen in a human mouth – there was a curious glow of excitement in his face'.[30]

In the following scene, Moreau notes Ouran's desire for Ruth and lets him into the compound. The threat is clear: having failed to make Parker mate with Lota, he will now attempt the same experiment with Ouran and Ruth, setting up a sequence that Williams describes as 'evocative of screen stereotypes of interracial rape going back to *Birth of a Nation*'.[31] Ruth retires alone to bed.

In a typical pre-Code moment, she undresses in front of the camera, peeling off her stockings and stripping to a silk chemise before falling asleep enshrouded in a mosquito net. Ouran climbs up to her window and breaks apart the bars, staring at her with an exaggerated wide grin and displaying his white teeth. As Ruth screams, Parker runs in and shoots at Ouran as he flees into the night. While the act may be formulaic for the 1930s – the sexual threat to a woman in her bedroom occurring in *Dracula* and *Frankenstein* to name only two examples – *Island of Lost Souls* re-appropriates the trope through interspecies and interracial rape. This is evidently an intention on the part of the filmmakers to shock, as Angela M. Smith reveals in her study of the film's pressbook. She notes that while the majority of the suggested posters were of Lota, reinforcing the panther woman angle, there was a single poster framed entirely around Ouran's attack on Ruth, promoted with the headline 'TERROR! Stalked the Brush-choked Island – Where Men Who Were Animals Sought the Girl Who Was All-Human!'.[32]

The equation of miscegenation and horror with Ouran's attempted rape then casts Lota's seduction of Parker in a new light. It is probably no coincidence that the puma of Wells' novel (also known as a cougar, typically with brownish-grey fur) becomes a panther in the film, a deadly big cat with a jet-black coat. Lota is a racialised hybrid monster, a sexually alluring and desiring tool by which Moreau can (by proxy) seduce Parker, but the film's lesson is that she can never be a human because of her mixed inheritance. Hence, while the story foregrounds her animal genetics as a barrier to finding love and happiness with Parker, it is also a question of race, a reading reinforced by the Ouran–Ruth narrative thread. Indeed, while we cannot know the many and varied audience responses to her character, there is certainly something of the 'race horror' in the film's critical reception. *Variety*'s first and (at the time) sole female critic Cecelia Ager published a lengthy analysis of Burke and her character in late January 1933. It is worth repeating at some length as it reveals much about received ideas of race, sexuality, gender and horror:

Nobody need be frightened of Panther Women as Kathleen Burke portrays them. They are really frightened little girls... There is but one ferocious thing about her – the violent make-up around her eyes. She dresses like any other native of picture tropics, in skilfully draped scarves and beads. Her riotous black hair assumes becoming outlines about her gentle face – Panther Women have excellent figures; it's hard to tell about their faces, however, for they obscure them with so much make-up. Leila Hyams' wholesomeness has never been more welcome as in this murky island – she illuminates the dank proceedings with her good common sense and clean cut Nordic face. Her nice American girl yachting clothes and sports dresses are as refreshing here as her nice normal reactions and level-headed outlook.[33]

An important and influential critic of the 1920s and 1930s, Ager often wrote on fashion in film, and hence the overall angle of the piece, with its emphasis on the female star's character and appearance, is understandable. Ager's article also functioned as somewhat of a slur on Burke's acting ability and appearance, with particular venom saved for her seeming inability to be monstrous. This aspect of the review is something I will revisit later in the chapter in relation to Burke's next horror film, *Murders in the Zoo*, and her legacy as the panther woman; but what I am concerned with here is the notably racial undertone in the reading of Burke's character. This is made most apparent in the comparison with Hyams' character Ruth, whose wholesome American-ness 'illuminates' the island with a notably 'clean cut Nordic face'. Ager's reading depicted Lota as a non-white character born into a foreign (non-American) environment, and provided a contemporary reading of the film that reinforces the reading of *Island of Lost Souls* as conjoining bestial characters with negative connotations of race. In a similar vein, the *Chicago Daily Tribune* noted that Moreau 'lives with another white man'.[34] While the reviewer was referring to race (and possibly sexual preference), it is clear that the costume of the characters further emphasises the film's split, where civilisation is white, and savagery is black. Moreau and Montgomery wear colonial all-white costumes, Parker is resplendent in a pressed white linen suit, and while Lota gets by in long beads and scraps of fabric, 'Nordic' Ruth wears a white pencil skirt and blouse.

Ager claimed that Ruth illuminates the film, but Lota also gets her moment in the spotlight. After the failed rape, Ouran murders Donohue and the beast men revolt, capturing Moreau and then torturing him to death in his House of Pain. Meanwhile, Parker, Ruth, Montgomery and Lota make their way through the jungle to Ruth's boat. Lota realises that Ouran is following them and attacks him. Parker hears a single, sharp cry and doubles back to find Ouran dead and Lota dying. As Parker shines his torch on the ground, Ouran's corpse gazes blankly, blood daubed around his mouth. The light then falls on Lota, breathing faintly. Parker picks her up and the two characters are united once more, framed together in a single romantic close up. In a melodramatic whisper, Lota says, 'go back to the sea' and her eyes roll back. She is engulfed in strong white torchlight as she dies in Parker's arms. Lota avenges her bestial nature by killing one of her own kind then dies under a bright white key light that creates an angelic glow.

With the deaths of Ouran and Lota, the film dispenses with the two beast folk that yearn for the gentle caress of a human hand; their aberrant interspecies and interracial proclivities die with them. The final shot of the film shows the three remaining human beings adrift in a boat as the island burns behind them. 'Don't look back', Montgomery advises, calmly smoking a pipe as the screen fades to black. The escape of Parker and Ruth, assisted by Montgomery, represents the restitution of patriarchal society and heterosexual coupling, an ideologically comforting South Seas Adam and Eve. To return to Wood, if the basic formula of the horror film is that 'normality is threatened by the monster', the film offers a perfunctory conclusion without much self-belief; the monsters (whether they be Moreau or the beast people) are destroyed and normality (with the attendant caveats that Wood brings to the term) is restored, blackness fades out to reveal only white.[35]

SHUDDER MOVIE: CRITICAL RECEPTION

There is no fooling about *Island of Lost Souls*. It is a genuine shocker, hard to shake off afterward. As art, it begins and ends with Charles Laughton.[36]

Philip K. Scheuer, *Los Angeles Times*, 10 January 1933

Island of Lost Souls is a very nasty film. When it went on general release it encountered state-specific censorship issues, the director of the Virginia censorship division twice rejecting it as being 'too extreme' a horror film. Paramount threatened legal action so the censorship board swiftly cut the film and passed it the same month.[37] This was small-scale, however, compared with the problems with its international release. It was banned in, among others, Latvia, the Netherlands, India, South Africa, Germany, Tasmania, Holland, New Zealand, Singapore, Sweden and Denmark; in Australia, people of Aboriginal origin were forbidden to watch the film.[38] As discussed in more depth in Chapter 6 in relation to the censorship practices of the BBFC, it was also banned outright in the UK. The ban was not rescinded until 1958 when it received four further cuts and was certified 'X', but it was still not screened in public until 1967.[39]

The extensive and international banning of this film, often for many decades, says much about the film's ability to arouse horror in its viewers. Its explicit attempts to shock were picked up in a number of American newspaper and trade journal reviews. Reviewing for the *Atlanta Constitution*, Elizabeth Thompson stressed that 'theatregoers addicted to nightmares or who naturally shrink from dark corners, should arrange to attend an afternoon performance', while *Variety* described it as a rather debased 'freak picture' as can be found in 'the cheaper magazines with the greater circulations', no doubt referring to the banning of *Freaks* (1932) the year before.[40] Yet the idea of the 'freak' picture was not the prevailing critical response: *Island of Lost Souls* was usually and explicitly defined as a horror film, or for fans of horror. This can be seen in trade reviews and newspaper reviews alike, the *Hartford Courant* commenting, 'out of such stuff as nightmares are made of is fashioned *The Island of Lost Souls* [sic] – here is a horror film that out-chills all others', while *Film Daily* advised that it 'probably has its appeal for horror fans but as family entertainment it is not a pleasant order'.[41] The *Los Angeles Times'* Scheuer described it as 'horrible to the point of repugnance' – that it stood apart from the other 'pseudo-horror films to date' in its casual horribleness.[42]

If we look more closely at the critical reception and attempt to unpick precisely what constitutes horror for the reviewers, something very odd happens. The panther woman, so heavily publicised, so integral to the film, was not – for these writers – what made the film nightmarish. Instead, they were preoccupied with contrasting the talents of British character actor Laughton, playing Moreau, with the film's 'distasteful' attempts to terrify. Describing the film as a 'shudder movie', Mae Tinee (a staff writer pseudonym for the *Chicago Daily Tribune*) argued 'minus the presence of absolutely convincing Mr Charles Laughton, this gruesome picture would be too utterly improbable'.[43] Merrick, writing for the *Los Angeles Times* preview, said that Laughton's 'incomparable artistry' saved the film.[44] In the *Atlanta Constitution* Thompson echoed this, suggesting that 'the powerful personality of Charles Laughton, almost hypnotic in its force, dominates the picture and the actions of the characters'.[45]

This focus on Laughton makes sense if considered within the wider context of his film career. He began working in Hollywood in 1932, making *Devil and the Deep* for Paramount (released in August), *The Old Dark House* for Universal (October), *Payment Deferred* for MGM (November) and Ernst Lubitsch's *If I Had a Million* for Paramount (December). Critical acclaim followed every screen performance; the *Film Daily*'s review by Phil M. Daly (another pseudonym) of *Devil and the Deep* being typical, where Laughton 'supplies one of the most unusual characterizations of the year. His acting carries an uncanny fascination. He makes everything count – his voice, his laugh, his remarkable facial expressions. He easily steals the picture'.[46] Furthermore, just before *Island of Lost Souls* went on release, Paramount premiered *The Sign of the Cross* at the Rialto in New York, an event attended by Jack Alicoate of *Film Daily*. Alicoate could not praise it highly enough, describing it as the 'spectacle of the year', writing that 'they will rave over the Nero characterization of Charles Laughton'.[47]

Laughton's rapid and starry ascent to the heights of Hollywood in just a few months before *Island of Lost Souls* helps explain why so many of the reviewers focused on Laughton and yet seemed bewildered at a particularly shocking example of the horror genre: it is by some distance a far more extreme film than Laughton's previous 'horror' turn in Whale's *The Old Dark House*. This is never clearer than in Mordaunt Hall's response, writing for the

New York Times. In the first of two reviews, Hall clearly struggled with the 'quality' signifiers of *Island of Lost Souls*, which include Laughton's performance and the film as literary adaptation – the latter point made by Hall in the first sentence of the first review. The production design is also carefully crafted and beautifully shot, a point Hall conceded, for 'although the attempt to horrify is not accomplished with any marked degree of subtlety, there is no denying that some of the scenes are ingeniously fashioned and are, therefore, interesting'.[48] Most importantly for this analysis, Hall emphasised Laughton as the best actor, arguing that he greatly enhanced the film. The second review, which focused entirely on Laughton, was published as part of a film round-up column nine days later. In it, Hall wrote: 'the outstanding feature of this film is the fact that even in such a role as Doctor Moreau, Mr Laughton never for an instant is off key'.[49] He elevates this film to art, for 'this film, with all its uncanny and unpleasant ideas, is worth an hour of anyone's time, if merely to watch Mr Laughton'.[50] A general consensus emerges: while the attempts to shock are crass and the horrific elements are unpleasant, the involvement of Laughton means the film is worth watching. Thereby, with a clear conscience, reviewers were able to recommend a most debased and disreputable film through their marshalling of star status and 'worthy' cultural connotations.

So where did that leave the panther woman? Somewhere near the bottom of the critics' reviews. In the 1930s, the typical format of an American newspaper film review comprised an introductory paragraph and the subjective experience of the reviewer, a pronouncement on the success of the leading actors, an extended plot summary and two final paragraphs, the first of which noted the minor actors and their roles and the last the other films or vaudeville acts playing at the theatre as part of the bill. In such configurations, the discussion of the panther woman was invariably located in the second-to-last paragraph as part of the minor actor's list, often with a simple acknowledgment that Burke won the panther woman competition and/or was a newcomer. She was reduced to several pleasant, harmless adjectives: 'decidedly alluring' in the *Atlanta Constitution*, 'a bit of grotesquerie' in the *Los Angeles Times* preview and 'vivid' in the same paper's review a few weeks later, as having 'weird makeup' in the *New York Times* and being 'beautiful' in the *Hartford Courant*.[51] Burke's most extensive review comes from the newspaper of her home city, Chicago. The title of the review is promising enough, 'Chicago Sees "Panther Girl" in First Film', yet the analysis of the panther woman still only amounted to a handful of words at the end: 'she hasn't much more to do than crouch and run and open her eyes wide, but she is agile and camera conscious, and very well suited to the part she plays'.[52] Despite the extensive pre-production publicity generated through the national competition for the role, the interviews with Burke during filming, and provocative posters printed in regional and national press in the opening weeks, the writers focused on the mad scientist narrative and Laughton, the man at its heart. For the critics, the panther woman was marginal to the film. It was the female audience, not the (predominantly male) film critics whom the nationwide competition appealed to; it offered the 'it could be you' promise to whisk the reader away from her humdrum life and to start again in the glittering world of Hollywood.[53] In the film itself Lota is marginalised in the male-centred narrative, a puppet of Moreau's desires; in the critical reception she was similarly unassuming, a passing footnote in a *New York Times* review.

This echoing absence also says something more about the representation and perception of female characters in 1930s horror film. Women were accepted as beautiful victims, like Lucy and Mina in *Dracula* or Joan in *The Black Cat*; they could be feisty reporters like Fay Wray in *Mystery of the Wax Museum*, reincarnated Egyptian princesses in *The Mummy* and even sharp-witted scientists in the (rather progressive) *The Man Who Changed His Mind*. But crucially, in fact quite decisively, they could never be truly monstrous. Even Madeline of *White Zombie* explains away her temporary 'undead' nature as a dream and falls thankfully into her husband's arms. Furthermore, if women became monsters and articulated horror through sexual desire, they were simply not accepted; the critics looked away. If we return to Ager's article and her reference to Burke's heavy make-up, we can see that the cult of the make-up chair was inverted by gender: while male monsters might spend hours sitting still and were then applauded for wearing thick and disfiguring make-up – which everyone agreed enhanced their performances greatly – female monsters should not wear any heavy make-up of any kind. Indeed, it would have been preferable if they did not actually exist at all.

'HURRAH AGAIN FOR AN AMERICAN GIRL'

Following the release of *Island of Lost Souls*, Burke accepted a continuing $200-a-week contract and hotel accommodation and started shooting *Murders in the Zoo*, a film that caused the *New York Times'* Andre Sennwald to bemoan 'just as it seemed that the cinema's experiments in sadism were ended for the season, Paramount disclosed a particularly gruesome specimen'.[54] In it, Burke plays doomed wife, Evelyn Gorman, whose life is brought to an abrupt end as her evil husband, sadistic millionaire sportsman Eric, throws her into an alligator pond. Burke was keen to leave the panther woman tag behind, revealing that 'I want to get as far away from panther woman as possible. Look at Mr Laughton – he played a madman in his first talkie – and has been playing mad-men ever since'.[55] Nonetheless, Paramount inevitably promoted her as 'Kathleen Burke (The Panther Woman)'; a number of crit-ics referred to her as 'Kathleen Burke (panther woman)' and at the same time Gail Patrick, the runner-up in the panther woman contest, attracted far more praise for her role in the same film.[56] *Murders in the Zoo* was released in late March 1933 and reviewed in major city newspapers in early April. Later that month *Variety*'s Ager returned her perspicuous attention to Burke, writing:

> It's not so easy to shake off a sobriquet like 'The Panther Woman', Kathleen Burke is finding out. Starting as an innocently friendly intro-duction to picture audiences, it has developed, in *Murders in the Zoo*, into well nigh a dastardly curse. After all, if a girl keeps on being called 'Panther Woman', she's got to do something about it no matter how gentle and domestic her real instincts may be – [Burke] has therefore to keep pulling herself together trying to fix a wild gleam in her eyes, trying to slink with feline stealth, trying to flare up with savage fire. All this panthering to do, when plain facing the camera is hard enough![57]

Albeit with an acid tongue, Ager was the only writer who really attempted to grapple with Burke's roles: it is telling that it took the lone female film critic on *Variety* to do it. Her comments stripped back the layers of meaning evoked in the original *Island of Lost Souls* pre-production campaign: despite being ostensibly a search for a female monster, this was really a beauty contest by another name and, as the winner, Burke was ill-equipped to live up to the symbolic demands of the female monster. Indeed, her absolute obedience and supplication in the film towards her torturer Moreau reveals just how much *Island of Lost Souls* is a traditional male-centred mad scientist narrative. This problem follows Burke to *Murders in the Zoo,* as Ager noted, where she simultaneously attempts to live up to the panther woman monicker that brought her into the pictures and at the same time attempts to transcend it as an actress in her own right. Ager's repetition of the word 'trying' in her review suggests that Burke strives and fails, that her efforts are so obvious that she does not inhabit the character at all; the audience is more likely to notice her inadequate efforts in front of the camera than become immersed in the plot. This brings us to the conflict at the heart of this chapter: to what extent is the panther woman actually a monster? On the one hand, the film depicts her as a hybrid, dark skinned and exotic beast from the South Seas, whose intense sexual desire results in claws erupting from her fingernails. On the other, she is spirited and friendly, self-sacrificing and heroic, beautiful and loving – not really evil at all. Is she, more simply, 'pretty Katie Burke from Chicago', a girl who happened to hitch a lift on the horror train as it rolled into Hollywood? While we can debate this endlessly, a letter written to the movie page of the *Chicago Daily Tribune* in July 1933 reveals what at least one actual fan thought:

> Dear Miss Tinee: I was so delighted to see our own Kathleen Burke in another picture. Though *Murders in the Zoo* was a rotten picture, the good acting of everyone in the cast partially redeemed it...The Panther Woman was such an ugly part for this beautiful girl and she is beautiful. I say hurrah again for an American girl, and especially a Chicago girl.[58]

For 'Mrs W.', writing to the letters page, Burke is not expected to be foreign, or monstrous, or ugly. She is a beautiful American girl who deserves better parts in better pictures. Never achieving more success or notoriety than in her first film, Burke worked in Hollywood until 1938 in minor supporting roles, before turning to theatre work and eventually moving out of the public eye. After her death in April 1980, obituaries referenced her as the panther woman.[59] The beast flesh crept back; she was never entirely free of her feline alter ego.

In exploring the relationship between the film and its intertexts – the nationwide audition campaign, on-set reports, publicity posters, film reviews, star journalism and fan letters – this chapter concludes that the relationship between the initial pre-production campaign and the film itself was flawed. The panther woman as represented in the pre-production campaign struggled for a meaningful place within the mad scientist narrative, and despite posters of her stamping on Broadway and its male patrons, she remained virtually invisible in the film reviews that turned with interest to Laughton. The female monster in this horror film was a façade; to many critics and some fans she was the end product of a beauty contest, her horror diminished by her attractiveness. Indeed, in the *Variety* review of *Island of Lost Souls*, the writer suggested that Lota 'is too much like a girl to even suggest transformation from a beast. Her part is little more than a *White Cargo* bit'.[60] Yet if we take a longer view, perhaps acknowledging the shift Klinger suggests from the synchronic approach (how history appears at one point in time, in this case 1932–3) to the diachronic (the study of history over a period of time) we can still salvage her importance.[61] As Tim Snelson and Mark Jancovich have both pointed out in their respective studies, it is not until the 1940s that Hollywood horror films position the woman as both monster and victim; Snelson pinpointing *Cat People*'s popularity in 1942 as inspiring 'a cycle of female monster films – in hope of also imitating its phenomenal box office success'.[62] Notably, as part of his preparation for *Cat People*, producer Val Lewton screened *Island of Lost Souls* and closely analysed the panther woman.[63] While her meaning in 1932 and 1933 may have been muddled, by the early 1940s she was evidently already recognised as an important progenitor of the female monster, an important part of horror film history. Reading the film in this manner, Burke's spirited performance then offered an early opportunity for the audience to engage with a warm-blooded and vivacious female monster who stood apart from the compliant female victims and inadequate male monsters populating the horror landscape of the 1930s. Rather than being the 'only woman on the island', she became 'the only woman in the genre', for this decade at least.

3

WHITE ZOMBIE AND THE EMERGENCE OF ZOMBIE CINEMA

White Zombie (1932) is the first zombie film, but it is not about the zombies that roam across our screens today. Richard Matheson's novel *I Am Legend* (1954) and the film *Night of the Living Dead* (1968) depict these monsters as rampaging in infectious hordes and hungering for human flesh; they have little in common with *White Zombie*'s black slaves toiling in the sugar mill and working the plantation fields.[1] Discussing the popularity of sequels and remakes of zombie films, Meghan Sutherland asks 'why they are at once so repeatable and so specific – so timeless and so timely?'[2] While Sutherland focuses on contemporary zombies, I want to consider how *White Zombie* can be usefully understood along similar principles, for while the modern American zombie may make the earlier ones look old-fashioned, they have a politic of their own.

Eschewing the gothic horrors of a dim and distant Europe, *White Zombie* is set in a contemporary Caribbean location with its own specific historical resonance. In 1932 the US military entered its thirteenth year of Haitian occupation and the film depicts black zombies labouring in sugar mills and on plantations for white owners, a point noted by Tony Williams in his review of the film, where the plight of the zombie mill workers not only echoes 'the earlier forced labour system that the US imposed on the native population but [also] the contemporary miserable servitude of Negro Haitians'.[3] As a result, much critical scholarship on the film explores colonial discourses and the zombie as a slavery metaphor; the film's timely qualities then emerge through a socio-political reading and a different context from the other films discussed in this book.

While allegorical readings are important, the slavery of the Haitian zombie has only ever been half of *White Zombie*'s story and its timelessness emerges in its dubious gender politics. When plantation owner Beaumont falls in love with the sole female character, the blonde American Madeline Short, he arranges for local *bokor* Murder Legendre (Bela Lugosi) to transform her into a zombie and stop her marriage to her beau, Neil Parker.[4] The poor woman experiences marriage, death, burial and resurrection in a matter of hours, and is carried off in her coffin to Legendre's home, the Castle of the Living Dead. Race horror remains, even with this abrupt shift of focus, for the idea that a white female could be subjected to the same sexual and bodily slavery as a black man is intended to shock; it is explicitly invoked in a 'catchline' in the *White Zombie* exhibitor pressbook: 'they knew that this was taking place among the blacks, but when this fiend practiced it on a white girl – all hell broke loose'.[5] Similarly, when the film was released in Baltimore, the local exploitation involved a 'living tableau': a trolley street car driven on railroad tracks was decorated 'with the negroes in the background of the jungle [sic]' while 'the menace made passes at the blonde girl dressed in clinging white muslin'.[6] This chapter, then, considers the idea of the timely and the timeless in relation to the black male zombie and the white female zombie, situating the reading within its historical, industrial and production contexts, where *White Zombie* belongs to a series of group of independent 1930s films, including Frank R. Strayer's *The Vampire Bat* (1933) and *Condemned to Live* (1935), that create horror outside the constraints of the studio system.

DIGGING THE GRAVE

White Zombie was based on an original screenplay by Garnett Weston, cost less than $100,000 to make, and was shot over 11 days in March 1932. The first cut of the film was previewed in New York City on 16 June, the Halperin brothers signed a distribution contract with United Artists on 13 July and premiered the film at the Rivoli Theatre in New York City on 28 July.[7] Price and Turner point out the prestige of the distribution deal: United Artists 'was owned by and released the product of a select group of top independent producers' (including Samuel Goldwyn,

Douglas Fairbanks, Mary Pickford and Charles Chaplin).[8] At the same time, the Halperin brothers also signed a contract with Amusement Securities Corporation, a New York firm that specialised in financing films whose producers were unable to raise the necessary capital upfront.[9] United Artists then registered the film at the Library of Congress on 1 August, and over the remainder of the year the film began to play across America and Canada, arriving at London's Dominion theatre in September 1932.[10]

The film was a cheap one by Hollywood standards, on a par with Edgar G. Ulmer's two-week quickie *The Black Cat*, yet it transcended the limitations of its production contexts. Producers on poverty row often capitalised on the financial problems of the Depression-era studios and rented their old sets and penniless crews, and brought in their actors for several days' work. In *White Zombie*'s case, studio sets were rented from Universal Studios and the RKO Pathé lot in Culver City, while some location shooting took place at Bronson Canyon in California.[11] According to George E. Turner, Michael Price and Gary D. Rhodes, the production team filmed on the following Universal sets: Castle Dracula's hall and stairway from *Dracula*, the pillars and hanging balcony from *The Hunchback of Notre-Dame,* and the dark corridors, wine cellar and dungeon set from *Frankenstein.* The chairs in Legendre's hall are taken from *The Cat and the Canary* (1927), and some of the rooms in Beaumont's mansion had an earlier incarnation in *Dracula* as the Seward house. The RKO–Pathé lot provided Legendre's rooftop veranda, formerly the Garden of Gethsemane set from *The King of Kings* (1927).[12] Castle Dracula was itself already a combination of expensive permanent sets that Universal had standing at the time of filming, but there is something about *White Zombie*'s use of old sets that creates an atmosphere of déjà vu; actors wander through rooms that occasionally tug at the memory in moments of uncanny recognition.[13]

White Zombie begins late at night on the island of Haiti as a group of black mourners dig a roadside grave. Its purpose is ghoulish; the grave stands aside a busy highway so that the passing traffic will regularly see it, reducing the likelihood that the corpse will be stolen for nefarious purposes. As the mourners toil, the credit sequence is superimposed through a series of diagonal wipes, aurally accompanied by chanting and drumbeats.[14] A horse-drawn carriage appears containing Madeline and Neil, and the mourners move out of the way to let the carriage pass. A racial hierarchy is explicitly manifested in shot length and lighting: the black actors are in extreme long shot, *en masse* with indistinguishable features, while the couple are in medium close up, encompassed in a white light and wearing white clothing. Such a demarcated presentation of characters accords with Steven Jay Schneider's reading of race and American horror cinema, that until the 1970s 'almost all horror films with a discernible racial component kept the black presence contained within narratives featuring exotic island locales, white interlopers, and uninhibited natives ("savages") practicing voodoo and experiencing zombification'.[15] *White Zombie* depicts black people in extreme long shot so that individual figures become an amorphous mass, chanting and wailing and evoking atavism.

Two glowing white eyes are superimposed over the carriage as it continues through the forest. A man walks alone on the path, and as the driver stops to ask for directions, the stranger is revealed as *bokor* Legendre. As the carriage slows, the superimposed eyes shrink. They recede into the rear of the image, eventually disappearing into Legendre's skull, signalling that he literally has eyes in the back of his head. Legendre leans into the carriage, gazes at Madeline, and grabs the white scarf tied around her neck. As the driver whips the horse and speeds away into the night, Legendre watches the fleeing carriage, stroking the white scarf with his pale hands. The couple arrive safely at the mansion of Beaumont, who has offered his house as the wedding venue for the couple. Neil harshly reprimands the driver for driving off with such haste after meeting Legendre, but the driver then slowly explains the powers of the *bokor* and the zombie to the horrified hero. The driver's explanation is a necessary expositional device, as the idea of the 'zombie' was only just beginning to permeate American popular culture in the early 1930s.

Unlike the vampire, werewolf or mummy, the zombie film is the only subgenre to have sidestepped a prior literary fiction incarnation, and one of its most distinctive qualities is the folkloric source of its origins, emerging from the tradition of voodoo in Haitian culture.[16] This is evident in *Variety*'s fairly long review of the film, which included a detailed explanation of what a zombie is and then noting 'it is the highest form of obi. [obeah], which in turn, is a super development of the voodoo of the Southern States'.[17] In the nineteenth and early twentieth centuries, voodoo was often a feature of racist and sensationalist poems, short stories, plays and novels set in the Caribbean and Louisiana. Non-fiction accounts of Haiti during this period were for Kyle Bishop, 'decidedly nega-tive and one-sided, focusing on primitive and taboo behaviour', and it wasn't until J.N. Léger published *Haiti: Her History and Her Detractors* (1907) that a sympathetic text could be found.[18] In his book-length study of *White Zombie*, Rhodes notes that the novel *The Maroon: A Tale of Voodoo and Obeah* (1883, Captain Mayne Read) is unique in its combining of voodoo and the living dead, but that the figure of the zombie was yet to explicitly materialise.

In fact, zombies were not clearly articulated in popular culture until the publication in 1929 of William B. Seabrook's sensation-alist Haitian travelogue, *The Magic Island*. Seabrook recounts a conversation with Polynice, a Haitian farmer, about the local folklore and belief in the supernatural. As Polynice recites stories of werewolves, vampires and demons, Seabrook shows little inter-est, seeing easy parallels with white European folklore. Yet his curiosity is piqued as Polynice mentions the zombie, a figure that returned from the grave but was 'neither a ghost nor yet a person who had been raised like Lazarus from the dead'.[19] According to Polynice, the zombie is a:

> soulless human corpse, still dead, but taken from the grave and endowed by sorcery with a mechanical semblance of life – it is a dead body which is made to walk and act and move as if it were alive. People who have the power to do this go to a fresh grave, dig up the body before it has had time to rot, galvanise it into movement, and then make of it a servant or a slave, occasionally for the commission of some crime, more often simply as a drudge around the habitation or the farm, setting it dull heavy tasks, and beating it like a dumb beast if it slackens.[20]

Seabrook is further confounded when Polynice explains that the zombie cannot be explained away as superstition, that 'at this very moment, in the moonlight, there are zombies working on this island, less than two hours ride from my own habitation'.[21] Polynice also reveals the Haitian practice of roadside burial, as evidenced in the opening sequence of *White Zombie*, where the regular passers-by 'assure the poor unhappy dead such protection as we can'.[22] The idea of the living dead had instant appeal to cinemagoers, and despite generally poor reviews the film proved very popular upon its Broadway release. As a *Film Daily* writer commented at the time:

> here is a feature that possesses elements that the critics seemed to entirely overlook. It is based on the supernatural, on superstition, and the Mob is swayed by superstition. While most of the Intelligentsia are interested in the supernatural along with the Mob so *White Zombie* starts off with a basic appeal that intrigues practically everybody.[23]

White Zombie's narrative emerges from a socio-political and contemporary context quite distinct from other American films appearing in the horror cycle at a similar time, such as *Doctor X* (released August) and *The Most Dangerous Game* (September). In its exoticism of 'native' practices and beliefs, the description of the 'undead' and the use of the zombie as a slave, Seabrook's travelogue provided the discursive context for the film, a point confirmed by the extensive reprinting of extracts from *The Magic Island* in the film's pressbook. His writing was cinematically reappropriated as a supernatural horror story grounded in a colonial discourse: the allure of Haitian voodoo offering the seemingly 'new' figure of the zombie to engrossed film audiences.

SUGAR AND SLAVERY

In the following sequence, the local missionary Dr Bruner arrives at Beaumont's mansion to conduct the forthcoming nuptials, and Madeline and Neil retire to separate rooms to prepare for the wedding ceremony. Beaumont leaves his mansion and travels to Legendre's sugar cane mill, a sequence best understood by locating the 'timely' qualities of the film within the context of

Haitian history and slavery. From the mid 1930s, the five leading Haitian exports were coffee, cotton, sugar, sisal and bananas, which accounted for over 90 per cent of exported commodities.[24] The largest proportion of sugar crops were produced on plantations run by foreign companies.[25] Black slavery comes to light in this history, as Laurent Dubois points out that 'sugar was the economic miracle of the eighteenth century [and] – slavery was deemed essential to the production of sugar'.[26] Sure enough, the zombie mill workers are black. In a very long shot inside the mill, zombies carry baskets of cane to the thresher, and the grinding wooden machinery emits an animalistic roar, an aural shock in a film that contains only the sparsest dialogue and sound effects. The zombies trudge in a circle around a large wooden grinder *en masse*, moving in uncanny automation. Beaumont sees a zombie dressed in white with a basket on its head. The creature loses its balance and falls off the balcony into the grinder. The camera tracks down the exterior of the grinder and comes to rest upon the zombies rotating the machinery below, with the implication that the fallen zombie is being torn to pieces in the grinder.

Haiti was built upon slavery. Christopher Columbus claimed the island of Hispaniola for Spain in 1492 and, from as early as 1510, Spanish colonisers uprooted Africans from their homes.[27] They sold them as slaves and shipped them across the Atlantic to endure inhumane conditions in the mass agricultural development of mines and sugar plantations. France and Spain divided Hispaniola in 1697, and France named her colony Saint Domingue, which according to Kieran Murphy became integral to the global 'slave trade triangle', a 'modern system of subjugation that was geared toward the complete commodification and alienation of its workforce in order to maximise productivity'.[28] The slaves' revolt began on 14 August 1791, and over a decade of violence followed before the establishment of Haiti as the first Black Republic in 1804. Yet it remained politically unstable, 'largely due to international cold-shouldering, power-hungry leaders, and recurrent clashes among the Haitian colour-coded classes'.[29] The invasion of the US marines on 1 September 1915 compounded the island's troubles, as did the ensuing instigation of martial law and forced labour until the US withdrawal in 1934.

One side effect of the occupation was an increased interest in accounts of voodoo and zombification in American media, a curiosity that *White Zombie* hungrily feeds upon. The fascination with Haitian culture (filtered through a sensationalist American lens) was present in contemporary accounts of the film. Announcing that the film had finished production, the *New York Times* eagerly explained the film's context as 'the "living dead" of Haiti, stories of which have been trickling back to these shores for years'.[30] When the film was released the reviews were muted, the same paper going as far as to say there was not, 'to be candid, much reason for *White Zombie*'; yet there was a positive response to the depiction of Haiti as overrun with the living dead as it confirmed widely held suspicions about the island.[31] Indeed, in Boston, the *Daily Globe*'s review discussed how 'the voodoo ceremonies of Haiti, harking back to the primitive savages of Africa' were 'fascinating to everyone', while the *Washington Post* mistakenly claimed that *White Zombie* was filmed on Haiti and for most of the review quoted Seabrook material from the pressbook.[32] Despite the poor critical reception, *White Zombie* was a financial success. It grossed $1,750,000 and because of its very low production costs it produced a higher net profit than *Dracula* and *Frankenstein*.[33] This success prompted further cinematic outings for voodoo and zombies throughout the decade, including *Black Moon* (1934), *Ouanga* (1936) and the Halperins' sequel *Revolt of the Zombies* (1936).

An element of the film's uniqueness, then, emerges from the interplay of gothic and colonial horror: the military occupation of Haiti is never explicitly alluded to in the film, yet is central to understanding its contemporary discursive context. Part of the American response to the occupation was to re-present Haiti as populated by a primitive and frightening race governed by black magic, while the aforementioned lack of political critique in the text suggests a complicity in the ideology of occupation. As Lizabeth Paravisini-Gebert articulates:

> Pro-Western ideologues of "progress" and "civilisation" have derided ritualistic practices of African origin as proof of the Caribbean folk's inability to embrace "modernity", of their incapacity for emancipation and sovereignty. Given a glimpse of Caribbean people's

resolution to assert their autonomy, they are quick to invoke the titillating figure of the zombie as representative of the Afro-Caribbean
folk as bogeyman.[34]

The allure of the black zombie, then, cannot be understood neu-
trally; the zombie becomes an attempt to justify neo-colonial
rule, an example of the black magic that the enlightened occupi-
ers must stamp out. Indeed, 'the accursed fate conjured by the
myth of the zombie is that of the Haitian experience of slavery,
of the dissociation of people from their will, their reduction to
beasts of burden subject to a master'.[35] The black zombies may be
an allegory for slavery, yet the *dénouement* abandons them entirely:
once the white female zombie emerges there is no interest in the
black male zombies; after Beaumont's trip to the sugar mill they
are never seen again.

After witnessing the destruction of the zombie in the grinder,
Beaumont walks into Legendre's office and closes the door. He
turns around to talk to Legendre, who is off-screen but extends
his hand into on-screen space in a curious way, breaking the frame
edge. Beaumont turns away from the disembodied hand and
explains that he is in love with Madeline and wants to prevent
her marriage to Neil. Legendre nods towards the head white male
zombie Chauvin, who stands as a sentry at the side of the desk, and
then remarks, 'there is a way, but there is a cost...' to which desperate Beaumont replies 'you give me what I want, and you may
ask anything'. Chauvin is then displayed from Beaumont's per-
spective. He stands utterly still, as if hewn from golem stone, his
eyes wide open but unfocused. Legendre whispers in Beaumont's
ear, causing him to look stricken – we are not privy to whatever
horrors the *bokor* suggests (Figure 3.1). Legendre sits back in his
chair but leaves his hand gently trailing on Beaumont's body, to
which the frightened man mutters 'no, not that. . .'. Yet desire for
Madeline and his weakness overrides his sensibility, and Legendre
provides a potion that will transform Madeline into a zombie.

Legendre's whisper in Beaumont's ear is sufficiently ambiguous
to have generated a wealth of material in film analysis. Rhodes
notes a Faustian tinge to Beaumont and Legendre's deal, arguing
that 'the major plot device *White Zombie* adopts is the contractual

Figure 3.1 Charles Beaumont (Robert Frazer) is shocked at Murder Legendre's (Bela Lugosi) suggestion in *White Zombie* (1932, Victor Halperin).

bargain with a devilish figure and the tense relationship between Faust and Mephistopheles'.[36] For Rhodes, Legendre will separate Madeline and Neil in exchange for taking Beaumont as a zombie; Beaumont then recoils as he sees his future self in Chauvin. There is, however, more to Beaumont's shocked response than the threat of simply becoming a zombie; Harry M. Benshoff's reading suggests that Chauvin is used to 'mediate the homoerotic tension' between Legendre and Beaumont'.[37] The homoerotic dimension is certainly borne out later in the narrative as Legendre poisons Beaumont and laughs, 'I have taken a fancy to *you*, monsieur!'.

Yet Tanya Krzywinska argues that Benshoff 'does not really address the breadth and depth of Legendre's monstrous perversity'.[38] For Krzywinska, Legendre is a Sadean figure who desires Madeline and 'Beaumont will be forced mutely to watch as Legendre consummates his necrophiliac desire with the zombie virgin Madeline'.[39] This was also *Variety*'s interpretation in August 1932, albeit enunciated in simpler terms: Legendre 'has come under the spell of the girl and plots to make her his own'.[40] Certainly, a narrative conceit of the 1930s horror film is the monster's 'romancing' of the heroine, so to a degree Krzywinska's reading makes sense. With overtones of *Frankenstein*, Legendre scuppers the heterosexual romance between Madeline and Neil by poisoning her on her wedding night and then blocks a potential necrophiliac romance between Madeline and Beaumont, taking both of them for himself. Ultimately, his tantalisingly silent suggestion to Beaumont opens up a whole host of possibilities. Given the way the film develops, Benshoff's reading seems the closest to articulating the unspoken dynamics of the scene. The scene is explicitly homoerotic, mediated through the tactile performance of the male characters. A male body is the object of another male's gaze; Legendre's dialogue is delivered dripping with layers of insinuation, the two men touch and whisper. Beaumont's frightened 'no, not that' can be read as a rebellion against Legendre's suggestion that in order to have Madeline, Beaumont must relinquish himself, body *and* soul.

MADELINE, ALICIA, OLYMPIA, CAMILLE....

I thought that beauty alone could satisfy, but the soul has gone.
I can't bear those empty staring eyes!
Beaumont bemoans Madeline's transformation
into a white zombie

In charting her demise and transition into the afterlife, the film's attention now turns to Madeline, a character performed by actress Madge Bellamy in an uneasy, sexualised-yet-unavailable fashion. In the scene following Beaumont's pact, Madeline dresses in her bedroom for the wedding. There are four full-length shots in the sequence in which Madeline wears only a bra and knickerbockers; in one shot she turns front-on to the camera and poses, seemingly admiring himself in the mirror image as the audience looks back. The scene may have only seven shots but it lasts for 30 seconds. The languid, contemplative and erotic tone, commented on rather mockingly by the *Chicago Daily Tribune*'s reviewer, signals not only its voyeuristic purpose but also the film's pre-Code status, for such an overtly titillating display would not have been passed by the Production Code Administration a few years afterwards.[41]

Later, Madeline refuses Beaumont's marriage proposal and he gives her a flower tainted with the zombie potion, which she smells and tucks into her bouquet. She marries Neil and at the wedding breakfast Beaumont and Neil toast the new bride; at the same time Legendre stands outside the house, carving a wax doll draped with Madeline's scarf. She raises her goblet in response to the salutations for her good health, looks into its murky depths and stutters 'I see death'. In a shot from Madeline's point of view, Legendre's head and glowing eyes are superimposed within the goblet. Outside the house, Legendre burns the wax effigy and Madeline dies in Neil's arms. In a final moment of disruption, Legendre turns his assaultive gaze on the audience. In a lingering medium shot, he stares directly into the camera and walks towards it, the viewer becoming, like Madeline, another victim of his powerful look. The scene ends as Legendre's blurred face fills the screen, fading into an all-encompassing blackness.

There have been several interpretations of Legendre's stare. Rhodes argues that it constructs a unique identification point for the viewer, the 'spectator-as-character', a device that 'allows the spectator to become – albeit in a very limited fashion – a character in the narrative'.[42] For Rhodes, 'this cinematic device moves the viewer from a more traditional and perhaps more passive role as spectator to a more active role as participant/character'.[43] Arguably, Legendre's look suggests the opposite, commanding the most passive and masochistic of positions. Legendre's direct look into the camera is a violent act, unsettling and discomfiting; it assaults the audience, who does not expect its look to be turned upon itself. The moment also functions as a repeat of Lugosi's glowing eyes in *Dracula*, to which the *Film Daily* made extensive comparisons in its *White Zombie* review, beginning 'another variant on the *Dracula* theme and with the work of Bela Lugosi it has the same quality of spooky thrills and weirdness'.[44] Notably the review concentrated entirely on the Lugosi angle and the 'white zombie' element of the film; very little was made of the slavery or native component. The focus was on Madeline as the 'just married' girl and the only male zombies mentioned were the white servants at the Castle of the Living Dead.

The connection between Legendre's look and the zombie Madeline is central to understanding the gender politics of the film. Ellen Draper has defined a group of 1930s and 1940s American horror films, including *Svengali*, *Mad Love*, *Bride of Frankenstein*, *White Zombie* and *The Black Cat* as 'zombie women' films, so called because 'the heroine becomes, or is threatened with becoming, a zombie in conjunction with her enslavement by a villain'.[45] For Draper, they form a unique grouping of 'fully fledged villains' whose power is manifested through 'the film's equation of their gaze with the gaze of the camera', which then subdues the heroine and bends her to their will. There are several issues with this, not least that only one of the above films features a zombie, that Poelzig's gaze at the female characters in *The Black Cat* barely functions in this fashion, and that Imhotep's lustful gaze at Helen in *The Mummy* is surely one of the most powerful examples of the model yet is not mentioned. Nonetheless, Draper's broader point, that 'the zombie women films began appearing as soon as sound films did, as if an exploration of the camera's domination of women were an immediate and natural concern as Hollywood developed the classical studio style' is an important one.[46]

Of all the villains in 1930s horror films, Legendre has one of the most overtly powerful gazes, and of all the submissive heroines, Madeline is one of the weakest; when zombified her passivity only increases. After her funeral, Legendre and Beaumont return to the tomb to collect her corpse. The white male zombies lift up the coffin lid to reveal Madeline, who appears to be sleeping soundly in the sumptuous coffin; her head nestles softly on the quilted silk lining. Perhaps she is not dead after all; the zombie potion appears to have sent her into a state of catalepsy. This is something never made entirely clear in the film and nor was it questioned in the critical reception; the term 'living dead' at this time appears to have encompassed those who are treated as dead but who are yet, paradoxically, still living a kind of shadowed, half-life. With this revelation, Madeline's literary forebear is suddenly apparent. She is not the first fictional Madeline to be buried alive: that honour falls to Lady Madeline Usher in Edgar Allan Poe's story 'The Fall of the House of Usher'.[47] On closer inspection the women have more in common than name and premature burial, Poe's story prefigures many elements of *White Zombie*'s Madeline, a point possibly not lost upon the *Film Daily* writer who described the film as 'a morbidly gripping Poe-esque fantasy' and the *Chicago Daily Tribune* scribe who wrote of its 'eerily Poe-ish backgrounds'.[48] Poe's Madeline succumbs to a wasting disease which the doctors are powerless to control, characterised, as the unnamed narrator explains, by 'a settled apathy, a gradual wasting away of the person, and frequent although transient affections of a partially cataleptical character'.[49] Upon her inevitable death, her twin brother (the hypochondriac and hysteric, Roderick) temporarily entombs her body in the dank family vault. Yet as Roderick and the narrator remove Madeline to her temporary resting place, the narrator cannot help but remark upon the bloom of youth that stretches across Madeline's visage, 'the mockery of a faint blush upon the bosom and the face, and that suspiciously lingering smile upon the lip which is so terrible in death'.[50] A week after her internment, the two men hear scratching in the darkness of the tomb. Roderick realises he has buried her alive and screams 'oh, pity me, miserable wretch that I am! ...*We have put her living in the tomb!*'[51] He dashes to her aid too late. Her final exertions have ruined her and with her final breath she dies, a bloodied corpse in her brother's arms.

In Jean Epstein's film *La chute de la maison Usher* (1928), Madeline is the submissive, mute wife to her deranged and sadistic painter husband Roderick, who keeps her in seclusion. In a twist on Oscar Wilde's *The Picture of Dorian Gray* (1890), painting becomes a vampiric act; the more he paints her portrait, the closer she slips into death, each brush stroke stripping her of her life force. When she finally expires she does so in such a quiet and meek manner that the protagonist and Roderick do not even realise until they trip over her corpse on the floor. In all three fictional versions, Madeline is characterised with ethereal feminine passivity. When the narrator of Poe's tale first encounters Madeline, he tells us she '[passed] through a remote portion of the apartment, and, without having noticed my presence, disappeared'.[52] In each tale she drifts around the edge of the scenery, doe-eyed and acquiescing to men; in Epstein's film she is a tiny cowed figure, adrift and floating through vast baronial halls in a haze of dust motes.

When Madeline Usher returns from her premature burial, Epstein dresses her in a ragged white dress with a veil hanging over her face, her long black hair plastered against her feverish skin. She stretches out her arms, lumbering forward and swaying from side to side. Her head is tilted limply across her right shoulder, she remains struck dumb, her agony explicit yet incapable of being verbalised. It seems that Epstein's Madeline is closer to the zombie as we understand them today, for *White Zombie*'s Madeline is rather less ghoulish. When she is exhumed and taken to the Castle of the Living Dead, she appears, to all intents and purposes to be Madeline as she was before her burial. This is a major problem with Bellamy's performance; Madeline is as flat in life as she is in (un)death. Her demeanour remains mournful whether her soul is in this world or the next, facial expressiveness is absent and physical gestures minimal (somewhat surprising from a silent film actress). She is a blank object to be possessed as the male owner sees fit, wrapped in a veneer of white cloth.

The relationship between Madeline and Beaumont has further literary predecessors in the android Alicia Clary and Lord Ewald in Auguste Villiers de L'Isle-Adam's novel *The Future Eve* (1886) and Nathaniel and Olympia in E.T.A. Hoffmann's story 'Der Sandmann' / 'The Sandman' (1817), the latter famously analysed by Freud in his study of the uncanny. 'The Sandman' story begins as young student Nathaniel is infatuated with Olympia, a clockwork automaton built by Spalanzani, his physics professor. Even in the grip of his lust, she unsettles him. He spies on her at night and realises that 'her eyes had in general something fixed and staring about them, I could almost say she was sightless, as if she was sleeping with her eyes open. It made me feel quite uncanny, and I crept softly away...'.[53] Later, Olympia plays the piano perfectly for the assembled audience at Spalanzani's party. Nathaniel's friend Siegmund then counsels him that Olympia 'might be called beautiful if her eyes were not so completely lifeless, I could even say sightless – when she plays and sings it is with the unpleasant soulless regularity of a machine', that in fact she is 'only acting like a living creature'.[54] Beaumont gently places a necklace around Madeline's neck as she plays Liszt's *Liebestraum* at the piano (Figure 3.2). Distraught at her lack of response, Beaumont proclaims, as noted above, 'I thought that beauty alone could satisfy, but the soul has gone. I can't bear those empty staring eyes!' Olympia and Madeline are kindred spirits, automated, uncanny and soulless female bodies; docile and passive women as envisaged by their male creators. Nathaniel and Beaumont are also very much alike, obsessive men who desire the unavailable bodies of beautiful women, and meet a tragic fate as a result. Eventually, Nathaniel discovers the truth of Olympia and commits suicide. As we will see, Beaumont also meets a similarly unpleasant end.

Beaumont is not alone. The inability of men to possess women with their gaze abounds in 1930s horror films – they are 'failed gazers'. In *Mystery of the Wax Museum*, deformed sculptor Ivan Igor (Lionel Atwill) possesses women by embalming them in wax and

Figure 3.2 Charles Beaumont (Robert Frazer) is devastated: having brought his intended lover Madeline Short (Madge Bellamy) back from the dead as his zombie, she fails to respond to his amorous advances in *White Zombie* (1932, Victor Halperin).

exhibiting them in his museum. When Igor attempts to embalm the heroine, Charlotte Duncan (Fay Wray), the police rescue her and Igor is shot, falling into a vat of his own wax. In *Mad Love* Dr Gogol (Peter Lorre) desires actress Yvonne Orlac, but when she refuses his advances he steals a waxwork that she resembles. In a self-conscious referencing of Ovid's story of Pygmalion and Galatea, he names the waxwork Galatea and urges it to come to life. Inevitably the time comes when Yvonne must substitute herself for the waxwork, and when Gogol discovers that his Galatea is a real, breathing woman he is overcome with a deadly passion. He is shot dead by Yvonne's husband as he attempts to strangle her.

Perhaps Madeline also has something in common with these women. One contemporary reviewer described her performance as 'waxen'.[55] Igor, Gogol, Beaumont and even the mummy Imhotep are just a few examples of the 1930s horror film's failed gazers, bound up in sadomasochistic love and unrequited desire. Each man is doomed in his attempt to possess an unavailable woman, each fails and dies by the *dénouement*, via gunshot, suicide or, in Imhotep's case, crumbling into dust. Of course, this does not bode well for Legendre, and certainly not Beaumont: as the instigator of the male gaze he will suffer the worst fate of all.

Overcome with remorse, Beaumont appeals to Legendre to restore life to Madeline. The *bokor* proposes a toast and doses Beaumont's glass with zombie poison. A moment too late, Beaumont realises his drink is spiked, and silently backs away from his host. Legendre calmly states, 'I have taken a fancy to *you* Monsieur!', Beaumont weakly whispers 'No, not that, not that' and the ensuing fade to black insinuates everything. In the following scenes Beaumont has been struck dumb by the poison, slumping over the dining table and writhing in agony. Legendre sits opposite him and in a protracted static shot of over 30 seconds Beaumont slowly reaches across to his tormentor, knocking over his wine glass in the process. His hand comes to rest on Legendre's and he stares into the *bokor*'s eyes. The zombie master reciprocates; he puts his free hand on top of Beaumont's and says 'well, well'. Beaumont slumps back into the chair, defeated. His last important moment in the narrative has passed, and he doesn't arise from the table until the very last few frames of the film. Utterly submissive, his body given over to the whims of the *bokor*, he has become a white male zombie and his penance for taking Madeline is almost complete.

Neil has discovered that his wife's corpse has been stolen, and enlisting the aid of Bruner, has travelled to Legendre's castle. In a typically ineffectual manner, he passes out when they get into the grand hall. Legendre instructs Madeline to stab Neil but Bruner thwarts her. For a moment she returns to consciousness and finds herself privy to a rather Macbethian moment; she stands over her husband, confused, clutching a dagger. She runs out onto the veranda and tries to throw herself off the cliff, but is prevented by the suddenly recovered Neil. Legendre's henchmen surround him, and he shoots Chauvin, whose pop-eyed gaze never falters as he stares down the camera lens. A last moment of shock: the zombie finally addresses the audience in the same fashion as Legendre. Neil's escape from the white male zombies is hardly as thrilling: he scrambles past them as they walk off the side of the cliff: the very perfunctory nature of their deaths was picked up in the *New York Times* review, that when zombies 'have served their fell purposes, they can walk off high cliffs and out of the picture'.[56] Beaumont unexpectedly appears and throws Legendre off the cliff before committing suicide, launching himself into the icy depths of the sea below. Beaumont's final gesture completes his masochistic narrative: as we have already seen in *The Mummy*, *Mystery of the Wax Museum* and *Mad Love*, death is the only possible outcome for the failed gazer.

All monsters and characters of generally dubious intent have been despatched over the side of the cliff. Now, it merely remains for the uncanny female cadaver to be restored to life. In the various source tales this return can be dramatic. In Poe's tale, Madeline Usher's return is theatrical. The vault doors are flung open and she emerges in a bloodied shroud, her emaciated frame ruined by her struggle, and 'with a low moaning cry' she falls upon her brother and 'now final death agonies, bore him to the floor a corpse, and a victim to the terrors he had anticipated'.[57] Similarly, in another key source for the script, *The Magic Island*, the ending is equally horrible. *White Zombie* evidently borrows heavily from Seabrook's account of 'Camille', which Paravisini-Gebert argues is the proto-type narrative for female zombification. As she explains, the nar-rative of 'Camille' includes:

> The coveting of a beautiful, light-skinned or white upper-class girl by an older, dark-skinned man who is of lower class and is adept at sor-cery; the intimations of necromantic sexuality with a girl who has lost her volition; the wedding night (in this case it is the anniversary) as the preferred setting for the administration of the zombie poison; the girl's eventual escape from the *bokor* in her soiled wedding clothes (the garment of preference for white or light-skinned zombie women); her madness and ultimate confinement in a convent or mental asylum.[58]

On the evening of her first wedding anniversary, Camille dresses in her finest as she is instructed to join her husband Matthieu Toussel at a celebratory party. She is taken to an outbuilding where she is instructed to dine with four corpses, her husband explaining:

> 'I beg you to forgive my guests their seeming rudeness. It has been a long time since they have tasted wine, sat like this at a table with so fair a hostess. But, ah, presently they will drink with you, yes, lift their arms, as I lift mine, clink glasses with you, more they will arise and dance with you...'.[59]

Horrified, Camille escapes Toussel, and in the morning a group of peasant women find her lying unconscious on the road. With shock, they discover 'her filmy dress was ripped and torn, her lit-tle white satin bride-slippers were scuffed and stained, one of the high heels ripped off – she was only half conscious, incoherent', and with Toussel missing, Camille is left with a tale whose 'credibility depends on the evidence of a demented girl'.[60] Without proof, Camille goes mad. So, Poe produces a bloodied corpse, Seabrook offers insanity and delirium; but what does *White Zombie* give us? Much like the summary despatching of the villains, Madeline's res-titution is very simple. As Legendre dies, Madeline's eyelids flut-ter. She smiles at her husband and whispers, 'oh Neil, I dreamed...'. The couple embrace and the film fades to black for the final time.

This is, of course, entirely unsatisfactory. Madeline Usher and Seabrook's Camille haunt Madeline Short throughout the film, yet they fail to leave a trace upon the conclusion. Much of what is written on Haitian zombies suggests that the passive deadness that characterises their outward appearance is not replicated internally; that the zombie is aware of everything that is going on, but can do nothing to prevent it. Hence, if Madeline was cognisant of everything that happened to her, these final moments have the propensity to be the most appalling of all. They finally free her character and offer the opportunity to recount or relive, for perhaps just a few moments, the horror of being buried alive and then being disinterred in order to become a soft, accommodating plaything of an evil voodoo master. Her torment need not even be vocalised: in my alternative ending Madeline retreats from her husband's embrace. She steadily holds his gaze, represented through a big close up of her eerie, stricken eyes, her look a mirror image of Legendre's assaultive stare. This close up communicates everything, of the horror that she has endured, the mental and physical violations. Such is the nature of her degradation, it cannot be verbally expressed: silence beats on the soundtrack, the horror cannot pass her lips. In this silent yet heartfelt communication, Neil would know that life for the couple could never be the same again. Normality could not resume. Most frustratingly, the final few frames of *White Zombie* offer the opportunity to make a real statement, but instead the returned wife slumps into her husband arms, mutters the comforting, 'oh Neil, I dreamed', and the horror is washed away like the waves lapping at the shore beneath the castle.

Of course, the film's gender politics is not the only problem unresolved by its conclusion; the final fade to black eliminates any further discussion of race. The black male zombies are left toiling in the fields, the troubling image of slavery ignored to depict the solution of something more manageable: the restitution of the white heroine. Writing on Romero's 1970s and 1980s zombie films, Robin Wood points out:

It has not, I think, been sufficiently recognised that the meaning and function of the zombies changes radically from film to film. It is consistent, in fact, in only one way – that the zombies constitute a challenge to the humans, not merely to survive but to *change*. But the nature of the challenge differs from film to film.[61]

This astute observation has its relevance for 1930s zombies too, with their dual function as slavery allegory and alternative mode of gendered possession. But Wood's idea that the zombie challenges people to change – which in *White Zombie*'s case would apply to racial and gender politics – is not consistently worked through in the film. As Edna Aizenberg comments, 1930s and 1940s zombie films simply transpose 'the zombie from enslaved black victim vitiated by white colonisation to virginal white victim menaced by black erotic rites'.[62] *White Zombie*'s uniqueness emerges from the film's origins in Seabrook's outré travelogue, in which he reflects 'werewolves, vampires, and demons were certainly no novelty. But I recalled one creature I had been hearing about in Haiti, which sounded exclusively local – the zombie'.[63] Its interest for studies of 1930s horror film and the idea of a specific cycle of horror cinema during this period comes from its Haitian setting, which taps into public perception of the island's voodoo heritage, a cultural inquisitiveness charged by the bestselling *The Magic Island* and colonial ideologies of contemporary occupation. The 1930s undead were represented (and interpreted in the media) as an exciting glimpse into native voodoo practices quite distinct from America's gothic horror lineage. Yet the film's narrative structure draws heavily on the gothic canon (with a liberal dosing of Poe and Hoffmann) and contains many haunting, timeless moments. Former silent film star Bellamy is so incredibly dull that the audience is unable to differentiate between her acting living and dead, black actors are accorded screen time but disappear into the mist as the narrative dispenses with them, and a penniless émigré actor already famous for his portrayal of a vampire is drawn to the poverty row in order to capitalise on his success. He stares into the camera, carves wax dolls and performs on the same sets that made him famous a year earlier. The end result is uncanny, however you look at it.

4

VAMPYR AND THE EUROPEAN
AVANT-GARDE

Vampyr is a peculiarly difficult film to write about.[1]

Robin Wood, 'On Carl Dreyer' (1974)

A s Robin Wood suggests, *Vampyr: Der Traum des Allan Gray /
Vampyr: The Strange Adventure of David Gray (1932) is awkward.
It goes by a number of different titles, is often screened with several different language prints cut together, and nobody is entirely
clear what to call the lead character.[2] What is more, *Vampyr*'s narrative and visual composition is at times almost impossible to
interpret, the film refuses coherence and any sustained attempt to
explain director Carl Theodor Dreyer's unique world concretely
seems doomed to failure. It is a very different kind of film to the
others discussed in *After Dracula*, not only in its unorthodox production history (as discussed later) but also in its context as both
European art cinema and horror film. Ginette Vincendeau points
out that categorising works as 'art cinema' reduces the diversity
of European films and filmmakers to one aspect of the international markets and further entrenches Hollywood as the 'norm' of
filmmaking.[3] Similarly, in *Cutting Edge: Art-Horror and the Horrific
Avant-Garde*, Joan Hawkins lists *Vampyr* alongside *Nosferatu* as
'high-end' horror cinema, before arguing that 'avant-garde cinema is just as diverse in scope and quality as horror cinema. The
European art film is so diverse that it is generally not represented
as a genre at all'.[4] Nonetheless, when Vincendeau suggests that
across the decades, the 'typical' European art film is 'a different
kind of spectatorial experience – loose, ambiguous narratives,
characters in search of meaning rather than action, overt direc-
torial expression . . . and a slower pace', the positive aspects of
thinking of *Vampyr* as a kind of European art-horror film become

more evident.[5] As such, while *Vampyr* may not be the first film to resist interpretation, it is certainly one of the earliest horror films to create this sense of elusiveness. Consequently I do not attempt a definitive reading but instead consider it as a kind of cinematic dream-work, deploying psychoanalytic ideas and terminology. I argue that Dreyer's inimitable treatment of vampirism emerges from its indistinct narrative, slow pacing and appeal to the unconscious, all arguably present as a result of its art cinema sensibilities, private funding and interwar European cultural context.

THE EUROPEAN AVANT-GARDE

Vampyr's Danish director Dreyer had already found international acclaim with his previous film, *La Passion de Jeanne d'Arc*, produced by Parisian Société Générale des Films and released in 1928. Britain banned *Joan of Arc*, *Film Weekly* speculating at the time that the 'censor's main objection is believed to be the scenes depicting the burning of Joan at the stake, and to certain scenes in which Joan is seen partaking of the Eucharist'.[6] While *Joan of Arc* was a commercial failure, Ib Monty notes that it was critically 'considered the last of the great silent films, a summing up of the French avant-garde movement'.[7] It received only a very limited, non-commercial release in America, opening in New York in March 1929, at which point Mordaunt Hall of the *New York Times* proclaimed 'America benefits where Britain loses, for as a film work of art this takes precedence over anything that has so far been produced – it fills one with such intense admiration that other pictures appear but trivial in comparison'.[8] Yet it was generally received with little interest in the States as a whole, which Jean and Dale R. Drum posit is partially because 'by the time it arrived sound film had already become established, and silent films did not generate much interest'.[9] *Joan of Arc*'s financial failure led the funding organisation to refuse to honour its contract to finance another of Dreyer's films. Dreyer sued and won, but was embittered by the experience and also the changing climate of filmmaking.[10] As David Rudkin comments, Dreyer 'had always assumed as his right the absolute creative-critical control over every aspect of his work', but the increasingly industrialised film industry now did not agree.[11]

For *Vampyr*, Dreyer sought out private funding, and the film was a co-production between Tobis Klangfilm (Berlin) and Filmproduktion Carl Dreyer (Paris), financed by Baron Nicolas de Gunzberg, a young man from a wealthy Belgian family, who played the lead role of David Gray under the pseudonym 'Julian West'.[12] It was filmed over the space of a year on the outskirts of Paris; British film magazine *Close Up* enthusiastically reported on filming in the neighbourhood of Montargis between April and October 1930, which accords with de Gunzberg's memory of shooting sequences in the spring of 1930.[13] The timing of *Vampyr* is crucial as it emerges on the cusp of sound cinema and was simultaneously shot as a silent and a sound film. When dialogue was required, the actors did additional takes, miming their lines in English, French and German, with actual dialogue added in post-production at Universum Film AG (Ufa) in Berlin.[14] The horror elements did create problems for the production as the Berlin censorship board demanded cuts of 53 metres, including the vampire staking, and shortening the doctor's death scene. The BBFC passed it uncut on 31 January 1933 but it was held back until May when it received the new 'H' for horror certificate.[15]

The film did not premiere in Berlin until 6 May 1932 by which point, as Caspar Tybjerg points out, 'the title made some people worry that Dreyer had been swept up in the fashion for horror unleashed in 1931 with the release of the three great classics *Dracula*, *Frankenstein* and *Dr Jekyll and Mr Hyde*'.[16] But *Vampyr* offers a completely different context for horror unrelated to the American talkie cycle. *Dracula* was filmed between September and November 1930 and released in February 1931, long after *Vampyr*'s filming was complete.[17] Instead, Dreyer's vampire film arose from the commercial failure of his avant-garde production *Joan of Arc*, was funded privately by enthusiastic amateur de Gunzberg, and was pan-European, made by a Danish director (who had previously worked at Ufa alongside Thea von Harbou and Karl Freund), shot and funded in France, premiered in Berlin and produced in three different European language versions. Yet when asked whether *Vampyr* was regarded as French or German, de Gunzberg replies 'well, it was really regarded as a Dreyer film and no nationality seemed to be applied to it'.[18]

In a sense, de Gunzberg's idea of *Vampyr* simply being a 'Dreyer film' has its uses, particularly in relation to understanding its eclectic and avant-garde influences. A unique aspect arising from Dreyer's complete control over production is that *Vampyr* uses diverse European cultural sources without being wholly sub-sumed into any of them. For example, there are parallels with the preoccupations of the early Surrealists, particularly their pen-chant for daydreams, passivity and psychoanalysis; Dreyer also claimed to be influenced by Swedish director Victor Sjöström: certainly visual and tonal echoes of Sjöström's supernatural epic *Körkarlen/The Phantom Carriage* (1921) are marked upon *Vampyr*'s surfaces.[19] Des O'Rawe also suggests that the film chimes with the Weimar Bauhaus experiments with sound, drawing upon the work of Kandinsky and Moholy-Nagy, and 'the work of graphic filmmakers such as Hans Richter [and] Walter Ruttmann – who, throughout the 1920s, attempted to extend into film their experi-ments with sound painting, tone colour, rhythmical imagery and aural animation'.[20] The film also owes a debt to Epstein's *La chute de la maison Usher*, discussed in the previous chapter on *White Zombie*. The similarities are sufficiently explicit to be noted in the *Observer* review, which described *Vampyr* as 'a return to the early silent French films', and 'very similar in treatment to *The Fall of the House of Usher*: Mist swirling, heavily gauzed, and unfocused scenes'.[21] While Epstein's film is a specific visual point of refer-ence, the early stages of Surrealism (before Salvador Dalí joined the group in 1929) are arguably the major avant-garde influence on *Vampyr*. Emerging from the last vestiges of Dada in Paris in the early 1920s, and founded by André Breton, Surrealism emerged with an obsession for accessing the unconscious, initially through automatic writing.[22] To be an artist in Paris during this period must have been inspiring; as Malte Hagener notes, it was 'not only home to avant-garde filmmakers activists and theoreticians from all over France, but also from Spain and Italy, from Great Britain and Germany, from Brazil and Romania'.[23] Seeing *Vampyr* as influenced by and part of a product of this period is not a huge conceptual leap, as Dreyer explained:

> At the time I made *Vampyr* I had been living in Paris for four or five years. In Paris at that time, you couldn't help but be caught up in the excitement and the imagination which the various artists and movements created, whether 'cubism', 'Dadaism', 'Surrealism', or what have you. I knew several painters and I was involved in discussions with and about them. So, of course, I was influenced, but by the excitement, the energy, the variety of work, not by any particular painter or movement. At the time of *Vampyr* I was 'over head and ears' in interest in abstract art.[24]

The Surrealists attacked the films of Epstein and Dreyer, as they abhorred cinema that was deliberately intellectual, calling it pretentious. Indeed, when writing on Epstein's film, Robert Desnos snidely suggested that 'Epstein's lack, or rather paralysis, of imagination is revealed'.[25] Later, when the French Surrealist Group created a list of directors whose work should be seen, they included James Whale, Tod Browning and F.W. Murnau, director of *Nosferatu*, and emphatically positioned Dreyer in the 'Don't See' list.[26] Despite this there are clear parallels between the 1920s avant-garde and Surrealism, exemplified by texts such as *Vampyr* that combine the tonal qualities of Epstein with the spirit of *L'Âge d'Or* (1930). Indeed, as Ian Christie points out, despite the Surrealists' emphatic claims to the contrary, Surrealism 'could easily be seen – and was – as yet another faction in the avant-garde'.[27] The key connection here is the apparent fascination with the unconscious of both the Surrealists and *Vampyr*, the bringing together of waking and sleeping states, of irrationality and impossibility. As the founder of Surrealism André Breton stated in the first *Manifesto of Surrealism* in 1924, 'I believe in the future resolution of these two states, dream and reality, which are seemingly so contradictory, into an absolute kind of reality, a surreality, if one may so speak'.[28] While *Vampyr* is certainly not the only 1930s horror film to draw upon European art and design movements (as the following chapter on modernism and *The Black Cat* shows), it appears at a key moment in European film culture: the cinematic avant-garde came to prominence in the 1920s and peaked by 1930, synchronised sound emerging in cinema in the middle, the horror genre following closely after.[29]

The following analysis explores how *Vampyr*'s myriad artistic influences, unusual production context and historical positioning work together to create a spectacularly dense and haunting text, with staring characters, oblique narratives and a languid, almost somnambulant tone. The film begins as protagonist David Gray arrives at the village of Courtempierre and takes a room at an inn. He is confronted in the night by the châtelain, who gives him a parcel with instructions that it must not be opened until the châtelain has died. The next morning, Gray takes a stroll through the village and witnesses the village doctor working with the elderly female vampire Marguerite Chopin, then wanders up to the Château de Courtempierre. Peering in through a window, he witnesses the châtelain being killed by Peg Leg, a soldier in Chopin's service.[30] Viewed entirely in shadows, the châtelain opens a door to retire to bed, then Peg Leg steps forward and fires a gun into the châtelain's chest. David Rudkin notes, 'he is shot by a shadow – at least, that is how the shooting is dramatised onscreen. The shadow is that of the karporal moving aside a door and lifting the shadow of his rifle – Shadow or not, the shot he fires is real enough'.[31] It is an avant-garde murder. In addition to being depicted through shadows, the image is presented upside down through flickering candlelight. The majority of the frame is composed of white space with the shadows of upside-down characters presented on the edges of the frame. In addition, the actual shooting is hidden by the shadows of the chateau, further complicating and obscuring the moment of murder.

Gray witnesses the first death through a screened window, the lattice work barring him from the château interior and removing him from the narrative action. David Bordwell observes that Gray is curious in that 'he "does" comparatively little in relation to the principal story action' and that 'he exists less to act than to mediate'.[32] Mark Nash, too, remarks that Gray is continually excluded from the story and that the château manservant usurps him as the hero, relegating Gray 'to an auxiliary role'.[33] My reading of *Vampyr* is that even though Gray is at times 'distanced'

from the action through a variety of narrative and visual mechanisms, he still possesses an active gaze: something that is evident
through the recently released Criterion Collection film restoration that includes new scenes and will be analysed later in the
chapter. Nonetheless, in reflecting on the complexity of *Vampyr*,
I'm not suggesting that Gray can be read as an unproblematic
'hero' figure. Gray's observations are often from behind doors or
windows: he is an outsider peering in; he regularly finds himself
looking through a frame within a frame, distancing him from the
action. There is a constant tension between narrative and image,
between the need for Gray to move forward throughout the story
and the characters, props and buildings that block his way and
thwart his progress.

The opening credits of the film claim that *Vampyr* is 'freely
adapted' from Sheridan Le Fanu's short story collection *In a Glass
Darkly* (1872); the vampire story 'Carmilla' is often considered the
main influence. The scenes in *Vampyr* where a female vampire
bites an innocent young girl are, however, the only events that
draw, even loosely, from the original text.

The châtelain dies and a coach driver is sent to fetch the police;
Gray then opens the châtelain's parcel and finds a book entitled
The History of Vampires. As Gray reads, one of the châtelain's two
daughters, Léone, is drawn out of the house and into the clutches
of Chopin. An exterior long shot frames the scene: beneath a large
tree, Léone lies on her back on a stone slab. Black-robed Chopin
bends over her neck, but the distant framing denies the audience
the opportunity to see either a bite or blood. The single bite is
obscured in the haziness of the image, while the framing of the
shot means that it is impossible to see clearly. Chopin lifts her
head from Léone's neck, and hobbles away leaving her drained
and unconscious. When Léone is taken to her room, she moans
as the nurse sponges her neck: the implied penetration is apparent. Barbara Creed suggests that this moment suggests lesbian
desire between Chopin and Léone, and Robin Wood describes
it as a 'macabre lesbian seduction scene', yet the scene lacks the
intimacy of close ups and Léone does not respond, suggesting that
desire is not felt by both women.[34] Despite the promise made by
the opening credits, the story of 'Carmilla' is only a lure, and there

are few points of correlation between the novella and film. The narrative substantially increases the age of the female vampire, transforming her from a young beautiful woman into an elderly crone. This departs from the original lesbian reading of the text that charts the relationship between two young and beautiful women.

The servants carry Léone into the house and upstairs to her bedroom. She sits up in bed and cries for her 'damned' soul (Figure 4.1). Her sister Gisèle attempts to comfort her, but Léone suddenly smiles and gazes greedily back, in the grip of a vampiric and incestuous blood lust (Figure 4.2); she opens her black eyes wide and exposes her white glistening teeth. Léone's bloodlust is communicated through the smallest movements of the actor's face, Sybille Schmitz's unearthly and unsettling acting chiming with Dreyer's confession, some 35 years later, that what he ultimately seeks is to obtain 'a penetration to my actors' profound thoughts

Figure 4.1 'If only could die!': Léone (Sybille Schmitz) sits up in bed, distraught, as she realises she has become the vampire's victim in *Vampyr* (1932, Carl Theodor Dreyer).

Figure 4.2 The audience as vampire: the camera is positioned from Léone's point of view as she gazes with incestuous bloodlust, at her younger sister Gisèle (Rena Mandel) in *Vampyr* (1932, Carl Theodor Dreyer).

by means of their most subtle expressions. For these are the expressions that reveal the character of the person, his unconscious feelings, the secrets that lie in the depths of his soul'.[35] Vampirism is not evoked through the erotic representation of Sapphism or the detailed depictions of wounds, but through Schmitz's performance and the obtuse presentation of Chopin's assault. Writing on Chopin's attack in the mist, Rudkin suggests that: 'we have to strain to see this through the baffling haze – it is a moral effect too: by denying us what in a film we most need – visibility – we are metaphorically put into the predicament of the vampire herself, straining for what *she* most needs'.[36] Although Rudkin's alignment of spectator and vampire is excessive, his comments resonate with broader issues regarding the film's treatment of vision. The haziness of the vampire attack undermines the ability of the audience to see what is happening; the moment of horror is hidden away like the shooting of the châtelain.

THE DREAM OF LÉONE'S INJECTION

The village doctor (who secretly works for Chopin) arrives to treat Léone. She grimaces as she is examined, her countenance pale, her eyes dark and her large teeth exposed. Her eyes remain closed, and when the doctor pulls back her eyelid, her eyeball rolls back in her head. In a moment reminiscent of the eye and the razor-blade in *Un Chien Andalou* (1929), Léone's eyes reveal only a fleshy white opaque surface, while the horribleness of her medical examination bears similarities to Freud's story of his patient Irma. In *The Interpretation of Dreams* Freud recounts a morbid dream that centres on an unpleasant examination of Irma's diseased throat by Freud and his physician friends. In the dream Freud meets Irma in a great hall and realises she is ill. He peers into her throat, Irma initially resists and then her mouth 'opens wide, and I find a large white spot on the right, and elsewhere I see extensive greyish-white scabs adhering to curiously curled forma-tions, which are evidently shaped like the turbinal bones of the nose'.[37] Freud calls upon his colleagues to examine the unfortunate Irma, and the physician Leopold calls attention to 'an infiltrated portion of skin on the left shoulder (which I feel, in spite of the dress)'.[38]

In his analysis of the dream, Freud decides that the meaning lies in a desire for professional revenge against his colleagues Otto and Dr M., Freud's dream has, however, also been interpreted as a disavowal of potential connections between the body of the woman and abjection. In his seminar 'The Dream of Irma's Injection', Jacques Lacan re-reads Freud's dream for his students. Lacan reinterprets the central point of the dream, the revelation of the interior of Irma's throat:

> There's a horrendous discovery here, that of the flesh one never sees, the foundation of things, the other side of the head, of the face, the secretory glands par excellence, the flesh from which everything exudes, at the very heart of the mystery, the flesh in as much as it is suffering, is formless, in as much as its form in itself is something which provokes anxiety. Spectre of anxiety, identification of anxiety, the final revelation of *you are this – You are this, which is so far from you, this which is the ultimate formlessness.*[39]

For Lacan, Freud's unveiling of Irma's mouth is a moment of revelation, unnameable and unlocatable, 'the abyss of the feminine organ from which all life emerges, this gulf of the mouth, in which everything is swallowed up, and no less the image of death in which everything comes to its end'.[40] Lacan's 'ultimate formlessness' is then intrinsically bound up with the horror of the female body; Michael Grant argues that it is 'this equation between the abject and the feminine body that points most clearly to the source of Kristeva's concept, Lacan's interpretation of Freud's account of his dream of Irma's injection'.[41] The examination of Léone resonates with Irma's experience; the bodies of both women are opened up for the prying eyes of the (male) medical profession. The revelation of Léone's squishy, white eyeball, a pale smooth surface, marks Léone not only as monstrous, but also as the prey of the female vampire. There is something here that exists in the realm beyond the field of the visible; Chopin's figurative absence, her 'formlessness' extends beyond her physical presence, emerging in the moment of the examination of her victim.

The doctor insists that Gray provides a blood transfusion, but he intends to give the blood to Chopin, rather than to the sick girl. He then leaves a bottle of poison at her bedside and encourages Léone to commit suicide, thereby relinquishing her soul to the vampire. The doctor can be read as an inversion of Van Helsing, refuting the traditional gothic narrative in which the medical man, or man of great learning, is a positive force of correction. In *Vampyr* the doctor is a transgressor on a par with Chopin, aligned in their ability to extract blood from the living: where Chopin uses fangs, the doctor wields transfusion equipment. The doctor then penetrates Gray with his needles, and for the remainder of the film Gray oscillates between active and passive, alive and dead. He slumps on a chair on the landing, framed in medium close up with his eyes half closed, gazing into the distance. The camera slowly moves down his body to reveal his outstretched arm, punctured with transfusion tubes. Shortly afterwards, he falls unconscious.

Until this point, Gray has regularly read the châtelain's vampire book, and through him, the audience has learned how to identify and destroy the vampire. When Gray passes out, the responsibility of reading passes to the château's manservant, who then carries out the generically 'heroic' tasks of staking Chopin and killing the doctor. The vampire book is a destabilising force that problematises Gray as the traditional protagonist. In addition, it ruptures linear narrative and temporal relations. The book relates the story of Courtempierre, of Chopin the vampire and the intended suicide of her victim. Although created in the past, the book charts the present and future of the narrative, revealing what will happen next. Typically, film treatments that emphasise the printed word do so to compensate for a lack of concrete explanation in the narrative. Here, the book does not assist in unravelling the story; rather, its obtuse temporality confuses. This is typical of the film as a whole, as Jonathan Rosenbaum suggests: 'if there are few films in narrative cinema as inimical to the notion of a synopsis as Carl Dreyer's *Vampyr*, this is essentially because the narrative conventions that it uses are largely present only to be contested and dismantled'.[42] Through the medium of the printed word time is re-inscribed in an eccentric manner; the film rejects verisimilitude as the book describes the future as if it were the past.

THE EYES OF THE CORPSE

In *Vampyr* rationality rarely visits its explanations upon the text. The surreal, reality and the supernatural collide in a dream-work of unexplained and irrational events; shadows dance across the screen bereft of living bodies while the cries of farmyard creatures are often heard although we never see any. This is particularly apparent in the following section of the film, which arbitrarily divides up the body of its main protagonist in three different ways. The manservant awakens Gray and they stop Léone taking the poison; meanwhile the doctor absconds, kidnapping Gisèle. Gray pursues the doctor but soon collapses on a park bench. His body then divides into two separate entities, one translucent and one opaque. The opaque body remains slumped on the bench and the translucent double stands up and leaves. The translucent body's forthcoming escapades possess a hallucinatory and dream-like quality, yet later Gray acts upon information he discovers while in his ethereal form, so this additional character cannot be interpreted as an illusion or as imaginary.

Leaving the normal body asleep in the park, the translucent double wanders to a disused factory used by the doctor and Peg Leg. He finds an open coffin on the floor, with a blanket draped over it obscuring the identity of the corpse. The coffin lid, propped up against a wall, features the carved biblical reference *'Tu n'es que poussière et tu retourneras à la poussière'*, meaning 'Dust thou art, to dust shalt thou return'. Gray kneels down in front of the coffin and pulls back the blanket to reveal his own dead body: now three versions of Gray are incorporated into the narrative, the unconscious man on the park bench, the translucent wanderer, and the dead body in the coffin. The translucent Gray peers through a locked door and sees Gisèle tied up on a bed; he then hides when the doctor and Peg Leg return. He watches Peg Leg put the lid on top of the coffin, revealing a small glass window conveniently fashioned in the lid at eye level (Figure 4.3). As the lid goes down, the point of view switches from the translucent Gray to the cadaver in the coffin, creating a corpse-eye view. This is the ultimate frame within a frame, somewhat fitting for a protagonist who is forever peering through doors and windows.

Chopin then appears at the coffin lid window and stares directly at the camera. Chopin's presence is usually manifested through the actions of the doctor and Peg Leg and the reactions of her victims and her victim's family. She remains off-screen for the majority of the film and appears on screen for less than three minutes in total. It is notable that it is when the audience is doubly trapped – within the confines of a sealed coffin, looking through the eyes of a cadaver – that she appears. The vampire returns the look to the vulnerable audience. Nash interprets the shift of Gray's point of view from the translucent second body to the third dead body as 'Gray has somehow been transferred into the coffin alive'.[43] Bordwell argues that Gray is split into three separate bodies, where he is 'simultaneously frozen in death and fully sentient'.[44] Rejecting Nash's attempt to explain away the unexplainable, this reading follows Bordwell's point of view: the bodies in this film are not grounded in verisimilitude and do not always have a rational justification, they dissolve the boundaries of reality and

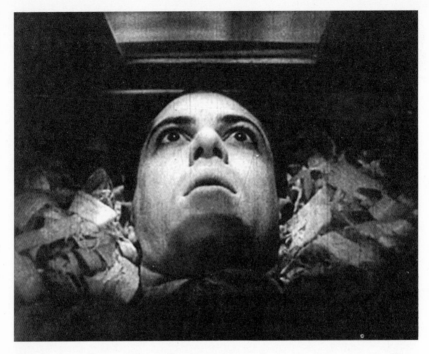

Figure 4.3   One of the most iconic images from the film: the 'dead' yet seeing protagonist David Gray (Nicolas de Gunzberg) is viewed from inside his coffin in *Vampyr* (1932, Carl Theodor Dreyer).

fantasy, death and life, sleeping and wakefulness. While attempts can be made to describe and analyse them, they often cannot be explained. Harking back to Wood's quote at the start of the chapter, *Vampyr* is difficult, awkward, ephemeral; it is polysemic and its meaning shifts, and the trebling of the male protagonist's body exemplifies the film's avant-garde nature.

The coffin is then carried outside and the procession passes the park bench where Gray lies unconscious. The *cortège* disappears, and the three fragmented bodies of Gray coalesce to become one. His reawakening signals the beginning of his final period of activity as protagonist. His function at the start of the narrative was to explore; but from the moment that his blood is taken Gray becomes as weak as Léone. Now returning from his coffin, his recuperation begins. Gray's first action is to kill the vampire: he sees the servant en route to the graveyard and follows him. They open up Chopin's grave and Gray peers in to the coffin. A pan shot reveals Chopin, seemingly asleep, her eyes shut and her face bathed in a strong white light. The servant picks up an iron bar and holds it over the vampire's chest.

This is a crucial moment at which to pause our analysis. Upon this single frame multiple analyses diverge, depending on which print, language version, or restoration is viewed. This is a crucial issue in reading *Vampyr* (harking back once again to Wood's acknowledgement of its inherent difficulty) as the staking scene fundamentally affects the reading of Gray's character. Until 2008, when Criterion and Eureka released the Martin Koerber restoration, composed of prints from Cineteca del commune di Bologna and Stiftung Deutsche Kinemathek in Berlin, the main DVD available for the home market was a poor amalgamation of several prints with dialogue dubbed in German and intratextual writing in French and Danish, as released by Image Entertainment in 1998. In the Image Entertainment version, the stake is not shown entering the body; instead the moment of penetration is suggested through an image of the sky, the camera perfectly static as clouds drift past the line of vision. The cloud movement confirms that this is not a photograph, but the product of an (undead) gaze, the crosscutting with the attack on the vampire unequivocally aligning with Chopin's point of view. A sharp, metallic clang is heard, repeating, as if a hammer strikes a blow upon the stake, but it is not shown. Most importantly, the cutting of the material implies that the servant stakes the vampire, but the recent digital restorations include the deleted scenes as extras, revealing a prolonged, brutal and quite beautiful staking, one reduced to its most essential components: a hand, a stake and a hammer. Framed in close up, in the bottom of the shot, the servant's pale hand holds tightly to the iron stake that dominates the image. With alarming speed, a heavy wooden mallet leaps down through the top of the frame and strikes down upon the head of the stake. The servant stands chest-deep in the grave, surrounded by earth and looking away from the supernatural carnage that is taking place at his feet. As the hammer rains down, Gray is revealed standing aloft of the graveside and swinging his hammer judiciously and confidently (Figure 4.4). The hammer hits the stake down through the bottom of the frame and the penetration of the vampire is

Figure 4.4   In a scene originally deleted by the censors in 1932, David Gray (Nicolas de Gunzberg) hammers the stake into the female vampire's body in *Vampyr* (1932, Carl Theodor Dreyer).

complete: Gray's victory as horror film hero is confirmed. The 'additional' scene ends and the different versions of the film re-coalesce (as much as they can). The editing, so important to the rendering of the staking scene, then offers an unambiguous link between female bodies and horror, connecting the demise of the old vampire with the recovery of her young victim. Chopin's body fades to a skeleton, and in a crosscut to the chateau, Léone sits up in bed. Her face, contorted by vampiric desire and human desperation, begins to soften. She smiles.

Shortly after Chopin's demise, the châtelain's ghost appears as a giant, moon-like face at a window and kills Peg Leg. The doctor flees to a nearby mill while Gray rescues Gisèle from the factory. Enveloped in a dense mist, the couple row across a lake and are then helped off the boat by a kindly man. They hold hands and walk through a beautiful luminous glade towards the sunlight. The remaining minutes of the film alternate between the increasingly naturalistic lighting that documents Gray and Gisèle's escape and a strange, creeping whiteness, characteristic of Dreyer's production design. As the young couple escape, the doctor steps into a large caged area in the flourmill. The door to the cage swings shut behind him and locks of its own accord. The cogs of the mill's machinery begin to grind, and the servant stands above him, working the machinery. The flour fills the cage and the doctor is buried alive. His final moments are awash with flour; his twitching hands feebly grasp at the mesh door in a desultory final attempt at freedom. The image gradually turns entirely white, its blankness signalling *Vampyr*'s final death.[45] The use of white as a dominant motif throughout the film appears to have been deliberate, although research into the production history inevitably unearths contradictory accounts. De Gunzberg contends that 'all the effects were completely natural – the mist and fog were real. Dreyer didn't use any gauze or other things in front of the camera lens at all'.[46] In a *Cahiers du cinéma* interview, however, Dreyer himself revealed that the whitewash was initially a technical error as a result of a false light being projected onto the lens. Dreyer liked the effect it created and 'henceforth, for each take, we directed a false light on the lens, by projecting it through a veil, which sent the light back to the camera'.[47] Regardless of the technical provenance, the important issue is the resultant effect: white renders the gaze opaque, another device that reinforces the impossibility of fully understanding the events on screen.

A FRENCH VAMPIRE IN LONDON

The public screening of *Vampyr* in the UK in the 1970s is a useful end point for my examination of the film, and for thinking about how and where the film might fit in a history of horror cinema. In 1976, the distribution company Cinegate reached an agreement with American film collector Raymond Rohauer to distribute his collection in the UK.[48] In June of the same year, Peter Howden, programmer at the Electric Cinema on Portobello Road, London, used the new Cinegate prints to stage a season of silent and early sound films. *Vampyr* was chosen to open the season, shown on a triple bill with two early American avant-garde shorts by James Sibley Watson, *The Fall of the House of Usher* (1928) and *Lot in Sodom* (1933).[49] *Vampyr* seems to be the obvious choice for such a theme, *The Times*' review of the season astutely noting that 'while *Joan of Arc* seems to be crying out (silently) for sound, *Vampyr*, which has sound, is essentially a silent film'.[50] The British broadsheets provided extended and quite poetic write-ups of the film, the *Observer* musing on 'Dreyer's gothic silhouettes and brilliant moonlight', while even the *New Statesman* was inspired to suggest that 'Dreyer somehow manages to imply horrors, evil wafts off the screen like a chill of bad breath'.[51]

Vampyr had reappeared at a pivotal point in the development of film horror. *The Exorcist* (1973) and *The Texas Chainsaw Massacre* (1974) had been in circulation for several years, while the Electric Cinema's screening took place in the same year that *Carrie* was released. The critics at the time explicitly stated that the film was different to modern American and British horror films; the *Financial Times* declared, 'what is remarkable about the film is how far it goes to the other extreme from the lurid Technicolour blood-letting of most modern horror films'; the *Sunday Telegraph* pleasured in a film 'in a week in which the few new films have been clotted with gouts of violent blood or grunting with animal sexuality'; while the *Sunday Times* put it more simply: '*Vampyr* makes our contemporary, explicit Draculas look like an advertisement for false teeth'.[52] Despite its seeming restraint amidst contemporary 'gouts of violent blood', *Vampyr* arguably does fall within a specific horror tradition prevalent during the 1970s, albeit a far more Continental version. *Vampyr* re-emerges at the same time as a wave of European art-horror preoccupied with the image of the woman and vampirism; this included some of the films of Jess Franco, Jean Rollin's French vampire films such as *Lèvres de sang/Lips of Blood* (1975), and Belgian director Harry Kümel's pan-European female vampire film *Les lèvres rouges/Daughters of Darkness* (1971), the latter described by Brigid Cherry (in what could easily be a review of Dreyer's film) as 'less a horror film (the blood-letting is far subtler here than in most vampire movies) than a portrait of psychic vampirism with a disturbing subtext and unsettling imagery'.[53] Therefore, if we follow Ernest Mathijs and Jamie Sexton's understanding of art-horror loosely as non-American art films that contain 'features of the horror genre' and make isolated appearances in the market, *Vampyr*'s art cinema qualities, cultural and production context and play upon the horror genre, mark it upon initial release as an early and important contributor to European art-horror, alongside *Nosferatu* and *Häxan* (1922).[54] When the film re-emerged in the 1970s, it then took its place alongside films made decades later, which its unorthodox and artistic ways had directly influenced. Whether it is the 1930s or 1970s, *Vampyr*'s unique qualities demarcate it as part of an alternative canon quite distinct from any American film discussed in this book.

The essence of *Vampyr*'s singularity is in its status as a silent/sound hybrid that can be placed contextually within the European avant-garde but that also maintains its own distinctive and elusive character. Despite this elusiveness, this chapter has attempted to pin down some of *Vampyr*'s unruliness; isolating moments that can be understood as part of the 'loose, ambiguous narratives' of European art cinema, as influenced by the interwar avant-garde and leaning towards psychoanalysis. Such mechanisms deny the viewer the opportunity to make sense of the events on screen, and this experience of the film is not limited to viewers today; the film's strangeness appears to have engendered equally odd audience responses at the time of its release. In Germany in 1932, it received 'a rather extraordinary reception – the audience evidently hissed and booed in equal mixture with hurrahs', while at its Parisian premiere at the Raspail 216 cinema on Boulevard Raspail in January 1933, the *New York Times* reported that the spectators were either 'spellbound, as in a long nightmare or else moved – to hysterical laughter'.[55] The use of the word 'nightmare' is particularly pertinent; Dreyer has explained that in creating *Vampyr* he wanted to make a 'daydream on film', suggesting that the sinister does not come from real things, but in fact from our subconscious, 'if we are, through some occurrence or another, brought to a state of great tension, there are no limits to where our fantasy can lead us or what strange meanings we can ascribe to the real things which surround us'.[56] *Vampyr*'s avant-garde roots can perhaps be found in a return to the first *Manifesto of Surrealism,* for its inexplicable horror chimes with Breton's claims for the purpose of the Surrealists:

> Everything tends to make us believe that there exists a certain point of mind at which life and death, the real and the imagined, past and future, the communicable and the incommunicable, high and low, cease to be perceived as contradictions. Now, search as one may one will never find any other motivating force in the activities of the Surrealists than the hope of finding and fixing this point.[57]

Arguably, Breton's desire for that 'certain point of mind' was found in this film, made only a few years after he wrote the manifesto: in the space opened up by the lack of 'contradiction' between the living and dead, real and imagined, the hero of *Vampyr* hunts for the vampire. In its amalgamation of 'high' art cinema and 'low' horror culture, combined with its 'incommunicable' nature, *Vampyr* remains slippery to demarcate, resistant to definition. In an interview with *Film Comment* in 1966, two years before his death, Dreyer pleaded for filmmakers to find their own style, to avoid following the standard form 'and we shall try to make more and more individualistic films, and on individualistic terms, so that we say that we *feel* the director and the style of the director in the film. Otherwise we will be making the same thing again and again'.[58] He had already achieved this in *Vampyr*, a inimitable contribution to European art film and horror cinema: his presence is felt in the film's unique qualities, and he is as much part of the film as Gray himself.

5

BAUHAUS OF HORROR: FILM ARCHITECTURE AND *THE BLACK CAT*

In a gleaming glass and steel house built on the remains of a wartime fortress, three men are drinking whisky, their images reflected in the gleaming Bakelite floor and long Corbusier ribbon windows. Crime writer Peter Alison (David Manners) makes small talk with his host, architect Hjalmar Poelzig (Boris Karloff) while psychiatrist Dr Werdegast (Bela Lugosi) comments on the 'atmosphere of death' that pervades the house.[1] Civility crumbles as Werdegast sees Poelzig's black cat. The tumbler falls from his hand and smashes on the floor; Werdegast throws a knife at the cat and kills it. Peter's ill wife, Joan, wearing only a thin white nightgown, then drifts into the room, and greets her host absentmindedly. Suddenly overwhelmed with lust for her new husband, she passionately kisses Peter, at the same time a focus pull reveals a bronze statuette of a naked woman in the foreground of the image. The woman is reclining with both arms stretched out behind her back, accentuating her physical form and suggesting sexual availability. Poelzig grips the arm of the statuette tightly, his desire for Joan relocated to the cold caress of the figurine.

As you can tell from the description of this intense and perverse scene, the primary way that horror is suggested in *The Black Cat* (1934) is from its modernist set design and the interplay of the characters with their surroundings. In their work on set design in 1930s cinema, Tim Bergfelder, Sue Harris and Sarah Street have argued that 'it is almost impossible to disaggregate the function of the set from a number of other constitutive parts of the *mise-en-scène*, including elements such as props and accessories, costume and make-up, and not least the performance of the actors'.[2] Bearing this in mind, this chapter discusses film and architectural space to explore the complex relationship between set design, modernism and horror. For Steven Jacobs, the re-evaluation of spatial perception inherent in modernist buildings can be understood as 'a new optical paradigm – often compared with the medium of cinema'.[3] Thus, film architecture may be fictional architecture, but for Hans Dieter Schaal the lack of reality is unimportant, for 'film architecture is an architecture of meaning'.[4]

In this spirit, I explore the spatial architecture of *The Black Cat* in order to work through its modernist sensibility. As in Chapter 4, this analysis will be worked through in relation to European influences, although the Surrealists and *Vampyr* are doing something quite different to the modernists and *The Black Cat*. As Ian Christie has noted, Surrealism was 'deeply anti-Modernist, rejecting the rationalism and utopianism that had inspired many Modernists during the inter-war years, and celebrating instead the "unconscious" and excess of popular culture, as found in genre films'.[5] So while *Vampyr* was understood through key Surrealist ideas of irrationality and psychoanalysis, this chapter locates another example of the 1930s horror film within a quite different Continental art context.

For Christopher Wilk, modernism in 'the designed world' emerged following the traumas of the First World War, with a determination to change society. It emerged as a socially and politically left-leaning 'loose collection of ideas' from across Europe which initially cohered around espousing the new, and often 'an equally vociferous rejection of history and tradition; a utopian desire to create a better world – an almost messianic belief in the power and potential of the machine and industrial technology – a rejection of applied ornament and decoration; an embrace of abstraction'.[6] This initial manifesto, prevalent until the worldwide economic slump of 1929, doesn't fully encompass how modernism found its way into Hollywood. Rather, the modernism that emerged in the cinema of the 1930s had lost its utopian ambitions and thrown off its political beliefs, becoming 'a style used to identify new and innovative design based on abstract, rectilinear geometry and the use of industrial forms and materials'.[7] Modernism met Hollywood in a commodified, mass-market style, emblematised by the architecture of Poelzig's house, a diffuse collection of Bauhaus, art deco and Corbusian visual tropes. Despite peaking during the interwar period, art deco is not usually considered part of modernism; its pragmatic and fashionable decorative approach is at odds with functional utopianism, leading Charlotte Benton and Tim Benton to describe art deco as modernism's 'contemporary, and rival'.[8] Definitions slip and slide, however, and as the Bentons note, 'works that have been generally accepted as Modernist are frequently included in books on art deco, or employed in other media to connote art deco attributes'.[9] 1930s set design can then be understood as part of the broader architecture and design interwar crossroads, 'a free-wheeling eclecticism that borrowed liberally, and often simultaneously, from traditional and modern sources of architecture and design'.[10] In *The Black Cat* we witness the coming together of 'modern' styles, the occasional decorative impulse of the art deco lamp, set atop the austere black Bauhaus desk. In doing this, we will see how modernist set design works within a horror context; in so doing we will ruminate upon *The Black Cat*'s uniqueness in 1930s horror film.

AILOUROPHOBIA

Edgar Allan Poe's short story 'The Black Cat' (1843) is the first-person narrative of an alcoholic predisposed to murderous rages. He gouges out the eyes of his beloved cat Pluto, hangs it and then kills his wife with an axe. He buries her corpse in the wall, accompanied by the very much alive replacement cat. The narrator's ailourophobia (his fear of cats) is unbounded; in describing his emotions towards the replacement cat his disgust oozes from the pages: 'I did not, for some weeks, strike or otherwise violently ill use it; but gradually – very gradually – I came to look upon it with unutterable loathing, and to flee silently from its odious presence, as from the breath of a pestilence'.[11] When reworking the story for cinema, however, it seems that director Edgar G. Ulmer was not too concerned about Pluto. In February 1934 he worked on the story draft with mystery writer Peter Ruric, who then produced the completed script.[12] The film was scheduled for a 15-day shoot, beginning on 28 February at Universal studios. It was initially completed on 17 March, only one day over schedule, but Ulmer was forced to film retakes over three and a half days in March, bringing the total cost to $95,745.31.[13] This is testament to Ulmer's speed: Gregory William Mank notes that a two-week shooting schedule was about half the time expected for a moderate 'A' production film, and compares this with *Dracula* (planned 36 days, took 42) and *Frankenstein* (planned 30, took 35).[14] When the film was released in May 1934 it was quickly revealed to be an adaptation in name only as the *New York Times* wryly noted: 'the acknowledgment which the producers of *The Black Cat* graciously make to Edgar Allan Poe seems a trifle superfluous, since the new film is not remotely to be identified with Poe's short story'; the *Chicago Daily Tribune* punned upon the lack of feline presence with the review title, 'Scenarists Go Poe One Better in *The Black Cat*'; while the *New York Daily News* disdainfully commented, 'the new story that was written to fit the title is so fantastically unreal that it is more apt to make one laugh at its absurdities than quake from its effects of horror'.[15] Perhaps the *Hollywood Reporter*'s review summarised the situation most succinctly. Addressing an intended trade audience of theatre managers, the writer claimed that the film managed to make Poe dull, continuing:

> That's not quite fair to Mr Poe, either, because outside of the title and the fact that a black cat does stalk around every once in a while, this is not the story your customers may have thrilled to in their reading days. Take full advantage of the exploitation possibilities and your fans' love of the Karloff–Lugosi brand of horrors, and sell it fast. It won't hold up on a long run.[16]

As Kyle Dawson Edwards has usefully demonstrated, the notion of adaptation in the case of *The Black Cat* is more profitably located within Universal's broader corporate strategies in the 1930s. Universal 'adapted' two more Poe texts as horror films during this period, the short detective story 'Murders in the Rue Morgue' (1841) as a Lugosi vehicle with the same name in 1932, and the poem 'The Raven' (1845) as a Karloff and Lugosi double-header the year after *The Black Cat*. Edwards argues that

Universal identified 'the works of Poe as fitting the horror cycle it had begun in 1931' while also more broadly exploiting 'the cultural discourse that had accumulated around Edgar Allan Poe and his literary works by the 1930s'.[17] Indeed, the potential profitability in adapting Poe wasn't only noted by the American studios: as discussed in Chapters 3 and 4, Epstein adapted Poe's gothic tale of intense sibling love in *La chute de la maison Usher*. In the UK, Brian Desmond Hurst directed the equally artistic *The Tell Tale Heart* (1934), a film described by *Kine-Weekly* as 'an extraordinarily interesting, if not commercial, essay in the macabre', while the *Picturegoer* proclaimed it to be an 'ingenious British contribution to screen art'.[18] In his book on the history of exploitation cinema, Eric Schaefer has also usefully explored how the exploitation film *Maniac* (1934) borrows 'liberally from mad scientist films, with bits of Poe's 'The Black Cat' and other stories, as well as nudity and gore added to the concoction'.[19] Poe's stories were evidently good horror currency in the 1930s, during the first cycle of horror films, the writer's name alone being enough to create interest in the product. Indeed, Ulmer himself admits that it was Junior Laemmle – the greatest supporter of the film – who came up with the idea of taking the title and using the author's name, as 'the Edgar Allan Poe story is not a story you can dramatise'.[20]

The choice of adapting a story by an American author may have been commercially driven, but arguably the film's aesthetic soul is European and is particularly influenced by the artistic traditions emanating from the Weimar Republic. Ulmer was born in Olomouc, Czechoslovakia and grew up in predominantly in Vienna, where he enrolled at the Academy of Fine Arts before working as a set builder for the Max Reinhardt Theatre and assisting in set design on a number of German films through the 1920s, including *Der Golem*.[21] In 1924 he worked in New York for Reinhardt's theatre company, then moved back and forth between America, Vienna, Berlin and Austria for much of the decade.[22] Ulmer settled permanently in America in the early 1930s, forming part of an ever-growing European émigré community of directors and designers in Hollywood. Noah Isenberg notes that unlike his contemporaries Billy Wilder, Fritz Lang and Robert Siodmak, Ulmer chose to leave Austria rather than being forced to flee after

Hitler's ascent to power. He argues that Ulmer 'maintained a similar state of in-between-ness, between old world and new, Europe and America, high culture and mass culture'.[23]

The interplay between European and American cultures is evident within the visual design of *The Black Cat*, where, owing to his background in set design and art direction, Ulmer was to have an unusually strong influence. The American horror genre may provide certain necessary narrative tropes for the film, but it is the Bauhaus that provides a physical frame for the building, while art deco inspires the decoration.[24] In addition, German expressionism infiltrates the set design, reflecting Dietrich Neumann's argument that Weimar's silent cinema even led some to hope 'for a "rebirth of architecture" through the collective experience of space made possible by the lens of the camera'.[25] Nonetheless, it is not only Robert Wiene's *The Cabinet of Dr Caligari* that I am thinking about here; Wiene's later film *Genuine: Die Tragödie eines seltsamen Hauses/Genuine: The Tragedy of a Strange House* (1920) is an important antecedent, which a contemporary reviewer for *Der Film* described as featuring 'a subterranean glass house filled with magic trees, the splendour of glittering mirrors, luxurious beds, strange furnishings – extensive halls, quiet enclosed gardens, dark rooms full of fabulous knick-knacks, and exotic curios'.[26] The following film analysis will demonstrate how European modernism, Weimar cinema, the shadow of the First World War, and a burgeoning émigré culture in Hollywood coalesced to create *The Black Cat*, engendering a distinctly European sensibility on the spaces of American horror film.

THE BAUHAUS OF HORROR

The film begins as newlyweds Peter and Joan Alison travel by Orient Express to their honeymoon in Visegrád, Hungary. Werdegast is forced to share Peter and Joan's carriage on his way to reclaim his wife and daughter from Poelzig's clutches. The film plays upon the audience's expectations of Lugosi's character. His creepiness – in part deriving from the fact that it is Lugosi and in part from his behaviour – is an aspect of the film's uneasy atmosphere, quite different from the more obvious visual monstrosities shown elsewhere in the American horror talkies. He may be polite and well-dressed, but his slicked back dark hair, heavily shadowed eyes and thick Eastern European accent relate his character to not only Murder Legendre in *White Zombie* but also the more famous Count in *Dracula*. This was emphasised in the film's publicity: a Universal poster in the *Hollywood Reporter* published a month before the film's release listed the cast as 'Karloff (*Frankenstein*), Bela Lugosi (*Dracula*)'.[27] Werdegast trespasses on the intimate moments of a newlywed couple, accidentally knocking their gramophone and turning off their record. Despite their ominous companion, Joan falls asleep, leaning against her husband. Werdegast leans across the carriage, smiling, and slowly caresses her hair. He apologises to her disgruntled husband, revealing that Joan reminds him of his own wife, the woman he left behind 18 years before when he went to war.

It is late, on the darkest and stormiest of nights, when the three travellers alight at the same station and share a carriage with Werdegast's servant Thamal; but the bad weather precipitates an accident and all four are forced to seek refuge at Poelzig's nearby house. This is no ordinary house but something far more sinister, built atop the remains of Marmaros, a fortress from the First World War where thousands of prisoners died (but also a distinctly modernist home). As the travellers approach the front door, the camera roams around inside the house, thus revealing and dwelling upon the strikingly modernist design: expanses of plate glass, chrome and Bakelite move into view, reflecting some of the most popular new building materials of the 1930s (Figure 5.1).[28] A gleaming curved glass staircase is fixed in place by striking scalene triangular supports scored with concentric holes. The walls are studded with small square boxes, providing a contrast to the stainless steel banister and smooth black floor, while the open-plan living space is separated from the dining area by a wall of glass.[29] The design is reminiscent of the typical style of the Hungarian Bauhaus artist, László Moholy-Nagy, whose *Untitled* (1926) is composed in black and white with a mere smattering of colour and strong, clean, abstract lines. Each light switch in the house is composed of brushed steel, each internal

Figure 5.1 The modernist home of Hjalmar Poelzig (Boris Karloff) in *The Black Cat* (1934, Edgar G. Ulmer).

door framed with a decorative horizontal strip of chrome running across its centre, encasing the door handle in shining metal. The very explicit attempts to 'design' the film with architectural form were not lost upon reviewers at the time. The *Daily Boston Globe* remarked upon Poelzig's 'chateau of sliding doors, modernistic rooms and electrically controlled dungeon'; the *New York Daily Mirror* described the film as 'a very modern horror thriller with a post-war period and bizarre modernistic setting'; while the *Washington Post* framed Marmaros as the 'ultra-modernistic castle of Boris Karloff'.[30]

The contemplation of the dramatic asymmetry of the set design is broken when the guests arrive; the white front door slides open and then disappears into the wall writing more generally on film and architecture. Edwin Heathcote has suggested that the symbolic significance of the door is that 'it represents the threshold, the entrance to another realm; whether that realm is sacred or profane, public or private, the door is the guardian. It is one of the most powerful of architectural symbols; if the anthropomorphic house has a mouth, then it is the door'.[31] In the case of *The Black Cat*, the front door does function in this fashion; the boundary between sacred and profane is breached as the group enter the property. They leave behind the safety of the outside world and enter a realm of satanic ritual and sadistic torture. Joan and Peter do not leave until after the deaths of everyone around them; Poelzig's property swallows them up. The doors are locked as they enter and the couple only escape at the film's conclusion when the house explodes.

As the bedraggled company are ushered into the house, Poelzig awakens in his boudoir, a room intersected by oversized and angular steel struts. Shadowed in darkness, and veiled by the gauze draped over the four-poster bed frame, Poelzig slowly sits up in bed. He switches on a small bedside light that illuminates the room but casts his own body in even deeper shadow. Silently, he leaves the room and goes to greet his guests. Poelzig's slow and stiff initial movements reference the Monster in *Frankenstein* and the resurrection of Imhotep in *The Mummy*, yet horror film fans may be breathing a sigh of relief, for the architecture of the building makes clear that Joan and Peter have not mistakenly stumbled upon a traditional old dark house. Art and design historians know better, however: as Joseph Rosa reveals in his study of contemporary cinema, there is a long-standing relationship between modern houses and evil characters in film:

> In recent Hollywood movies, modern domestic architecture has become identified almost exclusively with characters who are evil, unstable, selfish, obsessive, and driven by the pleasures of the flesh. Were they still alive, this might well shock the pioneers of modernism, who envisioned their movement facilitating a healthy, honest, and moral way of life. Nonetheless, filmmakers of late have chosen modernist works as the sites for murder, gangsterism, adultery, and a catalogue of other illicit and otherwise unsavoury behaviours. Bad guys may no longer wear black, but they do live in white-walled modern homes.[32]

Similarly, Gabrielle Esperdy notes that in Hollywood set design, 'modern equals bad; traditional equals good', and that melodramas in particular, 'equated modern design with sin, immorality, and even the extremes of inhumanity and evil', a pointed echoed by Jacobs, who suggests that despite its utopian aspirations, architectural modernism in American popular cinema has been 'practically always associated with cruelty, control and vanity'.[33] Rosa relates this inclination to an essential moral conservatism in America towards modern architecture: while accepting of it in the workplace, Americans have never embraced it for the home, where the preference has been for a traditional-style build. For Rosa, film is both reflective of (and further reinforces) this tendency.[34] While much of the writing on the relationship between 'bad houses' and horror has been on contemporary cinema, we can see here that the 1930s film makes an important contribution to this tendency. *The Black Cat* articulates an explicit relationship between modernism, houses and horror, a connection reaffirmed in Peter's comment that 'if I wanted to build a nice, cosy, unpretentious insane asylum, [Poelzig would] be the man for it'.

CUM GRANO SALIS

Werdegast tends to Joan in a guest bedroom as she recovers from the accident, reassuring Peter that she will recover. As he soothes the worried husband, the bedroom door swings open and Poelzig appears behind it. Without a word of greeting, he stares menacingly at Joan, the desire for the virginal newlywed burning in his eyes. He only relinquishes his gaze when Werdegast engages him in discussion, but now that both Werdegast and Poelzig have indicated their craving for Joan, the battle between the rivals commences. Having established a strong relationship between film architecture and horror, the narrative then incorporates sexual desire into the equation, manifested in a lengthy speech shortly afterwards by Werdegast when he confronts Poelzig in his study. He accuses Poelzig, former commander of Marmoros, of selling the fortress to the Russians and abandoning his men, leaving them (including Werdegast) to die: 'is it to be wondered that you should choose this place to build your house, a masterpiece of construction built upon the ruins of the masterpiece of destruction, the masterpiece of murder?'. Werdegast reveals that he spent 15 years as a prisoner, where he 'rotted in the darkness' and waited, 'not to kill you, to kill your soul'. It is not until this impassioned speech that Werdegast is finally shown as the nominal 'good guy', and the narrative slowly reveals that while Werdegast was incarcerated, Poelzig murdered Werdegast's wife and married his motherless daughter.

Design doubles as a prison cell: the past wartime horrors of Marmoros are embedded within the hard modernist architecture; the stark Bauhaus lines taking on a fortress-like quality that symbolically reflects Werdegast's prior incarceration as well as physically trapping Peter and Joan within the interior space. Perhaps the most terrifying incarnations of design's dance with death come in Poelzig's hidden space beneath the house, where dingy dungeons give way to shining glass cabinets displaying female corpses.

After Werdegast's confrontation with Poelzig, the household settles down for night, with the exception for the master of the house, who gathers up his black cat in his arms (mysteriously resurrected after Werdegast killed it) and takes a promenade through his exhibits. In a wide-angle long shot, he stops at his first display, lit in a chiaroscuro style to emphasise the female cadaver inside, shining in a sea of darkness. He stops directly in front of the angular cabinet, shaped as an inverted isosceles triangle, and his physical presence bisects the thick dark lines of the glass frame. The woman is suspended in the air, her head at least ten feet from the ground. She wears a fitted, low-cut white dress with a plunging scoop neckline, her eyes are closed and her pale arms hang loosely by her sides. Without comment he moves forward to his next display cabinet, this time framed in medium shot revealing another dead woman wearing a ragged, white dress, with an ethereal light surrounding her corpse. Poelzig's face is reflected in the glass: while he may be doubled in his reflection there is no doubt that it is the women who are uncanny: in addition to their suspension in mid-air their long hair stands on end, giving a giddy sense of viewing them upside down. The third cabinet reveals a change of angle — this time the camera is the left hand side of the cabinet and shoots through the pane, encompassing the woman and, through another layer of glass, Poelzig, in the same frame. He looks with great desire upon the corpse, slowly holding his hand up to the glass and pressing it gently. Now her face is reflected in the glass instead. Later that night, Werdegast demands to see his long-lost wife Karen (Lucille Lund, who also plays Werdegast's daughter, also named Karen) and Poelzig concurs. He leads Werdegast through a sliding white doorway and down a winding spiral iron staircase, explaining that it was the entrance to the gun turrets, referring to the house's previous incarnation as a wartime fortress. Poelzig pushes aside a thick stone door and enters a former chart room for long-range guns. The guns may be gone but the eight-foot charts of graph paper remain, adorning the walls and pro-viding a unique backdrop to his most awful glass cabinet, which contains Karen, Werdegast's wife (Figure 5.2). Poelzig whispers 'doesn't she look beautiful? I wanted to have her beauty always'. Karen wears the same ragged white ankle-length cotton dress, her

Figure 5.2 'I wanted to have her beauty always': Hjalmar Poelzig (Boris Karloff) reveals his favourite dead female exhibit, Karen Werdegast (Lucille Lund) in *The Black Cat* (1934, Edgar G. Ulmer). Her husband, Vitus Werdegast (Bela Lugosi), is not pleased.

long blonde hair, set in waves, stands straight up at the roots, yet she is utterly still. Deborah Jermyn has argued in relation to contemporary Hollywood cinema that the 'female corpse becomes such a disruptive presence in the text that any accusations of mere salaciousness are made redundant'; certainly in this case the scopophilic potential of the exhibit is undermined by the corpse's incorporation into a ghoulish and necrophiliac set design.[35]

Lit up in stark opposition to the shadowy darkness of the basement, Karen and her fellow female corpses are unsettling and bizarre museum pieces. Poelzig's dead women hang suspended, the shadows hiding any structural support and giving the impression that the bodies float outside time and space. These two scenes contain no real narrative impetus. Poelzig's initial sortie lacks purpose, while Werdegast's discovery of his embalmed wife only reinforces his hatred towards a man he has already sworn to kill. Nonetheless, these moments are deeply disturbing and by far the most uncanny passages of the film; it is noticeable that the set design turns to the extremes of cinematic expressionism to achieve this effect. Much of *The Black Cat* revolves around the relationship between set design and horror, and Poelzig's collection of cadavers takes the artistic theme in the realms of the unreal, transforming the archetypal horror dungeon into a bizarre and unsettling gallery space.

On discovering the death of his wife, Werdegast elects to play a game of chess with Poelzig, with Joan as the prize (Figure 5.3). The game takes place in the open-plan living room, the two men leaning toward the circular high-gloss black table, and teetering on the edge of tubular metal chairs that echo Marcel Breuer's famous *B3/Wassily* design for Wassily Kandinsky at the Bauhaus.[36] The design of the room includes long, horizontal ribbon windows, noted above, that owe more than a little to Le Corbusier's Villa 'Le Lac' and his new form of architecture.[37] This design is subverted slightly for its horror setting: the influx of light is tempered by long curtains of white gauze. Even the most modern of horror homes requires its dark corners. The chess set that the two men play with is ornate and expensive-looking, but the wooden box that holds its contents has been deeply and roughly cut into, creating a set of jagged letters whose message cannot be deciphered. These markings, while

Figure 5.3 Hjalmar Poelzig (Boris Karloff) challenges his enemy Vitus Werdegast (Bela Lugosi) to a game of chess, with Joan Alison (Julie Bishop) as the prize in *The Black Cat* (1934, Edgar G. Ulmer).

they are shown in only one or two shots, add a ghastly *punctum* to proceedings; they are a detail that once seen draws the spectator into a moment of appalling contemplation and causes them to question the defacement of the box. While the chess set and the gallery of cadavers serve to disconcert, the narrative itself dissolves into a series of vignettes with only the loosest sense of causality to advance the plot. Soon after the chess game, the local *gendarmerie* arrive at the house to investigate the accident, and a lengthy (and very jolly) dialogue-driven scene unfolds that has no further bearing on the plot. Scenes do not build in the classical Hollywood sense; as the daily New York paper *The Sun* commented, 'the less closely you look at its plot the more chance you have of enjoying it. It won't stand much inspection'.[38] For example, later in the film Joan will faint again and when she awakens she will find herself in the company of Madame Karen Poelzig, Werdegast's daughter (for Poelzig has married his stepdaughter, after murdering her mother, who shares the same name). With a crown of waist-length frizzy golden hair, Karen Poelzig is not only ethereal but fairytale-like, a dreamy Rapunzel roughly extracted from the Brothers Grimm. Joan reveals to Karen that her father is still alive and in the house, but the joy of the women is short-lived as Poelzig finds the women together and takes Karen into their bedroom (and off the screen) and then murders her without compunction. Her next moment on screen is in death when Werdegast and Joan find her corpse laid out on a mortician's slab.

The dream-like narration and disquieting visual motifs have a European tone to them; shades of *Vampyr* come to light. Indeed, in its freewheeling, uncanny atmosphere (if not its artistic influences), *The Black Cat* is arguably closer to Dreyer's film than its Universal stablemates *Werewolf of London* and *The Mummy*. It is haunting, intellectually driven (plots cohere around chess, classical music and architecture) and it is suffused with a sense of the European, a point not lost upon British film critics at the time. Reviewing *The House of Doom*, as it was released in the UK, the *Monthly Film Bulletin* acknowledged the attention to set design in a negative manner, describing the outcome as 'forced' and 'the setting artificial' (perhaps acknowledging its debt to expressionism) and dismissing the plot, for 'there is mystery, which remains a mystery to the end, many of the incidents having, apparently, no rhyme or reason'.[39] *The Times* was rather more pleased with the film, describing it as a success, having 'well designed sets' and rather astutely commenting, 'the direction owes more to Germany of the silent film days than to Hollywood'.[40] The cerebral quality of the text is reinforced when, having won the game, Poelzig unleashes his diabolical plans, accompanied by classical music. Peter discovers that the car is not working and they cannot be driven to the station, and, as Poelzig dryly quips 'even the phone is dead'. The writer is then locked in a pitch-black circular revolving cell, echoing Poe's 'The Pit and the Pendulum' (1842), while Joan faints and is locked in a bedroom. Having secured his female sacrifice for his forthcoming black mass, the triumphant High Priest Poelzig takes to his organ to play Bach's 'Toccata and Fugue in D Minor'. Even as early as 1934, classical music would have had resonance with the horror film audience, as *Dr Jekyll and Mr Hyde* was heavily scored, and Tchaikovsky's *Swan Lake* ballet suite featured in

Dracula, Murders in the Rue Morgue and *The Mummy*. *The Black Cat*'s musical director Heinz Roemheld, who reportedly used a 50-piece orchestra to score the film, drew on a number of composers, including Liszt, Tchaikovsky, Chopin, Schumann, Bach, Brahms and Beethoven.[41] Like Poe's own stories, classical music was in the public domain and therefore free to use, but Roemheld insists that Ulmer stipulated a classical score, 'partly because Ulmer was portraying the satanic character in the story, Hjalmar Poelzig, as an *arbiter elegantiarum* – possessing refined taste', lending what William H. Rosar describes as 'an air of sophistication or class to his film'.[42] Like *Dr Jekyll and Mr Hyde* before it, *The Black Cat* then uses Bach's 'Toccata and Fugue in D Minor' to create an intellectual atmosphere of horror, its effect so powerful that it was repeated again the following year in next Karloff–Lugosi horror vehicle, *The Raven*.[43]

Evening arrives, and Poelzig prepares a black mass to sacrifice Joan. The sequence begins as Poelzig's congregation gathers in the living room. He wears the garments of the High Priest, a long black loose robe with voluminous sleeves and contrasting cuffs and neck, a rope is loosely tied at his waist to gather together the material (but which also signals his role as executioner); around his neck rest two pieces of jewellery, a simple five-pointed star and a long chain composed of links. The robes are segmented with sharp diagonal lines in the white piping of the gown. Poelzig's make-up, created by Jack P. Pierce, is a white-powdered face in sharp contrast to his large black eyebrows, which in turn stand out against his grey receding hairline. Heavy black eye make-up and whitened lips then complement each other and suggest the walking dead. He slips across the Bakelite floor; his smartly attired guests slowly follow as he moves towards the camera. A spatial dislocation then occurs; a straight cut from the modernist living room goes directly into a room built for the black mass. While Poelzig's living and sleeping quarters would not look out of place at Walter Gropius's office at the Dessau Bauhaus, the hidden ritual room take on a baroque sensibility, the Bauhaus aesthetic overtly refracts the iconography of the old dark house while keeping the function the same: the property is littered with trap doors, hidden rooms and secret passageways.[44] The ritual room is spatially and stylistically disconnected from the rest of the house and is built as a theatre set, highly artificial and painted entirely black. Vases of drooping and dejected lilies hang from the walls and silver girders provide structural support in the enclosed, claustrophobic space. Its hand-crafted fakery is paramount to the effect, harking back to the painted expressionist sets of Wiene and Paul Wegener in the Weimar: it is here, in the flat surfaces and painted depths, that the horror lies, echoing Myron Meisel's assertion that Ulmer's set design is so powerful, that 'a few sticks of wood in primary shapes, dressed with a modicum of essential props, when photographed in shadows that respect no natural light, can create a world cognizant of the legitimacy of nightmare'.[45]

Similarly, the following moments combine the fantastical style of *Caligari* and *Genuine* with *Faust* (1926), where the commanding figure of Poelzig becomes akin to Emil Jannings' Mephisto. A giant broken crucifix sits upon a platform, and its crossed shape provides an ideal lectern for Poelzig's satanic incantations. He lifts his hands to his face and covers his eyes; a panning wide angle reveals his congregation changing into hooded black ceremonial robes. The ceremony begins: with a chillingly impassive face, Poelzig begins his Latin chant. He raises his hands to the (black painted) skies and his congregation flock around his pulpit, while the flat black background, the silver girders literally pointing up to the sky and the twisted crucifix – revealed as a double cross – creates an occult setting (Figure 5.4). Five women kneel down in front of the altar and drop their robes to reveal the same cotton white dresses worn by the cadavers in the gallery.

The action then moves to Joan's bedroom, where she is forcibly held down by two women and dressed in sacrificial garments before being dragged to the altar, her desperate screams echoing in the room. On witnessing the diabolical congregation, Joan faints once more, conveniently draping herself over the centre of the crucifix. Poelzig moves slowly towards her inert body, delicately brushing aside the gauzy fabric of her puffed sleeves, and tracing the contours of her skin. The tactility is sickening, an awareness that at any moment this tenderest of touches will transform into murderous brutality. At that moment, one of the congregation turns around to look towards the back of the room (at what, we never learn), screams and faints. Distracted, Poelzig tends to his flock, while Werdegast

Figure 5.4 High Priest Hjalmar Poelzig (Boris Karloff) presides over his Black Mass in *The Black Cat* (1934, Edgar G. Ulmer).

and Thamal liberate Joan from the crucifix. As she wakes up, she informs Werdegast that his daughter is still alive, but his sorrow quickly comes as he finds Karen on the slab in the dungeon.

Poelzig arrives, dashes Joan to the floor and tries to strangle Werdegast, beginning the final and inevitable physical confrontation between the two men. Like so many of 1930s horror films, *The Black Cat* concludes with two men bound up in an intimate and bloody *dénouement*, echoing *White Zombie*, *Werewolf of London* and *The Ghoul*, to name but a few. This film is more overtly sadistic and horrible than most though, perhaps channelling the gruesome powers of Poe. Werdegast straps Poelzig to an outsized torture rack, chanting 'how does it feel to hang on your own embalming rack Hjalmar?'. In a moment of pure homoeroticism, Werdegast tears off Poelzig's clothes to the sounds of the *sempre forte ed agitati* section from Liszt's 'Sonata in B Minor', revealing his thin and sunken chest. Wild-eyed and wild-haired (always a sign in the 1930s that a character has lost his mind), Werdegast grins maniacally as he grabs a sacrificial knife; his intentions mirroring the bloody conclusion of *Island of Lost Souls* when the beast men eviscerate Moreau in the House of Pain. Werdegast slits Poelzig's throat and skins his nemesis alive; close-ups show Poelzig's hands squirming in their restraints.[46] Peter finally escapes from his cell (when he discovers he needs to turn on the light and press a button to open the door), shoots Werdegast, and the newlyweds escape from the house, leaving the dying psychiatrist to flick the convenient switch that will detonate the property. Although Lugosi was playing the nominal 'good guy', his character was lecherous, looked like a vampire and skinned alive his son-in-law: such transgression cannot go unpunished.

The final scenes of *The Black Cat* are thus a spectacular riot of (implied) brutal torture and homoerotic violence, which were described at the time by *Variety* as 'a truly horrible and nauseating bit of extreme sadism'.[47] Yet *The Black Cat* got past the censors and survived contemporary critical reception. In his study of the film's PCA files, Mank reveals that on 26 February 1934, Ulmer and Ruric had a pre-shooting meeting with Joseph Breen, who advised of two major problems: the skinning and the killing of the cat, as well as cautioning them on a further 19 points, including Karen in the glass cabinet, the inverted cross at the black mass which was 'definitely inadvisable', and the need to 'avoid any suggestion of a parody on any church ceremony'.[48] As this chapter has demonstrated, many of these suggestions were ignored; and somewhat incongruously when the Breen office passed the completed film on 2 April, it sent Universal a letter 'congratulating the studio and Ulmer on the finished product'.[49] *The Black Cat* came out a few months before the official enforcement of the Production Code Administration, and was one of the last horror films to be made before the censors' suggestions had to be shown to be adequately addressed. Its horrors, therefore, remain intact. Beyond issues of censorship, the exhibition and audience reception of the film in America is also intriguing, not quite what one would expect. Gary D. Rhodes' illuminating survey of Universal Studios' in-house magazine *Universal Weekly* and industry trade publications reveals several significant points. Despite Universal's ballyhoo, the draw of a Poe 'adaptation' and the Karloff—Lugosi pairing, exhibitors approached the film with caution and often placed it on a double bill, lessening its impact and spreading the cinema's financial gamble. This perhaps says more about the cautious way that theatre exhibitors approached horror films; what is more intriguing – Rhodes demonstrates – is that the explicit representation of Satanism, torture and other 'potentially explosive' topics, had 'little-to-no effect on audience reaction' and that 'recorded responses' simply didn't take the representation of the topics seriously: perhaps referring to *cum grano salis* ('with a grain of salt'), a phrase oft-repeated in Poelzig's Latin incantation.[50]

REINVENTING THE OLD DARK HOUSE

Heathcote suggests that film architecture criticism tends to concentrate on the visionary: 'In these films, directors have the chance to achieve whole new worlds, or at least cities, in a way that most architects can only dream of'.[51] In creating *The Black Cat*, Ulmer has done something quite different. His world draws us into the past, is set in Hungary, draws upon European arts and culture popular in the 1920s and is framed by the unacceptable horrors of the First World War: the émigré returns to his roots. His set design is crucial to this: architectural modernism reinvents the old dark house; form follows function as the geometric Bauhaus lines capture and restrain Joan and Peter. Each of the three main types of set is distinct: the cadaver-filled gallery that speaks of the old dark house, the nightmarish ritual room as an ode to the flat, painted sets of expressionism, and the Bauhaus-styled, art-deco ornamented modernist living space. While distinct, they do cohere in that they create an atmosphere of horror in a domestic space. For modernism's originators – architects in the 1920s – modernism promoted an egalitarian vision in which good design is available to the average person in a bid to improve the quality of life, yet, as Donald Albrecht notes:

Instead of workers' housing, many popular films depicted deluxe villas and rooftop apartments; instead of factories, they created executive offices for capitalist captains of industry – it is one of the ironies of the modernist movement that the cinema, the twentieth century's greatest egalitarian visual form, took modern architecture's collectivist agenda and transformed it into a fantasy of privilege to be enjoyed only by the celluloid wealthy – meanwhile broadcasting that message to an audience composed of the widest segments of society that the architects sought to reach.[52]

In *The Black Cat*, Poelzig is rich, privileged and professional; his home is a fantasy unavailable to the masses, yet a house built upon the sorrows of the First World War is not one sought after by the movie-going public anyway; its placement within the horror genre inverts its modernist intention. Architecture becomes a central (and essential) character, echoing French architect and occasional film set designer Robert Mallet-Stevens' famous article 'Le Cinéma et les arts: L'Architecture' (1925), in which he suggests that 'modern architecture does not only serve the cinematographic set [*décor*], but imprints its stamp on the staging [*mise-en-scène*], it breaks out of its frame; architecture "plays"'.[53] Ulmer plays with the set design; the design plays with the cinema audience, casually torturing it in the manner that a (black) cat may bat at a captured mouse. In its connection between highbrow artistic style and generic narrative expectation, *The Black Cat* is the most European of the 1930s American studio horror films. While praise continues to be heaped upon Ulmer's classic film noir *Detour* (1945), it is *The Black Cat* that will truly be his long-term legacy.

THE 1930S BRITISH HORROR FILM

Does the 1930s British horror film exist? Not according to Ian Conrich, who argues 'there was in fact no British horror cinema of the 1930s'.[1] Conrich is not alone, as several accounts of this period of British cinema dismiss its horrific possibilities, citing censorship issues and cultural taboos.[2] Peter Hutchings argues that in the 1930s, 'British cinema was strikingly deficient in horror production', and although sympathetic to the 1930s 'shocker', James Chapman similarly suggests that 'a British "horror cinema" did not really emerge until after the Second World War'.[3] In such a context, the title of this chapter might seem provocative but it considers the production of British studio Gaumont-British (G-B) during the 1930s in order to tell a different story.[4] During this period the director of production, Michael Balcon, used his Continental contacts and aggressively marketed British pictures to the US – part of the history of the internationalisation of British film documented elsewhere.[5] He was attempting to make G-B, in John Sedgwick's words, 'a major player in the world film industry and therefore to rival in scale and output the principal Hollywood studios', and to achieve this by 'sustained access to and penetration of the American market'.[6] Similarly, Tim Bergfelder positions Balcon as a producer keen to produce distinctive material for international markets by combining the 'fast-paced, fluid narration of American cinema with the *mise-en-scène* and visual craftsmanship of Ufa'.[7] Our interest in G-B and Balcon is thus because he made a clutch of horror films as part of his strategy for achieving American success. The three G-B horror films discussed in this chapter – *The Ghoul* (1933), *The Clairvoyant* (1935) and *The Man Who Changed His Mind* (1936) – expose the diversity of horror themes during this period; they depict old dark houses and raise the dead in *The Ghoul*, display psychic abilities in *The Clairvoyant* and condemn the mad scientist in *The Man Who Changed His Mind*. I am, however, equally concerned with their production contexts and the idea of transatlantic exchange: *The Clairvoyant* and *The Man Who Changed His Mind* were made by Gainsborough, which had been associated with G-B since 1928, and Balcon was the production director for both companies; indeed G-B released all three films in America.[8] These films star Boris Karloff, Claude Rains and Ernest Thesiger, the former two on loan from Universal to G-B; at the same time Balcon imported American stars such as Fay Wray on short-term (often one-film) contracts.[9] This chapter explores the idea of transnational exchange in relation to the formal and generic characteristics of the three films and locates them within their censorship, production, distribution and reception contexts. In the process it reveals much about British perceptions of the American requirements of horror films, and in the process, American ideas about the British film industry in the 1930s.

HOW TO MAKE A BRITISH HORROR FILM

From the 1920s onwards, film producers were required to submit their scripts to the BBFC before production and BBFC script readers then produced scenario reports, allowing the BBFC to pre- and post-censor films.[10] Between 1933 and 1951, when the 'X' certificate replaced the 'H' certificate, the BBFC certified 31 films 'H', including five 1930s British films: *The Man Who Changed His Mind*, *The Ghoul*, *The Tell Tale Heart*, the short film *The Medium* (1934) and *The Dark Eyes of London* (1939), the latter being the first film to be classified as horrific under the enforceable certificate. *The Ghoul* was the first British film to obtain the 'H' certificate, and as two of only five 1930s British films classed as 'horrific', *The Ghoul* and *The Man Who Changed His Mind* become an integral part of the history of British film censorship. To explore how the period's censorship practices influenced the creation of indigenous horror films, this chapter first analyses the BBFC scenario reports for the three films and contextualises them within the changes in film censorship in Britain in the 1930s.

Annette Kuhn has explored how, in the early 1930s, the British government came under increasing pressure about children viewing films with 'sordid themes', and that in 1932 the issue coalesced to become about 'frightening films'.[11] *Dracula* and *Frankenstein* were not initially categorised as horror films and, as Kuhn reveals, it wasn't until the BBFC's 1932 Annual Report that the 'horror' film was discussed for the first time. Having introduced in 1913 the 'U' for universal (suitable for all) and 'A' rating (more suitable for adults), in 1933 the BBFC introduced an 'H' for horrific advisory rating to sit alongside the 'A' certificate and eventually replaced the advisory certificate with a full 'H' certificate in 1937.[12] In June 1933 London County Council offered a definition of horror that was to become standard: 'one likely to frighten or horrify children under the age of 16 years'.[13] A number of American horror films had already been substantially cut or banned before the introduction of the advisory certificate. *Freaks* and *Island of Lost Souls* were banned, while *Dr Jekyll and Mr Hyde*, *Murders in the Rue Morgue* and *Doctor X* suffered huge cuts of 731 feet, 352 feet and 205 feet respectively.[14] Paramount had evidently begun to self-censor after *Island of Lost Souls*: for the UK release of *Murders in the Zoo*, the shocking opening scene in which Lionel Atwill sews a man's mouth shut must have already been cut as there is no mention of it from the censors or the trade show reviews in May 1933.[15] After the introduction of the advisory certificate, the BBFC did not reject a single horror film. While this suggests that the advisory rating allowed the censors to pass a broader range of films, it is equally apparent that film producers were simply responding to the increasingly strict censorship in Britain and America, courtesy of the machinations of the BBFC and the newly empowered Hays office.[16]

In *The Ghoul*, Egyptologist Professor Henry Morlant (Boris Karloff) purchases a jewel of everlasting life. After his (apparent) death, his nephew Ralph and niece Betty gather at his gloomy mansion in Yorkshire to hear his will. Morlant then returns from the dead to take back the jewel stolen from his tomb, however it becomes apparent that Morlant did not in fact die – and so is not resurrected. In the film's conclusion, it is revealed, almost in passing, that Morlant was a victim of catalepsy, and was mistaken in his belief that he had returned from the dead. This is a key point for the film censors. When reviewing *The Ghoul*'s scenario report, the BBFC reader commented 'though the appearance of Morlant may be "horrific" for the moment, there is nothing in either scene or dialogue that we are likely to take an exception to. The explanation of his reappearance is quite plausible and there is no attempt to portray the supernatural'.[17] By 'explaining away' the supernatural with catalepsy, *The Ghoul* is able to explore other avenues of horror, namely bodily violence. This is evident about an hour into the film: Morlant has returned from the dead, found the jewel and gone to his tomb to pray to the god Anubis. He rips open his shirt and carves a ritualistic symbol into his own body as a sacrificial gesture, blood streaming down his chest. Yet when *The Ghoul* was submitted to the BBFC on 14 July 1933 it was passed without deletions and with certificates 'A' for 'adult' and the advisory 'H' for 'horrific'.[18]

In *The Clairvoyant*, Maximus (Claude Rains) and his wife Rene (Fay Wray) perform a music-hall clairvoyance act, but when Max sees a sultry woman, Christine Shaw, in the audience, his real psychic powers ignite with catastrophic results. *The Clairvoyant*'s producers had a straightforward run with the censors, but it did encounter a few early issues. G-B submitted Ernst Lothar's original book to the BBFC in December 1934, stating their intention to film it. An extensive report followed, focusing in depth on the book, and concluding 'this story is in my opinion suitable for production as a film'.[19] Yet, when the film scenario was submitted two months later, the disgruntled censor commented, 'this play does not follow the book story at all', and then, while pointing out that it is 'a strong drama', demanded two, potentially loaded changes: that 'no reference should be made to the Carlton Club' and that because 'the dramatic words and action of Counsel recall the trial of Christ' some dialogue must be modified.[20] It is interesting to see that politics and religion remain so important: the long-established Conservative gentlemen's club is excised from a spiritualist script, while the writings of Matthew and Luke are removed to avoid offending Christian organisations. *The Clairvoyant* was then submitted on 22 May 1935, passed 'A' with no deletions, suggesting that its modifications and emphasis on melodrama outweighed its more horrific elements.[21]

The Ghoul and *The Clairvoyant* may have had relatively painless interactions with the censors but the passage of *The Man Who Changed His Mind*'s from scenario to finished film was far more complicated. The original synopsis for *The Man Who Lived Again* (its original title) was submitted to the BBFC on 11 October 1935. In the synopsis, the character Nagy murders Orlok and disposes of his body in an acid bath. Nagy then murders a police inspector and brings his dead dog back to life with an artificial electronic heart installed by Professor Manton. Nagy is executed for murder, and the professor fits an artificial heart in Nagy's corpse, resurrecting him in time to admit he murdered the inspector, thus freeing the police's main suspect. The first reader rejected this synopsis, suggesting that this was 'a "horror" film if ever there was one. In view of Mr Short's decision on such subjects, I consider it unsuitable for production in this country'.[22] The second reader is equally disgusted, commenting:

> this story comes under the criticisms of 'horror' films made by the President at Cardiff. I consider the methods used to destroy the bodies revolting, and I do not think it is a pleasant idea to hand over the body of a hanged man for experimental purposes – in my opinion this story could never be suitable for production as a film.[23]

Further notes were added six days later. The censor and 'J.B.W' interviewed 'Mr Meslie and Mr Kurt Siodmak', whereupon the writers explained that they did not want to make a 'horror' film, but a psychological story. Accordingly, they planned to revise and resubmit the synopsis.[24] Siodmak, famous for (among other things) creating Larry Talbot's *The Wolf Man* in the 1940s, worked for G-B from 1934 to 1937 and was clearly already writing horror stories before moving to Hollywood. The synopsis was revised on 22 October with the murders completely deleted. Script examiner Miss N. Shortt commented that 'the story remains the same with the elimination of the chief horrors. Providing the actual resuscitation of the dead body is more inferred than shown, I think there is now no objection to the story being produced as a film'.[25] The final screenplay was credited to English writers Lawrence du Garde Peach, Sidney Gilliat (the latter best known for his writer–director partnership with Frank Launder and as the screenwriter for Hitchcock's *The Lady Vanishes* (1938)) and American writer John Balderston. By 1936, Balderston had written a long list of successful American horror scripts, including *Dracula, Frankenstein, The Mummy, The Mystery of Edwin Drood* (1935), *Mark of the Vampire* (1935), *Bride of Frankenstein* (1935) and *Mad Love* (1935) and was reportedly paid $3,060 for an unfinished script for this project.[26] The final version of *The Man Who Changed His Mind* bears little relation to the gruesome original script. It follows brilliant young scientist Clare Wyatt, who returns to work with her former supervisor, maverick Dr Laurience (Boris Karloff), who transplants the 'souls' of chimpanzees into each other's bodies. Then, with the support of a scientific institute, Laurience begins to transplant human minds. He lures Clare's boyfriend Dick to his laboratory and transfers his mind into the young man's body. Clare realises what has happened and reverses the experiment, returning Laurience to his rightful form just before his body dies. Even with revisions and a BBFC approved script, the film was still rated 'H' upon release in 1936, and is by some distance the most 'horrific' of the three films discussed here. *The Ghoul* managed to sidestep the censors by proclaiming rationality in the script, *The Clairvoyant*'s melodramatic core dilutes its associations with the horror genre, but it is in *The Man Who Changed His Mind* that we see how fundamentally the pre-production scenario reading affects the final narrative. If Kurt Siodmak had his way, Gainsborough would have made a grotesque film about hanging, execution, and the murder and resurrection of animals and men, something surely on par with, or possibly exceeding, the pre-code horrors of *Island of Lost Souls*. Whether one considers it a good thing that British censorship restraints put paid to this is another matter entirely.

THE 'BRITISHNESS' OF HORROR FILM

The Ghoul is imbued with numerous moments of 'Britishness', from the housekeeper's opening jibe 'we don't want to buy no lino nor nuthin', to black cabs, chauffeurs who doff their caps with a 'very good sir' and delivery boys referring to all and sundry as 'guv'nor'. But there is more to the representation of national identity than colloquialisms and pertinent props. This chapter now considers how Britishness is marked within the formal qualities of the films, arguing that while it occurs in the locations and settings, what is intriguing is the quite different and unusual ways in which each film handles 'authentically' British moments, and places them within broader discursive patterns of European and American cinema.

In *The Ghoul*, cousins Betty and Ralph drive up to Yorkshire to Morlant Manor, an archetypal old dark house whose unpleasantness is signalled by Betty's friend Miss Chaney's exclamation, 'what a horrible house! I wish I was back home in bed'. There they discover family secrets, dark corridors and abandoned rooms, and when Morlant (eventually, inevitably) returns from the dead, the spaces of the gothic house become an integral part of the narrative drive. Sadly, the character of Morlant is woefully and unimaginatively underused: he spends most of his time entering and exiting doors at either side of the imposing staircase, staggering down corridors and peering into empty rooms. This is contrasted with the bland 'adventures' of Betty and Ralph, who also aimlessly wander around the neglected property. They survey abandoned bedrooms, build fires in the neglected fireplaces of damp sitting rooms and spend a lot of time being baffled as to what to do next. In this, the set up of *The Ghoul* is faithful in its mimicry of the 1920s American old dark house film; it follows the same conceit where the plot initially appears to be supernatural but succumbs to logical explanation when Morlant is revealed to be alive. But this is arguably also where its Britishness emerges, as these 'old dark house' narratives can be understood as emanating from the nineteenth-century gothic fictions of British writers such as Ann Radcliffe, with her decaying castles and ultimate recourse to rationalism. There is also an added transatlantic dimension: two years earlier, English director James Whale directed *The Old Dark House* for Universal, a horror adaptation of English writer J.B. Priestley's thriller *Benighted* (1928). Described by *Kinematograph Weekly* as 'Universal goes British!', it may have been an American production but it featured an almost entirely British cast, including

The Ghoul's Boris Karloff and Ernest Thesiger.[27] Indeed, the cast's seeming obsession with tea-drinking annoyed American co-star Gloria Stuart (who went on to star in *The Invisible Man* with Claude Rains), who complained that the English were 'clannish' and 'had tea at eleven and four, the whole English cast and Whale, and they never once asked me or Melvyn [Douglas] to join them'.[28]

Kim Newman points out that in 1933, the filmmakers could have seen only a couple of American horror talkies, and as a result some of the 'eccentricities' of the film relate to genre expectations of the time, that 'like *The Old Dark House*, it owes more to *The Cat and the Canary* or *The Bat* than *Dracula* or even *The Mummy*'.[29] While the old dark house is central to its construction, the film has more connections with *Frankenstein* and *The Mummy* than perhaps Newman acknowledges, and it is here that its American qualities (or aspirations) are most obvious. There is a clear expectation that *The Ghoul*'s audience will have seen *Frankenstein* and *The Mummy*; as *The Times* noted upon its release, Karloff 'has made a great reputation for himself in Hollywood as a player of parts in which a note of horror dominates'.[30] Several scenes are organised around this expectation, including Morlant's botched attack on Miss Chaney, a weak repetition of the Monster's assault on Frankenstein's fiancée Elizabeth. Miss Chaney stands alone at the French windows in the library, looking out into the garden for her intended beau, Aga Dragore. Morlant walks up behind her and grasps at her neck but, apparently without reason, he then walks away. Chaney turns and screams only when the door slams behind him. Such staging is symptomatic of the representation of Morlant. He fails to arouse fear in the characters, instead stalking the house unnoticed and unable to interact. If his victims do not know that he exists, how can he frighten the audience?

Morlant's resurrection, 46 minutes into the film, is likewise indebted to *The Mummy*, a fact identified by the American press, with one reviewer describing the film as 'a fast-moving exciting piece, which is "horror" to whatever extent one is susceptible to cinematic horror', and that the film is 'virtually *The Mummy* redivivus'.[31] The very small movements of the Egyptian mummification casket signal Morlant's return. A single hand slowly pushes the casket lid up. An exterior shot depicts a full moon casting light over the entrance to the tomb, and the door slowly opens. There is silence as Morlant leaves the tomb, mirroring the silence of the mummy when it is first resurrected. Morlant then discovers that his jewel of eternal life has been stolen, and the following close-up emphasises his face. As an aged professor, Morlant doesn't require particularly extensive facial make-up, but his visage is a work of art: it has the texture of crumpled paper and the unpleasant tightness of badly burned skin (Figure 6.1). His heavy brow and bushy black eyebrows overshadow his eyes to the extent that they appear to recede entirely into the back of his head. This was noted in the reviews, a writer commenting on Morlant's 'deeply furrowed face, his eyes veritably in pits, his whole body confounded almost beyond description – that is Karloff'.[32] Jack P. Pierce was not on hand for *The Ghoul* though – in a film awash with émigré technicians, including cinematographer Günther Krampf and art director Alfred Junge – German artist Heinrich Heitfield transformed Karloff into Morlant. When the *Picturegoer* went on

Figure 6.1 A close up emphasises the gruesome make-up of Professor Morlant (Boris Karloff) in *The Ghoul* (1933, T. Hayes Hunter).

a set visit during the shooting of the film in April 1933, writer P.L. Mannock described the makeover:

> [Karloff] was being tended by a brace of intensely serious German experts. The bottom half of his face was the swarthy, quietly genial Mr Karloff *au naturel*. His nose, however, had been distended into a semblance of an Australian bushman. Sagging pouches clung to his cheeks below his eyes; the eyelids were weighted with swollen pads; furrows of almost agricultural dimensions lined his brow. And the Teuton bending over him was snipping transparent wrinkled cellophane into patches and plastering it over the entire facial area. 'Leave the mouth till last' said the victim. It looked as though it must itch terribly. 'It doesn't really', Karloff reassured me. 'Just burns a bit, that's all'.[33]

As with *The Mummy* (and its references to Lon Chaney), make-up and appearance becomes a central signifier of the 'horror' quality of the film, one that trades upon Karloff's past work in America; yet again he is forced to endure a lengthy period in the make-up artist's chair. Not only does *The Ghoul* appropriate specific scenes from *Frankenstein* and the narrative of *The Mummy* and 'borrow' Pierce's make-up techniques, but also, in the pan-European play of the film, émigré workers apply them.

If you watch Karloff on screen, however, it is simply another film and another monster's face. The performance he gives in *The Ghoul* is imbued with weariness and pessimism as he re-enacts his already career-defining roles just a year or two after their release. By going through the motions with his head held low, he is literally acted off the screen by fellow Englishman Thesiger, who plays his mournful servant Laing. The limited writing on *The Ghoul* often focuses on the expressionist visual devices created by Krampf and Junge: unsurprisingly, as a number of the set designs, such as Broughton's office, come closer to *Caligari*'s carnivalesque than the dank London cityscapes haunted by Mr Hyde and Dorian Gray.[34] Nonetheless, there are definite Conrad-Veidt-like tendencies in Thesiger's acting style.[35] Early in the film, soon after Morlant's funeral, Laing appears at one of the windows of the manor. He presses his hand against the pane of glass and gazes out into the night, his eyes open wide in surprise. He silently backs away into the shadows of the room and then tiptoes towards a table stacked with towers of books. Having selected a tome, he stands tilted at a 45-degree angle, holding aloft an address book with an expressive flourish that would not be out of place in *Orlacs Hände* (1924). The camera lingers upon Thesiger's body and privileges his exaggerated facial expressions; at the same time Karloff, who (besides being off-screen presumed dead for over half the film) is abandoned to wide-angle long shots and flat static spaces.

The final moments of *The Ghoul* prove to be an uneven mix of *The Mummy* and 'old dark house' narratives. When Morlant slits his chest open the statue moves – yet again mirroring the final moments of *The Mummy* – but the supernatural is revealed to be a feint, carried out by a dastardly confidence trickster who has posed as the local helpful parson. In *The Mummy*, Frank and Muller are frozen by the monster's powers, and can only look on as Anckesenamon calls upon the power of Isis to crumble the mummy into dust. *The Ghoul* is rather less powerful. Morlant faints and Ralph and the fake parson argue. Dragore shoots at Ralph and Betty and then fights Ralph. The fistfight is utterly underwhelming, something apparent to the American director T. Hayes Hunter even as he filmed the scenes. In a second visit to the set, the *Picturegoer* watched Hunter film repeated takes of the fight between the actors Harold Huth (Dragore) and Anthony Bushell (Ralph). Privately, Huth claimed that he had been made to fall over 43 times alone in the previous 24 hours. According to the *Picturegoer*, the scene was rather difficult:

> 'Now you guys! This is no pink tea' exhorted 'Happy' Hunter, dominating everybody. 'All right, turn' em over'. Strenuously, grasping and snarling, the two men grappled fiercely, stumbling and hitting ... 'I'm afraid that's no good' was the director's comment. 'Just a couple of tame wild cats.'[36]

Dragore escapes and it is revealed that Morlant has suffered catalepsy. He has not resurrected, the 'old dark house' film triumphs and the supernatural is revealed as mere audience frisson.

Possibly the most overtly international of the three films discussed in this chapter, *The Ghoul* suffers as a result of an uneven combination of multiple sources. The British colloquialisms and fog-bound London streets bespeak the late Victorian gothic; the monster and the mummy tropes and heavy make-up refer to American horror talkies; the old dark house is a popular conceit taken from British literature and popularised in American cinema, and the perilously leaning bookcases, distorted set design and exaggerated gestures are beloved of German expressionism and reflective of the practitioners working on the film.

The Clairvoyant is quite different, and an important early contribution to a tradition of British horror film that explores psychic ability in relation to spiritualism, mediums and séances. It is preceded by Maurice Elvey's earlier film *At the Villa Rose* (1920; remade in 1930 by Leslie S. Hiscott) and *The Other Person* (1921), and made before *Night of the Demon* (1957) and *Séance on a Wet Afternoon* (1964) to name but a few. Notably, while *The Man Who Changed His Mind* tips over into science fiction and *The Ghoul* suggests resurrection, it is in fact only *The Clairvoyant*, the least 'horrifying' of the three, that actually depicts the supernatural as real. The film begins *in media res* in the music hall as blindfolded Max stands on stage, identifying for the audience objects chosen by Rene. The relationship between the music hall and cinema is lengthy and symbiotic, Sarah Street commenting, 'the West End provided the first film actors and scripts, and music halls were the earliest public arenas for cinema exhibition', while Andy Medhurst cynically describes the initial association as 'one of straightforward exploitation', noting that some variety acts, such as George Formby and Gracie Fields, had an extended life on celluloid.[37] What is relatively unusual, however, is the inclusion of the music hall as a narrative space in a film whose origins do not lie with variety, although Hitchcock's *The 39 Steps*, released in the same year as *The Clairvoyant* (and produced by G-B), notably uses the stage as a high point of suspense. One of the ways in which *The Clairvoyant* is made idiosyncratic is the yoking together of spiritualism and the British music hall in order to generate horror.[38]

The theatre audience is underwhelmed by Max; applause muted. Christine, daughter of an influential newspaper tycoon, is also in the audience and gazes sadly at Max as he sits down heavily at the corner of the stage and removes his blindfold. But as the black cloth falls from his eyes the scene becomes invested with supernatural power, a strong white light builds in intensity until Max's face shines bright white (Figure 6.2). He gazes at Christine and in close up as she returns his gaze without a shadow of a smile. The humiliated fake psychic and the sad woman are united in a single look and the psychic connection is complete. In a series of shot-reverse-shots, Max becomes suddenly invigorated, producing prophecy after prophecy and demonstrating true psychic ability. He then stumbles, 'I see – I see' before falling to floor. He remains in a trance until Rene returns to him, and Christine's bewitching spell is broken. Like *The Ghoul*, *The Clairvoyant* then leaves behind London for Yorkshire. Unlike Betty and Ralph, preoccupied with tiptoeing around Morlant manor, Max has the more down-to-earth premonition of a coal mining accident at the Humber Shaft. Max travels to the mine and speaks passionately

Figure 6.2   On-stage in the music hall, Maximus (Claude Rains) experiences his first real psychic premonition in *The Clairvoyant* (1934, Maurice Elvey).

to the workers about to go on shift. The sequence begins with stock footage of coal mining: drills bore into walls, bare-chested filthy men work cheek by jowl. The noise is overwhelming; the discomfort worsened when detonators explode. Max begs the men not to go into the mine, at the same time a harsh white light illuminates Max's rival, the foreman who threatens to sack anyone who doesn't work. The steam siren shrieks with increasing intensity as Max pleads with the men, but cowed by the foreman they return to work. Suddenly there is an explosion and debris and smoke fill the screen. Fires burn, ceilings collapse and the soundtrack rings with the sound of screaming men. The wagons used for leaving the mine are quickly filled with fleeing workers, and the frailty of human life is emphasised as men climb on and crush their colleagues below, scrambling aboard as great waves of water fill the cavern. Britain's industrial heritage is articulated in a dangerous and dramatic encounter with elemental forces, and the unsettling evocation of the supernatural found in the music hall is swept away on a tidal wave of horror; the film's darkest sequence is encapsulated in a single moment as pale, faltering arms disappear below the water's surface.

When Max's other-worldly skills are confirmed by his prophecies, success quickly arrives, and Max moves his family into a swish London hotel suite, all gleaming white *moderne*, straight out of a Cedric Gibbons MGM set design. At this point the film takes a melodramatic turn. With its penchant for horror, it would seem obvious for the narrative to mine the dreadful implications of Max's supernatural talent, to ruminate upon the downsides of being able to see into the future and to damn the God-like qualities that that could confer – after all, whenever a mad scientist decides to play God he always comes to a sticky end. In fact, the film places as much emphasis on Max and Rene's marital relationship and her jealousy at his connection with muse Christine, a relationship necessary for earning their living. This is evident in the final, rather flat scenes, which cannot match the brutal chest carving of *The Ghoul* nor the human mind transplants of *The Man Who Changed His Mind*. The film ends, as it begins, with a performance from Max; this time he is in the high court. He is accused of panicking the miners in order to generate publicity for his show; which it is argued led to the catastrophe. Max's psychic abilities only occur at moments of high stress and when he is with Christine: she sits in the pews watching him and his pupils glow with bright white light. A new psychic pronouncement emerges from his lips: the 200 men remaining trapped in the shaft have now escaped. The judge confirms the story and the film ends with Rene and Max eating popcorn as they watch a clairvoyant perform, suggesting that Max has forsworn his psychic powers and his marriage with Rene is reconciled. The slippage between melodrama and horror is exemplified by the *Rochester Journal*'s review, which described it as a 'deeply dramatic picture of a very human individual in the grip of a force he cannot understand' but the perceptive *New York Times* review is more useful for our purposes.[39] It homed in on how Rene's disapproval of Christine 'motivates the first two-thirds of the picture', and chastised the producers: 'had [they] elected to stress the danger of knowing too much about the future, rather than building so long upon the issue of the wife's jealousy, *The Clairvoyant* would have been more effective drama'.[40]

The Clairvoyant is a rather awkward film. Generically, it is an uneasy mix of horror and melodrama and, of the three films discussed, it is the most 'British' in its social and cultural context, with scenes revolving around horse racing, the high court and London's theatreland. There is even a lengthy scene in which Max and his entourage endure a long train journey and complain about the food, bringing to mind Philip Larkin's poem 'Dockery and Son' (1963) in which he catches a train to Sheffield 'where I changed, and ate an awful pie'.[41] Yet the European production context that underpins *The Ghoul* is also evident, albeit in a distorted fashion: the film employed Junge as art director but had him make art-deco-influenced *moderne* sets as popularised in American film productions.

Balcon also made unusual casting decisions. By 1934 *The Clairvoyant*'s lead actors Rains and Wray had already become famous through their roles in *The Invisible Man*, *Doctor X*, *The Most Dangerous Game*, *The Vampire Bat*, *Mystery of the Wax Museum* and *King Kong*. This was noted in the press, the *Washington Post* preview commenting on the prestige of twinning G-B with the two stars.[42] Yet the film ignores the expectations of an audience that would come from such casting; it dispenses with the gothic, monsters and mad scientists, indeed all the usual trappings of American horror talkies. Perhaps *The Clairvoyant*'s wayward and obstinate nature accounts for its lack of attention in existing histories of the horror film. Its value here then emerges in two ways: its contribution to an important horror tradition that explores spiritualism's relationship with British cinema, and from the way it locates its traumas within a specifically British social and industrial milieu.

The Man Who Changed His Mind is a very different proposition again to either of the two films already discussed. In the same way that *The Times* remarked that the casting of Karloff in *The Ghoul* gave the audience certain expectations, the *New York Times* comments of his casting in *The Man Who Changed His Mind*: 'knowing Mr Karloff, it is not hard to predict what this picture will be like, so indelibly is he typed in the public mind'.[43] The producers of the film were evidently disenchanted with *The Ghoul*'s gothic mode and demonstrated this by drawing upon and then mocking the 'old dark house' conventions, a point noted in *The Times* review, which describes the set-up as 'one of those sinister scientists who live in crumbling manor-houses surrounded by dangerous dogs'.[44] Unlike the other two films, there is little sense of 'European-ness' here; this film works through the British gothic mode at the outset in order to jettison it in favour of a straightforward American mad-scientist narrative. In the first half of the film, Clare abandons her surgical job in London and catches a train into the country in order to work at Laurience's private laboratory in his decaying manor house. It is here that the film particularly draws upon gothic themes, locations and settings, and is arguably influenced more by British literature than cinema. As Clare cautiously leaves the gloomy provincial station she becomes lost in a desolate rural space with a brooding atmosphere that owes more than a little to Daphne du Maurier's novel *Jamaica Inn*, published in the same year. A tall figure looms out of the darkness and ominously enquires whether she is 'for the manor'. This is the first instance of many where the film demonstrates its awareness of gothic mechanisms, only to undercut them for comedic purposes. The shadowy figure is revealed as Clare's would-be beau, the grinning newspaper reporter Dick Haslewood, son of entrepreneur Lord

Haslewood. Dick warns her not to work with Laurience, who has a terrible reputation, but his efforts are in vain as Clare blithely dismisses his protection and boards a horse-drawn carriage to Laurience's house.

The carriage pulls up some distance from Laurience's neglected property. It is shrouded in heavy shadow, the trees grow perilously close to the building and weeds choke the pillars that frame the grand doorway. The inhabitants of the house have clearly turned their backs on the outside world, a fact emphasised by the opaque white fabric that covers the windows: no one can see out, and no one can see in. The manipulation of the gothic suddenly becomes less arch: Clare is frightened as she is denied her request to be taken right to the door, and the driver abandons her. As she rings the doorbell, a crosscut reveals an empty hall bereft of adornment. Clayton, a small, thin man in a wheelchair, answers the door and introduces himself as Laurience's assistant. In Clayton, who is regularly experimented on by Laurience, the mad scientist narrative makes its first inroads into the film, Within moments of meeting Clare, Clayton verbally marks himself as monstrous, lingering with some relish on his description of his 'intercranial cyst' and remarking 'most of me is dead, the rest of me is damned. Laurience manages to keep the residue alive'. Clare meets Laurience in his laboratory; he emerges from behind a bench of test tubes and beakers, white chalk covering the back of his jacket and his grey hair knotted and wild. While his dubious character has already been hinted at, his horrific nature is manifested for a moment in the set design. He looks into an elaborate gilt mirror, scowling and showing his teeth, his visage paralleled with the face of a gargoyle that is sculpted into the mirror surround: the man and the monster aligned in the glass (Figure 6.3). Having met Laurience, Clare retires to her spartan bedroom high in the eaves and sits on an oversized wooden four-poster bed, brushing out her long blonde hair. There is a sudden noise and Clare looks up, brush suspended in her hand. A moment passes before she realises that Dick has followed her to the house and is throwing gravel at her window. He promptly attempts to climb the ivy that winds up the wall of the house, only to fall off and be chased by Laurience's dog. The film's parodic gothic form

Figure 6.3 Dr Laurience (Boris Karloff) scowls at his reflection in *The Man Who Changed His Mind* (1936, Robert Stevenson).

parallels Jane Austen's *Northanger Abbey* (1817), Clare embodying Catherine Morland, poised for danger at every turn only for the reality to be much more mundane.

Laurience then agrees to go to London to work at the Hazlewood Institute of Modern Science, which is owned by Dick's father. At this point, the film turns its attentions wholeheartedly to the mad scientist narrative, becoming a straightforward film whose sets, actors and plots are virtually indistinguishable from Karloff's previous work, including Universal's *The Invisible Ray* (1936), released only a few months earlier. Having previously experimented on transferring the minds of chimpanzees at the manor house, Laurience decides to go a step further in London and transfers Clayton's mind into Lord Hazlewood's body. Hazlewood dies in Clayton's broken body, and then Laurience murders Clayton when he becomes too demanding in his powerful new form. Laurience's future plans to experiment on himself are then revealed in his discussion with Clare, who remains unaware of the latest turn in his research. Laurience, with his heavy, dark eyes, wrinkled face and wild white hair stares at Clare, her youth and beauty reflected in her luminescent skin and shiny blonde hair. He begs Clare to understand, 'I understand, I'm old, but – I could take a new body, a young body, and keep my old brain! And you too, you won't always be young – I offer you eternal youth, eternal loveliness'. He then transfers his own mind into the body of Clare's boyfriend Dick, and the desires of the mad scientist are revealed.

The formal analysis of the three films reveals very different approaches to defining Britishness in horror film. They are united in using British locations and settings as markers of national identity, but it is in their interactions with European and American contexts that discrepancies occur. *The Ghoul* uses the 1920s popularity of the old dark house, drawing on its manifestations in British literature and American cinema. It employs émigré technicians, who give the production design an expressionist tone, and trades extensively on British actor Karloff's American film roles. *The Clairvoyant* similarly employs actors already established in the American horror film industry but undermines audience expectations by creating a film immersed in British heritage. Indeed, while the supernatural ability of the psychic may mark the film as horrific, the mining disaster is one of the darkest and most sombre moments of all three films. Similar disjunctions occur in *The Clairvoyant*'s production design, as it demands that its émigré technicians turn to the *moderne*, popularised in contemporary American cinema. *The Man Who Changed His Mind* parodies the gothic mode and discards it for a straight American mad scientist narrative, and notably it is the only film out of the three that had a good critical reception in both the UK and US. This suggests that for a 1930s British horror film to be internationally popular, its 'Britishness' must be quickly discarded in favour of American tropes. Hence, the final section of this chapter considers the films in light of their literal 'transatlantic exchange': Balcon's desire to internationalise his films and exploit the American market, the deals struck between individual American cinemas and British studios, the transfer of American and British actors between Hollywood and London and the critical reception of the three films.

TRANSATLANTIC FILM EXCHANGE

I'm not trying in any way to alter the national character of our pictures, merely to make them more readily acceptable to the point of view of American entertainment.[45]

Michael Balcon, Director of Production at G-B,
Interviewed by the *Observer* film correspondent, May 1935

In 1933, the *New York Times* outlined the need for an increased exchange of material between Hollywood and Elstree, partly owing to 'considerations evolving from the financial crisis and the present economic conditions in the world at large'.[46] It highlighted G-B as an organisation with 'its eyes wide open for the possibilities of the American market' and singled out *I Was a Spy* (1933), *Waltz Time* (1933) and *The Ghoul* as crucial to the company's bids for American success. Balcon's need for *The Ghoul* to have international appeal then generated interesting material in the critical reception. It was filmed during April 1933 at G-B's recently refurbished studios in Lime Grove, Shepherd's Bush.[47] It was trade shown in the UK on 25 July and premiered at the Capitol cinema in London on 7 August 1933 and then premiered at the Rialto in New York in January 1934.[48] In the UK, critics largely ignored it. The *Guardian* did not review it, *The Times* mentioned it very briefly as part of the influx of British cinema on London screens, while the *Observer* provided a cursory six-line review of its regional release over two months after its London premiere, in which it was dismissed as a 'muddled mystery story, which takes place mostly, and leaves the audience entirely, in a fog'.[49] This is fairly typical of the response of the *Guardian* and *Observer* to horror films during the 1930s; reviews of *The Mummy*, *Bride of Frankenstein* and *The Black Cat* were first covered upon regional release, and almost always in dismissive and disparaging tones.[50] The fan magazine the *Picturegoer* did offer a full review, but described it as 'undoubtedly poor', saying that the film concentrates 'neither on the macabre nor the melodramatic, but makes an entirely unsatisfactory compromise between the two', a charge to be laid against *The Clairvoyant* two years later.[51] To this extent, the UK broadsheet critics treated *The Ghoul* in much the same fashion as American horror films, as unworthy of detailed coverage.

The transatlantic reception of *The Ghoul* was varied. It played in Chicago but the *Chicago Daily Tribune* did not review it, and the *Washington Post* only provided a short preview, which focused on Karloff's star status.[52] In contrast, the *Motion Picture Daily* did enjoy it, suggesting that 'acting all round is topnotch and the photography and settings round out a swell contribution for thrill-seekers'.[53] The *Daily Boston Globe*'s brief review was also positive, describing it as 'an exciting horror film' and focusing on its Britishness as a key point of interest.[54] The Britishness was also crucial to the *New York Times'* analysis, but unlike the *Daily Boston Globe*, it saw the film's national origins as a point of ridicule. Damningly for Balcon, the *New York Times* specifically attacked both the British settings and the production context. Unsubtly, 'A.D.S.' (Andre Sennwald) lamented that Karloff 'has had the misfortune in his new picture to fall among amateurs at the game' then emphasised that it was 'British-produced'.[55] As such, the film 'has nothing like the hearty terror that the uninhibited script writers in Hollywood piled into *Frankenstein* and *The Mummy*'.[56] The final nail in the coffin emerges in the next paragraph, suggesting 'perhaps American audiences have been taught to expect too much from Karloff', and that they are more cultured, with higher expectations of films, than British audiences.[57] Here, *The Ghoul*'s (undoubtedly many) flaws are attributed squarely to its country of origin, that there is something *essential* in the British character, something repressed and inhibited, that directly affects the ability of a studio to produce a good horror film.

Over the next few years, Balcon repeatedly travelled to America to court US film markets, confessing to the *Observer* in early 1935 that 'as a result of the first visit I modified our plans, altered our production methods a little and tried to eliminate the more purely insular of our characteristics'.[58] *The Clairvoyant, Alias Bulldog Drummond* (1935) and *The 39 Steps* (1935) were the first three films made by Balcon under these new conditions. Wray became part of this drive and was interviewed by the *Picturegoer* while spending six months in London working on *The Clairvoyant*. During the interview she gamely tried to communicate her British heritage:

'it is my grandfather's own country. He was born in a little town – a seaport, I believe – by the name of Hull. You have heard of it?' – yet her antipathy towards the British film industry was apparent.[59] Four months later, when returning to America, she commented that the British producers didn't have the same 'rigid adherence' to schedule, and like Gloria Stuart made much of on-set tea drinking: 'everyone has tea. In fact, the whole atmosphere is redolent of tea. It's there in the morning and stays there all day'.[60] When asked to comment specifically on differences in working methods between G-B and Hollywood, she hesitantly admitted that 'one does not feel the same degree of efficiency in the superintending of the technical job. In Hollywood you just know that the set is right, that the lights are right, that the cameraman will do a perfect job. In England I was not sure about it'.[61]

Fifteen days after Wray's damning interview, G-B signed a contract with the Roxy Theatre in New York and opened its American season with Wray's *The Clairvoyant*. When the Roxy manager Howard S. Cullman signed the contract, he proclaimed 'there is no longer any distinction between Hollywood and British films'.[62] As Wray's interview suggests, this sentiment was not shared by everyone, including the *New York Times,* which argued that British producers such as Balcon were 'long the Cinderellas of the picture industry and relegated to second place even in their own backyard – the sprawling British Empire', and that it was only in securing American distribution that they had finally 'stepped up to the line with the announcement that they were out to get their place in the cinematic sun'.[63] At least the *New York Times* knew that the British film industry existed. Only five months earlier the *Chicago Defender* newspaper printed an eyewitness account of London's cinema scene:

> Perhaps the movies – cinemas, they are called in England – are the most notable example of the American influence abroad. There are practically no English motion pictures in England, so to speak. There are a few companies, but out of every ten pictures advertised about nine will be American-made built around American stars, or around English stars who work in Hollywood. Motion picture theatres are not plentiful – they haven't the motion picture mind yet.[64]

While the *Chicago Defender*'s nod to the transatlantic exchange of actors is pertinent, one can imagine that Balcon would be horrified at the article's sentiments. There is a sense here of 'damned if they do, damned if they don't' in the discourse around the internationalisation of British cinema in the 1930s. In the *New York Times'* view, the British film producers may have made amendments to their films to please transatlantic audiences, but this did not mean that their films would be as good as American ones; rather, Britain had accepted the need to toe the line with American policies. It is notable that this shift in policy came after *The Ghoul*, with all its European flourishes. Nonetheless, Balcon's desire to make his films more accessible to American audiences seems somewhat at odds with the very British tone of *The Clairvoyant*, which was distributed in America by G-B (as parent company of Gainsborough) and received its world premiere in New York at the Roxy Theatre on 7 June 1935.[65] It did not premiere in the UK for another two months, appearing at the New Gallery cinema in London on 9 August.[66]

Yet Balcon appears to have been on to something, because reviewing the critical reception of *The Clairvoyant* yields some rather unexpected results in the American reviews. The UK press were certainly largely unimpressed. *The Times* listed the range of locations, including the pit explosion, the Derby forecast and the 'provincial theatre' but argued that it was 'very melodramatic' and 'the story is unsound because it is the outcome of confused thinking'.[67] The *Monthly Film Bulletin* considers *The Clairvoyant* 'a dramatic treatment of the social problem provoked by the practice of public clairvoyancy', but damns it by saying 'it is not sufficiently dramatic to be just entertainment nor sufficiently thought out to offer any solution of the problem it chooses to raise'.[68] But in America, something quite different occurred. *Variety* was admittedly unconvinced, writing that '*The Clairvoyant* is an effort to fit material to Claude Rains but a mild excuse as screen entertainment', but on the whole the city newspapers were more forgiving.[69] The *Daily Boston Globe*'s review was typical, categorising the film in the first line as 'a motion picture made in Great Britain' but quickly turning to sing Rains' praises, 'in one of his best roles'.[70] Analyses of Rains' performance dominated; the *Spokane Daily Chronicle* described him holding 'the spotlight' and the *Chicago Daily Tribune* talked of his 'easy and skilled' and 'convincing' performance.[71] The response of the American city newspapers shows that despite its very British settings and links to British industry and society, the film's production contexts had little-to-no negative impact on its reception. Rather, Rains' performance and star status (having already starred in Universal's *The Invisible Man*) overcomes national specificities. We can perhaps partially account for the American response by acknowledging the stateside success of Alexander Korda's *The Private Life of Henry VIII* (1933), a film imbued with British traditions and culture which was nonetheless well received by American critics and at the box office.[72] So, to an extent, Balcon's gamble appears to have paid off – the British critics were unimpressed but the American writers were keen to see well-known stars in British roles.

The *Man Who Changed His Mind* was recorded at Gainsborough Studios and was trade-shown in London on 11 September, before being re-titled *The Man Who Lived Again* and released by G-B at the Rialto Theatre in New York on 15 December 1936.[73] The most Americanised of Balcon's horror offerings, it garnered positive reviews from both sides of the Atlantic. It is certainly the most accomplished of the three films, and British film reviewers were uniformly positive: *Kinematograph Weekly* gleefully proclaimed it 'as good a Karloff offering as the best the Americans have given us' and 'unquestionably a first-rate box office attraction'.[74] *Monthly Film Bulletin* categorised it as 'grand guignol melodrama', noting approvingly that 'it provides plenty of macabre thrills without descending to horrific sensationalism', while *Film Weekly* reads it as a 'pseudo-scientific thriller' and 'as good as most in this class'.[75] Unlike their treatment of *The Clairvoyant*, whose British settings were ignored in favour of Rains' performance, the American reviewers of *The Man Who Changed His Mind* decided to focus on the film's production context to frame their reviews.[76] The response of the *Chicago Daily Tribune*'s Mae Tinee is typical in this regard, beginning with what we can only assume to be an attempt at 'writing' an English accent: 'Gorsh! Here's that Mr Boris Karloff trying to frighten us again!'[77] The *New York Times'* review is almost pure gobbledegook with utterly incoherent sentences (describing the laboratory equipment as 'characteristic impedimenta of cinema alembic').[78] It appears to be an attempt to communicate in British English, which seems to be predicated in this instance upon archaic language and what the reviewer describes as 'Oxford pronunciation'. This is typical of the reception of British films in America following the introduction of sound. Sarah Street has noted that American reviewers became preoccupied with the 'comprehension of accents' in the early 1930s; regional accents were preferred to the 'potentially alienating' 'Oxford accents and use of long vowels'.[79] In the case of *The Man Who Changed His Mind*, the emphasis on the language play reveals American impatience with 'posh' British language and demonstrates the irreverence with which the material is treated. Such is the lack of serious consideration of the subject that the reviewer fails to spell out an opinion of the film.[80] The industrial and reception contexts for the three films illuminate something of the British response to 'internationalised' home-grown films, and American perceptions of the British film industry. To suggest, as the *New York Times* did about *The Ghoul*, that amateurish filmmaking practices were the defining characteristics of British industry in the 1930s accords with Wray's decidedly dour comments while making *The Clairvoyant*. Such responses were not unusual; the American *Film Daily* review of Gainsborough's *The Ghost Train* (1933) was similarly quick to note the drawbacks inherent in its British origins: that it was 'slow in getting started. Also the English accents are a trifle heavy for American ears'.[81] With hindsight, it is perhaps unfortunate that Balcon chose several horror films – often critically maligned at point of release – with which to penetrate the transatlantic market. Nonetheless, the critical reception alone does not provide a rounded understanding of the performance of these films in American markets, or how the audiences responded to them. For example, *Variety* reported on the exploitation activities, at the Majestic Theatre in Columbus, of Edgar Hart, who in a bid to promote *The Ghoul*, built a seven-foot canvas sarcophagus 'with blu-ish gray jewel sides and a greenish marble top':

At the back was a sort of headjewel carrying a blow-up of Karloff's face, spotted through with a green light through a small hole cut in the vault. The centre of the jewel was inset with a circular window to suggest cathedral glass in various colours with the lighter colours towards the centre. Through this could be viewed the body of a beautiful woman, represented by the prettiest figure Hart could coax from a local store, richly draped in silks and satins – and lighted by a strong white light.[82]

With its suggestions of *The Mummy*, the image of Karloff and the body of a beautiful woman, it is unsurprising that *The Ghoul* then 'did better business than anticipated', Hart's strategy producing 'a highly effective seller for a none too hot picture'.[83] Similarly, if any of the exhibitors followed the suggestions of *The Man Who Changed His Mind*'s American pressbook – which suggested procuring a local chimpanzee and display him in a cage in the lobby with a sign saying 'IS THIS CHIMP IN HIS RIGHT MIND?' – public interest would probably be aroused.[84] Without knowing the box office takings for individual American cities, it is hard to know how much impact, if any, the critical response had on actual audience figures. It could well be that the lure of Boris Karloff in *The Ghoul* and *The Man Who Changed His Mind*, and Claude Rains and Fay Wray in *The Clairvoyant* was enough to get the punters queuing at the cinema door.

This chapter has revealed that the combination of the horror genre and British filmmaking was not the easiest to sell in the 1930s. The positioning of the three films as 'horror' led many British newspapers simply to ignore or dismiss them. American actors who performed in them were often indifferent to their potential, while American film critics used them as a platform to make fun of 'Britishness' and the British film industry as a whole, reinforcing Hollywood's status as the producer of gold-standard cinema. Despite this, the material is valuable as it provides an alternative way of thinking about the initial horror film cycle of the 1930s. Balcon's productions are a discrete body of films at the centre of a fourfold moment in film history: the increasing internationalisation of the British film industry, the interwar transnational European émigré culture, the transatlantic passage of American and British actors, and the emergence of the horror genre in sound film. G-B's attempt to infiltrate American markets with British horror films may have had limited success (certainly critically), but the historical and cultural worth of the films comes from their telling record not only of the popularity and importance of horror films during this period but also of American attitudes to British film culture.

WEREWOLF OF LONDON AND THE ORIGINS OF WEREWOLF CINEMA

The gothic films of 1931 have cast a shadow over this book from its beginning. It is appropriate therefore that this final chapter deals with another film that harks back to 1931, namely Universal's *Werewolf of London* (1935) which draws much of its inspiration from Paramount's version of *Dr Jekyll and Mr Hyde* (1931). Both films feature an upper-class, educated protagonist who works in a private laboratory attached to his house and whose scientific endeavours unleash a murderous double. The man undergoes a physical and mental transformation into a monster, who then stalks the streets of London in search of innocent victims culled from the capital's underclass. Eventually and inevitably, he meets a horrible death.[1] Nonetheless, to reduce *Werewolf of London* to a mere furry copy of Robert Louis Stevenson's celebrated gothic novel *The Strange Case of Dr Jekyll and Mr Hyde* (1886) is to underestimate it. It is the only American horror film discussed in this book to emerge wholly after the inauguration of the Production Code Administration (PCA) in 1934, and an examination of the Hay's Office's correspondence with the film's producers during pre-production reveals a careful engagement with the figure of the werewolf and the problems inherent in depicting it on screen for the first time.[2] It is also a product of its time and contains many elements integral to the studio-produced 1930s American horror film, where the same plots and characters (and actors, directors and cinematographers) were used again and again. As we have seen in *Dracula* and *The Mummy*, such repetition is common, and while Dr Jekyll may provide the prototype for the tortured werewolf Dr Glendon, the film is in itself idiosyncratic and unusual, particularly in its exploration of gender, sexuality and the body. Cloning the mad scientist narrative is not the only accusation *Werewolf of London* has had to bear; it suffers the indignity of receiving only the most cursory of glances in accounts of werewolf cinema. Horror film histories commonly cite *The Wolf Man* as the first important silver screen werewolf and dismiss *Werewolf of London*, released six years earlier, as an ineffectual work in progress (although J. Robert Craig and Chantal Bourgault du Coudray point out that it is the first film to suggest that the werewolf bite transfers the curse to its victim).[3] By examining the representation of the werewolf in literature and culture before 1935, the PCA and Universal documentation, the distribution, exhibition and reception of the film, and of course the film itself, this chapter will provide a much-needed re-evaluation of the film and its context, while arguing for *Werewolf of London* to be understood as the true originator of werewolf cinema.

LONDON, PARIS, HOLLYWOOD: PREPARING *WEREWOLF OF LONDON*

I dream at night that I am drinking blood and it scares me to death.[4]
Nine-year-old Bertrand Calliet confesses in
The Werewolf of Paris (1933)

Stories of shape-shifting beasts have circulated in legends, folklore and superstition back to the first century AD, but there was a distinct increase in the circulation of such stories during the Victorian and Edwardian eras. These included Frederick Marryat's 'The White Wolf of the Hartz Mountains' (1839), Arthur Conan Doyle's 'A Pastoral Horror' (1908) and Algernon Blackwood's 'The Camp of the Dog' from his John Silence Collection (1908).[5] A number of novels also emerged during and after this period, including George W. M. Reynold's *Wagner: The Wehr-Wolf* (1846–7), Gerald Biss' *The Door of the Unreal* (1919) and Jessie Douglas Kerruish's *The Undying Monster, a Tale of the Fifth Dimension* (1922). Possibly the most well known and oft-cited novel is Guy Endore's *The Werewolf of Paris* (1933). The novel begins as the narrator stumbles upon the abandoned papers of Aymar Galliez, and uncovers a shocking story about Galliez's relationship with a werewolf, Bertrand Calliet. In the 1850s, a young servant girl,

Josephine, is raped by a priest and on Christmas Eve bears a child whom she names Bertrand. He grows up with werewolf inclinations, but believes his violent nightly activities are merely vivid dreams. It is not until he reaches adulthood and relocates to Paris, where he attacks a prostitute, rapes his own mother and murders his best friend, that he admits his condition, lamenting 'God, is it real?... Or will I yet wake up from this nightmare more horrible than any I have ever had?'[6]

The Werewolf of Paris has an interesting relationship with *Werewolf of London*. The main points of crossover can be found in the physical details of Calliet's transformation and the tragedy he experiences as he mournfully comes to terms with his own being. Yet the title *The Werewolf of Paris* is somewhat misleading, for author Endore shows little interest in the murderous shapeshifter. Once Calliet arrives in Paris the book changes pacing and direction, with whole sections of the novel barely featuring the werewolf and instead turned over to Parisian political history with a close focus on the Paris Commune of 1871. It is clear that Endore is at least partly aware of his deviation. Chapter 15 begins:

> The writer apologizes for the confusion of the last chapters. His excuses are that the chronology in the script is none too clear, and further that the elucidation of the events in the story was none too easy. Aymar, as we have said, first came face to face with Bertrand during the Pipcus affair, and though in our elaboration of the Galliez script we went off the track in the last chapter, we intend to come back to our duty in this one.[7]

Calliet's presence in Paris during the Paris Commune is a mere device to make a political point, Galliez proclaiming:

> Why should this one wolf be shut up for an individual crime when mass crimes go unpunished? When all society can turn into a wolf and be celebrated with fife and drum and with flags curling in the wind? Why then shouldn't this dog have his day too?[8]

Ultimately, *The Werewolf of Paris* suggests, perhaps obviously, that people are capable of committing worse atrocities than supernatural monsters. The novel was out of print for decades and when Citadel Press reissued it in 1992, Robert Bloch, author of the original *Psycho* (1959) novel, provided an ecstatic preface, explaining 'the commentary, the social criticism it contains, is as vital today as when it first appeared in print. These were the elements that raised *The Werewolf of Paris* far above its genre'.[9] Indeed the novel does seem very distant from the horror films of the period in both its desire to make a meaningful statement about the human condition and in what, to some at least, might seem a high level of pretentiousness. For all this, one might have expected that the book's publication in 1933 would have caught Universal's eye, if only for the title. In fact, for *Werewolf of London*, which began pre-production in late 1934, the studio created its own screenplay based on a story written by the film's associate producer, Robert Harris.[10] At first glance, the lack of interest in the novel seems curious, especially as – despite his Francophone name and grasp of nineteenth-century French political history – Endore was born Harry Relis in New York in 1900, and by 1934 was working in Hollywood providing original stories, adaptations and screenplays and specialising in horror films.[11] The *Los Angeles Times* film critic Philip K. Scheuer describes bumping into him with a fellow worker on the MGM studio lot:

> the author was of medium height but peculiarly frail and graceful, with mild blue eyes that seemed to reproach you. The other, the actor, was short and roly-poly, with apple cheeks and the smile of a baby. They spoke in such gentle tones that you had to lean close to hear them. In the bright sun, it was hard to believe that one was Guy Endore, author of *Werewolf of Paris* – the other Peter Lorre, murderer of *M* and diabolic surgeon of *Mad Love*.[12]

A perusal of *Variety* casts some light on the situation. Endore was contracted to MGM on 17 September 1934, where he worked on the sound remake of *London After Midnight*, entitled *Vampires of Prague* during production but released as *Mark of the Vampire*.[13] He then adapted Maurice Renard's novel *Les Mains d'Orlac* (1921) as *Mad Love* (hence the intimate chats with Lorre) and co-wrote *The Devil Doll* (1936) with Todd Browning and Garrett Fort.[14] In late 1934 Scheuer indicated that Lorre would be interested in performing in a film version of Endore's novel, but relayed Lorre's belief was that the censors would not allow it to be 'done right', no doubt because of the novel's themes of rape, incest and murder. One might also speculate that Universal would have baulked at adapting the work of someone contracted to another studio.[15]

Without Endore but with Harris' story, a script for *Werewolf of London* was completed in early January 1935 and sent to the Hays Office (as the Production Code Administration was colloquially known) for pre-production approval. As this was the only horror film discussed in this book to be made after the regulation of the Production Code in 1934, it is worth pausing to recall the origins of American film censorship, discussed in the introduction, before exploring how *Werewolf of London* was affected by changing censorship laws. The Motion Picture Producers and Distributors of America (MPPDA) was formed in 1921, and in 1930 its president Will Hays instituted the 'Production Code', also known as the 'Hays Code', a set of industry censorship guidelines established to deal with the increase in sex and violence in the cinema. In 1934, under public pressure, the Production Code Administration (PCA) was established to enforce the code. The Code was significantly overhauled by the head of the PCA, Joseph Breen, with the principle that 'no picture shall be produced which will lower the standards of those who see it'.[16] James Chapman explains that under the new enforced Code 'there was a list of prohibited subjects and an even longer list of subjects (including sex and crime) that needed to be treated with the utmost caution and restraint. Any form of obscenity, profanity or blasphemy was forbidden'.[17] New films required a PCA seal of approval to be distributed, and so the PCA tended to work on scripts with producers before actual filming. They then required approval before release; therefore the producers of *Werewolf of London* submitted the script before starting filming.

Bearing in mind the far stricter censorship guidelines that had come into force six months previously, the censors were inevitably concerned with a number of elements in the film. Getting final approval on the script involved two meetings, a number of memos, letters and a particularly pleading telephone call from

Stanley Bergerman (Carl Laemmle's son-in-law) to John Mc. H. Stuart at the PCA. The first meeting on 15 January involved Harry Zehner, a producer at Universal who liaised specifically with the Hays Office; Lilian Russel, who was Universal's assistant censor; Carl Lischka and Stuart from Hays; and Harris as the film's producer and story writer.[18] At this meeting and a subsequent one a fortnight later, two main issues were debated: the depiction of a soliciting prostitute and the depiction of the physical transformation from man into wolf. A letter from Breen to Zehner on 15 January reveals this, as Breen counselled 'we understand that you will not show the actual transvection [*sic*] from man to wolf, and that repulsive or horrifying physical details will not be used'.[19] The Universal team appeared entirely compliant, a letter from Harris to Breen on 30 January confirming that the prostitute would be rewritten as a beggar and the werewolf transformation would not be shown. As we shall see later, the compliance only ever took place in the memorandums, and both scenes remained intact. Harris and Harvey Gates contributed to the screenplay, but John Colton was tasked with delivering the final product.[20] He submitted the script on 26 January and the film went into production on 28 January. Director Stuart Walker did not have a background in horror films, but his successful Dickens adaptations for Universal, *Great Expectations* (1934) and *The Mystery of Edwin Drood*, demonstrated he was able to evoke a specific kind of gothic London. Hungarian Charles Stumar (who also filmed *The Mummy* and *The Raven*) was the photographer, and filming was completed less than a month later on 23 February, four days over schedule and $36,000 over budget at $195,000.[21] The film was screened to the PCA on 22 March and granted a certificate the next day subject to cuts being made in the final werewolf fight scene, including 'the shot in which Yogami's face is shown scratched and dripping blood, and second, the actual strangling of Yogami'.[22] No doubt Zehner agreed, and yet again we shall see that the shots – or at least a number of shots that exactly fit the descriptions above – remain.

Werewolf of London went on wide release across America in May 1935, and was screened at the Rialto Theatre in Times Square, New York. This cinema had a certain significance in horror film exhibition, nicknamed the 'cinematic chamber of horrors', the *New York Times* writing in 1941 that 'in the field of jitters, the Rialto is undoubtedly tops. A goose pimple is its trademark'.[23] By the 1930s Times Square was in serious decline, Prohibition and the Depression wreaking havoc on what was 'once a centre of upmarket cultural consumption'.[24] In February 1933, with a final screening of *Island of Lost Souls*, bankrupt Paramount relinquished ownership of the Rialto and handed over control to Arthur Mayer, who as Tim Snelson and Mark Jancovich explain, positioned the Rialto's programming in opposition to the post-1934 Hays Office:

> rather than playing to aspirational cinemagoers, Mayer cultivated an overtly disreputable image for his cinema, aiming to appeal to people slumming it. He publicly rejected notions of 'cultural uplift' precisely when the Hollywood studios, their exhibition chains and the administrators of the production Code were labouring to counter accusations of impropriety.[25]

Werewolf of London was the last screening at the Rialto before the building was demolished in May 1935.[26] Its significance emerges as not only the first werewolf film, but in its relationship to censorship and exhibition practices: it is the first film in this book to deal at pre-production stage with the Hays office, it is then marketed explicitly as a disreputable 'horror film' through its relationship with the Rialto; it also played an important part in the cinema's exhibition history.

FOREIGN HORRORS

As suggested by the censor's intended cuts, the film has a strong and sustained interest in the mutilation and dissolution of the male body, where the male werewolves – Dr Glendon and Dr Yogami – physically suffer and are eventually murdered. I now explore the sexual politics of the film in this light, suggesting that the representation of the werewolf is intrinsically linked to a presentation of horror and suffering as a masculine, rather than feminine, form. As I have suggested elsewhere, later werewolf films such as *An*

American Werewolf in London (1981) or *Dog Soldiers* (2002) are pre-eminently concerned with locating fear, trauma and death upon the male body.[27] Arguably, this preoccupation can be traced right back to the first werewolf film: *Werewolf of London*.

The film begins by zooming in on a map of Tibet and then dissolves to reveal a mountain base camp. The film's main protagonist, Glendon, treks across barren landscapes and scrambles down into an isolated ravine. He eventually locates his prize, a rare plant that only flowers by moonlight, the *marifisa lupina lumina* (an early link in the film between plant life and werewolfery, 'lupina' deriving from *lupus*, meaning 'wolf'). However, he is not alone. As he crouches over the plant he is unaware that a werewolf (later revealed to be Yogami) is spying on him. Glendon is framed from the monster's point of view, unusually for the period this aligns the audience with the aggressor: the werewolf then attacks, Yogami bites Glendon's arm viciously and Glendon responds by wielding a curved hunting knife and stabbing the monster. The attack is the first point of intimate contact between Yogami and Glendon, and one that resonates with Carol Clover's assertion that in horror films 'knives and needles, like teeth, beaks, fangs and claws, are personal extensions of the body that bring attacker and attacked into primitive, animalistic embrace'.[28] Indeed, this primitive communion sets in motion an intense and ambivalent relationship that lasts the duration of the narrative, conflating the (yet to be revealed) homosexual desires of the two male werewolves with violence.

Glendon crawls forward, bloodied and torn, and grabs at the *marifisa*. A quick dissolve reveals the scientist healed and tending to the plant at home in his London laboratory. A party is thrown to celebrate his triumphant return, but much to the chagrin of his wife Lisa, Glendon refuses to leave his laboratory. The first image of Lisa in the film is mediated electronically: she is shown on a video monitor designed by Glendon to screen people attempting to enter his laboratory. The image evokes the aloofness with which Glendon treats Lisa, and is representative of the distancing *mise en scène* between husband and wife. Having coaxed him away from his experiments, Lisa weakly jokes that he cares more for his plants than he does for her. Their exchange is filmed in medium shot from side on, both parties within a single static image; its significance marked by a lack of shot/reverse-shots that are later used to signal reciprocal sexual interest between Yogami and Glendon, and between Lisa and her childhood sweetheart, Paul Ames, with whom she eventually elopes. Glendon joins the party with notable displeasure, and witnesses his Aunt Ettie reintroducing Lisa to Paul. There is a significant difference between Lisa's earlier stilted conversation with Glendon, as eyeline matching, smiling faces and reciprocal gazing mark Lisa and Paul as a traditional heterosexual couple and reinforce her estrangement from her husband.

Yogami appears at the party in his human form and introduces himself to Glendon as a fellow botanist. Their intimacy is signalled by their twinned sartorial style: identical black suits, white shirts and matching white flowers in their jacket pockets. While Yogami, played by Swedish-born Warner Oland, doesn't appear here as a werewolf, he is still inscribed as monstrous through racial stereotyping. Despite Yogami's measured tones and affiliation with the University of Carpathia, Aunt Ettie pervades her references to him with Orientalist overtones, repeatedly referring to him by the Japanese-sounding 'Dr Yokohama'. The conflation of the Oriental and monstrosity is a relatively common fate for 1930s horror film monsters, particularly characters played by Oland, which include the 'Yellow Peril' figure of the 'Fu Manchu' series.[29] Indeed, it seeps into the critical reception of the film, with the *Motion Picture Herald* describing Yogami as 'a strange Oriental, in whom Glendon recognizes something strangely familiar', the *Hollywood Reporter* as 'the Oriental werewolf', and *Motion Picture Daily* as an 'afflicted Oriental scientist'.[30] Harry M. Benshoff has argued that the 1930s monster is often simultaneously racialised and sexualised, that 'frequently the queer couple is itself an inter-racial one, a trope that invariably recasts a light/dark racial hierarchy along with a gendered one'.[31] *Werewolf of London* follows this dynamic, for as I will show, Yogami is made monstrous not only by his foreignness but through his sexual proclivities.

Deep in discussion, the two botanists leave the party to speak alone inside Glendon's house. Glendon does not recognise his Tibetan attacker but he senses something of familiarity, asking Yogami 'have I met you before, sir?', to which Yogami replies 'in Tibet, once, but only for a moment in the dark'. Their close-up shot/reverse-shot then further reinforces the men's attraction to each other, contrasting with static long shots and the gap between Glendon and his wife from a few minutes before. Yogami recounts werewolf lore to Glendon, explaining that the sap of the *marifsa* will prevent transformation and that 'in workaday, modern London, at this very moment, there are two cases of lycanthropy known to me'. Having still not understood, Glendon asks how the werewolves contracted their disease and Yogami moves even closer, whispering 'from the bite of another werewolf'. He slowly and deliberately strokes his hand down Glendon's unresisting arm, feeling through the suit material to press upon the scars that he has torn into Glendon's skin. Unable to speak, Glendon walks forward into the foreground of the frame and Yogami moves in behind him, staring intently. The stillness between the two men is only broken by the sound of Lisa entering the room. Yogami whispers 'your wife?' into Glendon's ear, and Glendon nods briefly before turning to face Lisa, who walks into the middle of the frame and provides a physical point of separation between the two werewolves. By introducing four people into erotically charged relationships, rather than the traditional heterosexual couple who are forced apart by a single male monster, *Werewolf of London* is relatively unusual for a 1930s horror film. While Lisa initially serves as the triangular point between Yogami and Glendon, her childhood sweetheart Paul also woos her, and they grow intimately acquainted as the narrative progresses. The purpose of this four-fold relationship is revealed at the film's close: Glendon murders Yogami, Glendon is shot dead by Paul's uncle and the monstrous men are thus removed from the narrative, leaving Lisa a respectable widow and Paul free to pursue her.

The party ends and that evening Glendon works alone in his laboratory. As he tends to his plants, he glances at his right hand, which (through a series of lap dissolves) grows fur and transforms into a grotesque parody of a paw. Panicking, he wipes his hand with the *marifisa* bloom, and the transformation stops. Later that night, Yogami tries to get into the laboratory, desperate to halt his own transformation, but is confronted by Glendon. Yogami entreats 'tonight is the first night of the full moon', and stares knowingly at Glendon's bare right forearm. A close up captures Glendon's Tibetan injury revealed by his rolled-up sleeve: the

V-shaped wound is deep and is pulled together with thick, uneven sutures. Yogami begs for the blossom of the *marifisa* to 'save two souls tonight', but Glendon rejects him. Angrily Yogami stalks out into the night, but not before providing him with a warning that 'the werewolf instinctively seeks to kill the thing it loves best'. The heterosexually sanctioned reading suggests that should Glendon transform, he would attack his wife Lisa, but it can be read another way. In Yogami's warning is a less-than subtle reference to Oscar Wilde's poem 'The Ballad of Reading Gaol' (1898), written after his incarceration for gross indecency with another man. It includes the oft-quoted phrase 'yet each man kills the thing he loves'.[32] The reference to Wilde's poem and the performance of the two actors suggests that Glendon and Yogami when transformed will attempt to kill each other. Wilde wrote of a man walking to his death, in this case the prophecy indicates Glendon's doomed ending: both botanists are dead men walking.

'TRANSVECTION': MAN TO WOLF

The following night Glendon begins to transform once more. This time he cannot stop the change as Yogami has stolen the final blooms, and the scene then depicts a man changing into a werewolf for the first time in film history. The transformation is shown in a tracking shot of 20 seconds, comprising three separate shots with edits disguised by Glendon's disappearing behind a series of stone pillars. Each time he emerges from behind a pillar he is significantly advanced in his transformation. His hair is fuller and darker with a sharp widow's peak, thick-furred sideburns frame his face, his skin is significantly darkened, his nose flattened, his ears elongated and pointed and his mouth is filled with sharp white incisors. He holds his paws up to his mouth in horror, he chokes and scrabbles at his throat unable to verbalise the anguish of his transformation. Horror emerges not just from what we have seen – the transformation of man into werewolf – but from Glendon's realisation of what he has become.

Special Photographic Effects assistant David Horsley, interviewed by *Photon* magazine in 1935, explained that technical pre-production focused on how the transformation would occur, with the general consensus that a series of obvious cuts would spoil the flow and significance of the moment:

> It was decided to photograph Hull against a black velvet background and matte his figure onto the normal background scene. The pillars were separately photographed and further matted onto this composite, masking the precise instant where the alteration in makeup occurred, so that in its final stage there appeared to be no break in camera movement.[33]

In addition to the composite matte, Hull underwent a significant make-up transformation. In a story that sounds suspiciously like studio publicity material, *Variety* reported that there was nobody in Universal's make-up department with sufficient imagination to create the horrible face required for Glendon's transformation and so Hull was forced to craft his appearance himself.[34] The *Los Angeles Times* must also have been fed the same story, for it reported the same in greater detail, explaining that Hull 'planned his make-up by using portrait photographs of himself. On these photographs he drew in pen and ink the facial changes [he] wanted to look like a werewolf', then made himself up as he would if acting the part in the theatre, finally demanding of the official make-up artist Jack P. Pierce 'here's the way I want to look – now fix me up to look like this on screen'.[35] The article obligingly explains how the make-up maestro achieved this:

> Pierce framed his face with strips of long gray wolf hair. A set of pointed fangs like a wolf's were fitted over the natural teeth in Hull's lower jaw. His eyes were reduced to two-thirds normal size by pasting the corners tight. His upper lip was coated with absorbent cotton and collodion which gave it a wrinkled appearance. His hands were covered with hair and fitted with long claws. Six hours were needed to don this make-up.[36]

Whether or not this was just studio ballyhoo, the description reinforced the association of the werewolf with Universal's established horror film monsters; following Lon Chaney's masochistic

endeavours, each description in the press of Karloff's transformations was accompanied by a description of the length of time he
was bound to the make-up chair. With his six-hour stint, Hull was
now inaugurated into the Universal monster stable.

Having read the revised script, Breen wrote to Zehner on 28
January. He pointed out two instances of 'actual transvection from
man to wolf' in the revised script and then referred him back to
their first meeting, stating very clearly that they had agreed that
the transformation would not be shown.[37] In a wonderfully florid
response written two days later, Harris referred to Paramount's
Dr Jekyll and Mr Hyde in order to explain what will happen
on set:

> We quite agree with you in the point that you raise that the picture
> should not be unduly terrifying and we have eliminated from the
> script any transvections into the animal, wolf, and our transvections
> are merely from our normal players to people with hirsute tendencies
> with naturally a pointing of the ears and noses and a lengthening of
> the fingers, not dissimilar to what was done to the picture *Dr Jekyll
> and Mr Hyde*.[38]

Harris appeals to the prestige of Paramount's production in order
to allay the concerns of the censor, a canny move as *Dr Jekyll and
Mr Hyde* had been a particularly lauded picture. It had screened to
much critical success at the first-ever Venice International Film
Festival in August 1932 and had been included in the *Film Daily*'s
'Ten Best Pictures of 1932', voted for by national film critics and
editors.[39] The letter is also further evidence that Harris – as story
writer and contributor to the screenplay – was not only familiar
with the *Dr Jekyll and Mr Hyde* plot, but was actively seeking to
emulate the reputation of the 1931 film in his own production.
Harris' letter may have temporarily pacified the censors, but during filming the production team became increasingly concerned
about how the final product would be judged by the PCA. Filming
began at the end of January; on 7 February Bergman telephoned
Stuart to ask if the objections against showing a man turning
into a wolf still stood. As documented in the follow-up letter,
the censor smoothly responded that according to Harris' earlier

correspondence, the 'transvection shot' would simply be a change in make-up, and as such they did not foresee any problems.[40] As my earlier description of the moment of transformation reveals though, the final product was rather more than that, a complex combination of matte composition, make up and sharp editing, its horror compounded not only by the hirsuteness of Glendon, but Hull's anguished, desperate performance.

DR JEKYLL AND DR GLENDON

with a transport of glee, I mauled the unresisting body, tasting delight from every blow; and it was not till weariness had begun to succeed that I was suddenly, in the top fit of my delirium, struck through the heart by a cold thrill of terror. A mist dispersed; I saw my life to be forfeit; and fled from the scene of these excesses, at once glorying and trembling, my lust of evil gratified and stimulated.[41]

'Henry Jekyll's Full Statement of the Case'
The Strange Case of Dr Jekyll and Mr Hyde (1886)

Werewolf of London had already appealed to the make-up techniques of *Dr Jekyll and Mr Hyde* in order to obtain PCA approval. In the following section of the film, Glendon the werewolf goes on a murderous rampage in London and there are further resonances with *Dr Jekyll and Mr Hyde*, not least the conflicted protagonist: an educated man who cannot stop his dark side wreaking murderous havoc, who bitterly regrets his double's misdemeanours but is powerless to stop them. Despite being filmed in seemingly contemporary settings for the beginning and the end of the film, this section depicts the capital city as a Victorian urban space bruised by the aftershocks of Jack the Ripper. This change adheres to one of the prototype narrative structures of the late Victorian gothic novel, that Peter Hutchings describes as the 'Victorian Gothic' journey, which sees the protagonist move from 'comfortably bourgeois locations into London's dark side' redolent with 'encounters with anachronistic settings and types'.[42] Until now, Glendon's body has been victimised: brutally attacked, imbued with homoerotic tension, and transformed into the body of a hairy, homicidal beast. Upon leaving Glendon Manor, Glendon enters London where he conforms to the heterosexual murderous impulses of his forbears. He will murder two of the women, attempt to murder a third and be forced to fraternise with down-at-the-heel tripe-eating landladies, Mrs Whack and Mrs Mountcaster.

The remainder of the principal characters are also in London, socialising at Aunt Ettie's house party. Drunken Aunt Ettie is sent to bed and is thus alone and incapacitated when the werewolf comes calling. Glendon climbs up the wall of her house and onto the balcony outside her bedroom. As was the case in the depiction of the first werewolf attack the camera aligns the audience with the subjective experience of the monster, beginning with a close up of gnarled paws grasping at the *fleur de lis* iron balcony (Figure 7.1). The emphasis on the first-person viewpoint is not simply to represent the victimised woman in the most direct manner, but (as demonstrated through the emphasis on the paws

Figure 7.1 A first-person point of view shot: the viewer becomes the werewolf as it climbs onto a balcony and prepares to attack in *Werewolf of London* (1935, Stuart Walker).

at the beginning) to thrill the spectator in performing the role of monster. Nonetheless, generic expectations are then somewhat thwarted: Aunt Ettie is neither the beautiful young nubile virgin, nor sleeping in bed. As the French doors are opened and the werewolf enters, she sits on the edge of the bed fully dressed in the dark, turning slowly as she hears Glendon's approach. Fluctuating light levels cast dancing shadows on the walls and she screams at the werewolf (Figure 7.2). The action abruptly moves downstairs to reveal frightened guests reacting to her cries. At first glance, Aunt Ettie's attack appears to function as a gendered horror trope in which the (female) victim is menaced by the (male) monster, echoing Linda Williams' analysis that in horror 'the bodies of women figured on the screen have functioned traditionally as the primary *embodiments* of pleasure, fear and pain'.[43] Yet unlike Yogami's bloody assault on Glendon, Ettie's attack does not involve physical contact, and after the action returns to the bedroom it is evident that Glendon has fled before killing. The film is unusual for the 1930s in having a fairly large supporting cast of

Figure 7.2 Aunt Ettie (Spring Byington) screams into the camera as the werewolf approaches in *Werewolf of London* (1935, Stuart Walker).

predominantly middle-aged and older women who play comedic supporting roles. As one of these, Aunt Ettie cannot be categorised as a female victim, whose sole purpose – typically – is to look beautiful while screaming. Unsympathetic and 'stiff upper-lip' male characters such as Glendon and Scotland Yard's Captain Forsyth may drive the narrative forward, but strong female (and explicitly English) characters such as Aunt Ettie, her friend Lady Forsyth and landlady Mrs Mountcaster offer kindness, laughter and humanity and undercut the perception of women in 1930s horror films as commanding only a 'scream queen' role.

Glendon may have botched the first murder but now he goes to Goose Lane, intent on finding his second victim. The Goose Lane sequence begins with a low-angle, extreme long shot of a foggy street dimly illuminated by a solitary gas lamp, explicitly evoking the dangerous, run-down version of London inhabited by popular-culture representations of Jack the Ripper. Glendon hides in the background of the image, wearing a black overcoat, a cap and scarf, an outfit that mirrors the sartorial style of Mr Hyde and signals that murder is afoot. A woman walks under the bridge, her bleached blonde hair is curled and set beneath a jaunty black beret; a patterned scarf tied at her neck sets off her heavily made-up face. Her short skirt, heels and handbag complete the visual insinuation of prostitution. The censors frowned upon this even at script stage, and on 15 January Breen requested that a code violation be removed from page 'D-14 of the Blue Script', where 'one of Glendon's victims is shown as a prostitute soliciting him', emphasising that 'if this story is photographed in a fashion to create nervous shock among women and children, it might be held up as contrary to the good and welfare of the industry'.[44] In a letter responding to a later meeting on 30 January, Harris attempted some nifty political double-speak in order to keep the sequence in the picture:

> We see a girl of the poorer class walking down a dim street. She is naturally a little frightened because of the neighbourhood and the darkness of the street – the girl, being of the lower class, is wearing a skirt which is not too lengthy, possibly having shrunk when she herself washed it, being quite without money to send it to be

regularly cleaned, and carried a handbag such as is carried by millions of respectable women today, large enough to hold the miscellaneous vanities which women carry today.[45]

This is notable as another example of how the producers used prolix language in order to pacify the PCA thus retaining the intended content of their film. It also says much about American ideas about class and gender in Victorian London, for the werewolf has entered the world where poor 'working girls' can be found around every corner. Glendon refuses to look at the woman but she stops and stares openly at him. He raises his face to the lamplight and finally returns her look, then lunges at her, and chases her off-screen. Her screams ring out for two seconds as the screen fades to black, insinuating that Glendon has finally killed. The taboo is breached and his old life is forfeit. He plunges further into London's murky depths, eventually ending up at a nearby gin palace and trying to rent a room from Mrs Mountcaster, another anachronistic archetype described gleefully in the *Hollywood Reporter* as 'a gin-soaked cockney crone'.[46] It would not be fair to attribute the plot entirely to Stevenson though, for when Glendon retires to his rented room his actions closely mirror those of Calliet in *The Werewolf of Paris*. Surrounded by the detritus of the (imagined) East End, in a place awash with gin, economic deprivation and unpleasant old ladies, Glendon moves into the bare room and prepares himself for his next transformation. He locks the door, bars the window, and prays that he will not be able to escape. Yet stopping killing is not an option, as Calliet has already discovered in Paris:

> He knew when an attack was coming on. During the day he would have no appetite. It was particularly the thought of bread and butter that nauseated him. In the evening he would feel tense and both tired and sleepless. Then he would arrange his window and lock his door, and having taken his precautions, he would lie down. Frequently he would wake in the morning, in bed, with no recollection of what had happened at night. Only a wretched stiffness in his neck, a lassitude in his limbs, that could come from nothing but miles of running, scratches on his hands and feet, and an acrid taste in his mouth argued that he had spent the night elsewhere.[47]

Physical enclosures cannot contain Calliet nor Glendon, who transforms, smashes a window and escapes into the night, leaving frightened Mrs Mountcaster to fret about her latest lodger. His next kill takes place at London Zoological Gardens, and again the narrative insinuates that the woman deserved her death for being out at night and returning the monster's look. The scene begins at the zoo as a heavily made-up, drunken blonde woman appears. She is having an affair with Al, the married zookeeper. She holds up her compact to powder her face and as she looks into the mirror, Glendon is captured within the reflection. She screams and flees off-screen with Glendon in pursuit, the scene quickly fading to black. Al and the blonde become the mirror image of Paul and Lisa's (insinuated) adulterous upper-class affair; they are working-class and sordid, drunkenly kissing late at night in a public place and an easy target for moral retribution. The lesson here, about which Breen was so keen, is that adultery should be punished. Indeed, Glendon's despatching of the blonde allows Paul and Lisa to find happiness at the film's conclusion, once Lisa is a widow. While alcohol may be a London vice, it is the advertising of sexual availability that must be condemned.

This section of the film echoes both *Dr Jekyll and Mr Hyde* and *The Werewolf of Paris* in depicting the conflicted male protagonist at the mercy of his bestial impulses. As this analysis has revealed, however, it has a somewhat uncomfortable fit with the rest of the film; its preoccupation with murdering young women and interacting with older ones stands in direct contrast to the beginning and end of the text with their resolutely male-centred narrative. It suggests, in a slightly uncomfortable fashion, that urban lower-class locations bespeak heterosexual violence while the safety of upper-class country abodes allow homosexual desires to run unchecked. Yet, in keeping with the theme of the film as a whole, the final section will reveal how the end of the film returns to Yogami, Glendon and (referring to Wilde once more) 'the love that dare not speak its name'. The *dénouement* takes place in one of the most common backdrops of the 1930s American horror film: the mad male scientist in his laboratory.[48]

HOMO HOMINI LUPUS

I only knew what hunted thought
  Quickened his step, and why
He looked upon the garish day
  With such a wistful eye;
The man had killed the thing he loved
  And so he had to die.[49]

Oscar Wilde, 'The Ballad of Reading Gaol' (1898)

As with so many 1930s 'mad scientist' films, the final act of *Werewolf of London* concentrates on concluding the monstrous homo-social male narrative and restoring the heterosexual relationship. Glendon leaves London and travels in secret to Lisa's family home, an imposing country manor, where he instructs the groundskeeper to lock him up in a suitably cobwebbed crypt. Lisa and Paul also arrive at the estate, whereupon the transformed Glendon breaks out of the crypt, attacks Lisa and fights Paul, who recognises him before he escapes once more. With a werewolf for a husband, Lisa is legitimately able to fall into Paul's arms. Glendon's assault on Lisa represents the proper dissolution of the 'rectangular' relationship: the four characters are split evenly into two couples, Paul and Lisa set as the heterosexual norm, Yogami and Glendon as the doomed werewolves, set to pursue (to the death) their bestial homoerotic bond. The fight to the death takes place as Glendon escapes Lisa's family home and sneaks back to his laboratory. He leans eagerly over the *marifasa* as the final bud flowers, but his much longed-for temporary respite from werewolfery is not to be: Yogami appears and takes the sap for himself. Transformed, Glendon grabs him and locks him into an intimate, violent embrace, their faces almost touching. He then throttles Yogami, bends him backwards over a bench, and tears at his blood-streaked face, while his victim beats him in vain with a silver-tipped cane. The Tibetan assault is reversed and the logic of *Frankenstein* comes into play: Yogami is now the helpless victim assaulted by his own creation.

Glendon pins Yogami to the floor by his neck, killing him. He then looks directly into the camera in an extreme close up: at first, his face is still, then he whimpers and howls, his distress echoing Yogami's warning that the werewolf instinctively seeks to kill the one it loves (Figure 7.3). When Yogami warned of this, an image of Lisa was superimposed over Glendon's face offering a socially sanctioned heterosexual reading. This reading was reinforced in publicity for the film, as demonstrated in a poster for Chicago's New Palace Theatre: Lisa's eyes are wide open with fear and her arms wrapped around Paul, who manfully holds her close to his chest and quizzically stares off-screen. The tag line: 'ever meet [*sic*] a werewolf? Well, you don't want to. But these people have – Valerie Hobson and Lester Matthews have reason to look afraid. Because in *Werewolf of London* something awful is after them'.[50] This reading was made by a number of contemporary newspaper, trade journal and magazine critics on both sides of the Atlantic, including writers at the *Atlanta Constitution*, *Monthly Film Bulletin* and *Harrison's Reports*. This was typified by the *Motion Picture Daily*'s explanation that Glendon 'is about to kill the one he loves best, Valerie Hobson, his wife'.[51] Only the *New York Times* hinted at potential subversive

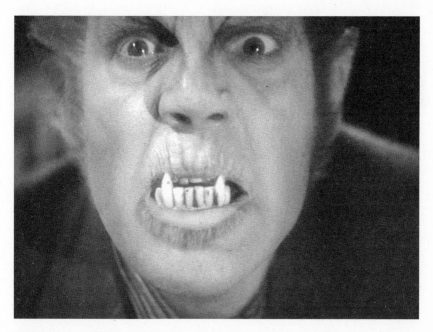

Figure 7.3 The werewolf (Henry Hull) howls in anguish as he realises he has murdered Dr Yogami (Warner Oland) in *Werewolf of London* (1935, Stuart Walker).

activities in describing how Glendon 'may be driven to the murder of his wife and others "whom he loves best"'.[52] Despite two attacks on his wife (one of which is still to come), however, Glendon never kills Lisa. The editing of the sequence reinforces this: Yogami and Glendon's fight and Yogami's death in Glendon's laboratory in the basement of the manor are juxtaposed with crosscuts to Lisa hiding in her bedroom on the first floor. Lisa's isolation on the marital bed as her husband strangles his homoerotic love interest several floors below makes a rather forceful point.[53] Thought of in this way, the death of Yogami might be seen as the culmination of a narrative of male homosocial desire, a narrative which, in the case of this film, has particular resonance with the figure of the werewolf. In 'Civilisation and its discontents', published five years before the film's release, Freud has much to say about the wolf's relationship to the man:

> ...men are not gentle creatures who want to be loved, and who at the most can defend themselves if they are attacked; they are, on the contrary, creatures among whose instinctual endowments is to be reckoned a powerful share of aggressiveness. As a result, their neighbour is for them not only a potential helper or sexual object, but also someone who tempts them to satisfy their aggressiveness on him – to use him sexually without his consent – to humiliate him, to cause his pain, to torture and to kill him. *Homo homini lupus.* [54]

Freud's description of man's instinctually aggressive nature, of his desire to torture, sexually attack and to kill others says much about the psyche of the werewolf. Glendon then tries to attack Lisa again, but the Chief of Scotland Yard (and Paul's uncle), Colonel Forsyth, arrives and shoots Glendon in the chest. As he dies, he apologises to Lisa saying 'I'm sorry I couldn't have made you – happier', as if to acknowledge their sham marriage. In the film's final moments a series of lap dissolves depict his return to his human form. Paul stares at Lisa intently as her husband dies; waiting for the moment when they can legally be together. The final image of the film is a plane flying into the distance, implying that they have eloped to his flying school in California. Indeed, *Harrison's Reports* explains that 'Miss Hobson later marries Matthews', even though this is never shown or discussed in the film.[55] For all this film's gendered and sexual subversions, its Freudian drives and Wildean references, the 1930s horror film has two final demands: the vanquishing of the monster(s) and the union of the heterosexual couple by the time the credits roll.

Werewolf of London is a film composed of violence, homoerotic relationships, a not-insignificant debt to *Jekyll and Hyde*, and of course, for the first time in the cinema, the werewolf. It did not receive entirely positive reviews: *Jekyll and Hyde* references certainly abounded, as noted in *Time*, *Variety*, the *New York Times* and *Photoplay*, while a few also commented on similarities with the premise of *The Invisible Man*.[56] The *Hollywood Reporter* advocated the film, demanding that it 'takes its place on the horror picture roll of honour beside *Frankenstein*, *Bride of Frankenstein*, *Dr X*, *Dracula*, *Wax Museum* and the rest of the better spine vibrators'.[57] *Photoplay* argued that the film was 'another good old Universal shocker – chock full of screams and howls and murders – if you like to be subjected to chills and the creeps, you'll enjoy it'.[58] The *Motion Picture Daily* described it as 'acted in a manner calculated to bring a maximum of thrills and chills, this picture maintains the horror pace set by Universal'.[59] What is notable is that the more upbeat reviews cohere around the idea of the werewolf as the cinema's newest monster; evident in Mae Tinee's enthusiastic review in the *Chicago Daily Tribune*:

> Good morning! Have you a werewolf in your home? Probably not. BUT – if any male connected with your establishment starts acting funny when the moon is about to be at its full; if he cultivates strange flowers in a conservatory; if he disappears mysteriously; or if howls are heard coming from the place where you saw him last; why – beware![60]

Tinee is a staff writer pen name (matinee), and the many reviews quoted from Tinee in this book are undoubtedly from a number of different reporters. What is, however, particularly pleasant about a Tinee review is the almost universal enjoyment of horror films (as well as the very bad jokes – when reviewing *Doctor X* s/he puns 'if you liked *Dracula* and *White Zombie* you'll probably get a kick from *Doctor X*. But don't X-pect too much! Forgive me!').[61] While many newspaper critics during this period not only disliked horror films but also refused to engage with them in any meaningful way, Tinee can always be relied upon to delight at the new monsters and to peruse the macabre depths to which the narratives will go. As Tinee so thoroughly enjoys the horror cycle, it leads me to wonder if the veil of anonymity afforded by the nom de plume is what makes the horror film an acceptable pleasure to a film critic during the 1930s. Consider *Island of Lost Souls*' reception (Chapter 2) and how Mordaunt Hall of the *New York Times* tied himself in knots trying to dismiss the film while simultaneously acknowledging its quality signifiers. This contemptuousness is certainly still evident in *Werewolf of London*'s reception: Scheuer of the *Los Angeles Times* and Andre Sennwald of the *New York Times* managed only moderate approval, the former grudgingly describing it as 'a good picture of its kind', with the latter admitting it was a 'pretty valiant bit of gooseflesh melodrama'.[62] And again, as with *Island of Lost Souls*, many reviewers struggled to reconcile the film's intentionally horrific sensibilities with its possibilities of being a good film. This is typified by the *New York Herald Tribune*'s response, which admitted 'strong nerves are needed to cope with the Rialto's new offering' and criticised the plot (weak with 'too many loose ends') and 'stereotyped' direction.[63] This was also the response of *Monthly Film Bulletin* and *Film Daily*, the latter arguing that the acting ability of the cast made the film 'better than it actually is from a story standpoint', but as a horror film it 'well acted and calculated to satisfy fans who like this kind of hoke'.[64]

In 1935 Universal released four horror films in quick succession: *The Mystery of Edwin Drood*, *Werewolf of London*, *The Raven* and *Bride of Frankenstein*. The last was a prestige production with a respected director and a popular lead actor. Its A-picture status is evident in production statistics: it took 46 days to shoot and ran more than $100,000 over budget at $400,000, more than double *Werewolf of London*'s $195,000.[65] The differences in budget and production were not the only points of contrast between the two films. The British settings of the werewolf picture, so important to the middle section of the film, are also lacking when held up for comparison with Whale's film, which was made by a prestigious English director who commanded an all-British cast of main characters including Boris Karloff, Colin Clive, Valerie Hobson, Elsa Lanchester, Una O'Connor and Ernest Thesiger. As Alberto Manguel has pointed out, the Britishness was 'a feature the publicity department endlessly exploited by having the cast photographed endlessly drinking tea', an American grumble already heard in relation to Whale's previous 'British' horror film, *The Old Dark House*, and Wray's experiences of working on *The Clairvoyant*.[66] Indeed, the werewolf film's weakest moments come from the middle third of the film and its very limited production design: the sets create only an indistinct and intangible city, merely a series of impressions of late-nineteenth-century urban English gothic. Reviewing the film's release in London at the Capitol, the UK trade paper *Kinematograph Weekly* dismissed the setting, as 'the London atmosphere is marred by many inexcusable incongruities', while *The Times* criticised Walker for his inability to adequately capture the capital city.[67] Discussing the *marifisa*'s lack of response to laboratory conditions, the reviewer continued:

> Not even the artificial moonbeams created by the doctor could restore the plant to life. Artificiality is not confined to these moonbeams, and throughout the film the terror which London is supposed to experience on account of the doctor's ghoulish murders never becomes more terrifying than the headlines in the more sensational Press – and newspaper print is inevitably cold.[68]

Universal chose to release *Werewolf of London* and *Bride of Frankenstein* almost simultaneously. In Los Angeles *Bride of Frankenstein* opened on 22 April, while *Werewolf of London* followed on 6 May.[69] In New York, they opened a day apart, *Bride of Frankenstein* on 8 May at the Roxy and *Werewolf of London* on 9 May at the Rialto.[70] Competition was made even tougher in New York with the release of MGM's *Mark of the Vampire* in the same week. Contemporary reviewers certainly noted the ill-timing of the werewolf film, the *Philadelphia Exhibitor* commenting that 'it is being released too closely on *Bride of Frankenstein*'s heels' and the *Los Angeles Times* bemoaning, 'Hollywood audiences are never let off anything. Scarcely recovered from the horrors of the recent *Bride of Frankenstein*, they were scared all over again yesterday when *Werewolf of London* had its premiere at that theatre'.[71] It appears that *Bride of Frankenstein* was the primary draw, and that audiences were not sufficiently recovered to stomach a second horror film (from the same studio) so soon afterwards.

The unfortunate comparison between the two films is exemplified by *Variety*'s reviews, published side by side on 15 May 1935. *Variety* describes Glendon's story as 'neither sufficiently gripping nor more than moderately shocking', adding that the 'name value is slight', and 'the picture is a distinct takeoff on *Dr Jekyll and Mr Hyde*. But without the kick of the original'.[72] In contrast, Whale's picture is 'an imaginative and outstanding film', and 'one of those rare instances where no-one can review it, or talk about it, without mentioning the cameraman, art director and score composer in the same breath as the actors and director'.[73] Valerie Hobson featured in both – playing Lisa in the werewolf film and Elizabeth in the Frankenstein film – having flown over from England on a four-picture contract to Universal.[74] But rather than being an asset that elevated the B picture, she performed weakly in both films, described by *Variety* as a 'comely girl with few opportunities' as Lisa, and 'not at all convincing' as Frank's fiancée in *Bride of Frankenstein*.[75]

The *New York Times* hinted at 'a change in plans' that had brought *Bride of Frankenstein* forward to replace *Mister Dynamite* (1935) in the release schedule, but perhaps the simultaneous release date suggests a lack of faith in *Werewolf of London* itself.[76] In being released with *Bride of Frankenstein*, *Werewolf of London* can be seen as a sacrificial gesture for the film critics who, by 1935, had tired not only of Universal's output but also of the film cycle as a whole. Whether planned or not, this is certainly what happened. *Bride of Frankenstein* was very positively received yet *Time* described Walker's film as a 'nasty little fantasy' that was 'sillier than *Bride of Frankenstein*' and 'more alarming for small children than *Mark of the Vampire*'.[77] *Picturegoer* was entirely venomous, shrieking about 'a thoroughly preposterous story, which presents you with macabre thrills without attempting either to justify them or make them really convincing. This is an example of the "horror for horror's sake" picture which appeals to many'.[78] William Troy's review for *The Nation* was the most overtly negative, placing it within the 'deluge of horror which has been gathering in Hollywood studios since the success of *Dracula* and *Frankenstein*'.[79] *Dracula* inaugurated the sound horror film cycle in 1931 and four years later critics had had enough; by the time of *Werewolf of London*'s release they appeared to be holding up their hands in despair. For years previously they had complained about these films; in 1932 a critic for the *Washington Post* described *Murders in the Rue Morgue* as a tribute 'to mass morbidity' and a 'thoroughly conventionalized form of emotionally perverted appeal'; the following year the *Los Angeles Times* began its *Island of Lost Souls* review by describing it as 'horrible to the point of repugnance'.[80] Walker's film was released at a crucial point in the sound horror cycle, right at the end of the first wave when there was a clear sense of the tide turning for production and critical reception of the genre. Familiarity had undoubtedly bred contempt, and the new lifeblood of the werewolf did little to impress the reviewers.

This chapter has sought to illuminate *Werewolf of London* as the first, the most important (and yet most overlooked) werewolf film. Its production and release in 1935, coming after the inauguration of the PCA, makes it particularly important in the context of *After Dracula*. I hope that the censorship material discussed goes some way to changing our understandings of the relationship between horror film producers and censorship bodies in the 1930s: while the producers of the film negotiated with the PCA on a certain level, they ultimately ignored many of their requests yet the PCA passed the film anyway. These findings accord with Eric Schaefer's analysis of the PCA during this period; he quotes Geoffrey Shurlock (who worked under Breen before being put in charge) who explains: 'we never refused seals. We were in the business of granting seals. The whole purpose of [the PCA's] existence was to arrange pictures so that we could give seals'.[81] This leads Schaefer to point out, 'once created, the PCA worked in the interest of the majors, taking a proactive position of suggestion and negotiation rather than a reactionary stance of restraint'.[82] While Schaefer is concerned with exploitation films, his point is equally valid for horror films: my analysis of *Werewolf of London* suggests that the relationship between the PCA and Universal's producers wasn't quite as straightforward as a decree to follow the enforced code or face being banned; there are many shades of grey in creating and censoring the 1930s American horror film. These findings can be contrasted with British production censorship: a comparison of *Werewolf of London* with *The Man Who Changed His Mind* suggests that the BBFC appears to have had a far stronger and more sustained impact upon horror filmmaking practice.

At the outset of the chapter I noted the critical neglect of *Werewolf of London* in favour of the later *The Wolf Man*; a typical example of this can be found in Reynold Humphries' *The Hollywood Horror Film,* where he writes of *The Wolf Man*, 'this latter film is of importance historically inasmuch as, far more than *Werewolf of London* in 1935, it "codified" the werewolf movie, therefore looking ahead to later developments'.[83] In researching and writing this chapter I have sought to overturn this common assumption, revealing production, censorship and reception contexts that both complicate and illuminate our understanding of the film. In addition, I have argued that some of the film's distinctiveness comes from the text itself, in its unbridled passion for homoerotic bestial encounters and its fascination with destroying the male body. The former theme is central to the 1930s horror film, the latter sets in motion a central trope that remains significant in werewolf cinema to the present day. Nonetheless, in attempting to extricate this wonderful film from triviality, I have realised that *Werewolf of London* was damned to obscurity even at the time of its initial release. Its narrative debt to *Dr Jekyll and Mr Hyde* undermined it critically, and it was unfortunate that MGM rather than Universal contracted Endore, author of *The Werewolf of Paris*, to write horror films. It was finally eclipsed by its dual release with *Bride of Frankenstein*, and forced to shoulder the burden for the critically unpalatable horror cycle. When Glendon apologises to Lisa with his dying breath he could in fact be apologising for the production and horror cycle as a whole, for those whom he (and the film) were never able to truly please.

(RE)MAKING FILM HISTORIES

I first started writing about horror films when I was a PhD student at Lancaster University. My thesis explored how the writings of Jacques Lacan, Julia Kristeva and Sigmund Freud could be brought together to illuminate the aesthetic experience of horror cinema. I loved the theoretical incursion into film genre, the cool intellectualism of reading demanding material and ruminating upon what it could bring to my film analysis. Yet when reflecting on this, what really stands out to me is how a theoretical study can be researched and written anywhere. In my case, it often was. Because I lived some distance from my university office, my thesis was written in pubs, cafés, at other people's houses (I never worked well at home), on trains, and on occasion in the bars of airports. Theory is an eminently portable methodology, and it reflected my needs and interests at the time. There was a single trip to the BFI National Archive in London, to use its research viewing facilities, and a couple of slightly aimless visits to the British Library Boston Spa in West Yorkshire, where I wandered around randomly picking up bound issues of *Moving Picture World*, not really sure what I was doing. Throughout, I remained entranced by theory, my research turned inward, forming part of a discourse around the limits of psychoanalysis for understanding the address of horror cinema.

The sealed-off world of my graduate study will probably come as a surprise to those of you who have read *After Dracula* and who (I hope) sense my passion for researching and interpreting the past. While I still champion the importance of psychoanalysis for understanding some of the mechanisms of horror cinema, this book is as much a cultural history, an excursion into not only film texts but also film intertexts. Much of the shift in my methodological approach can be mapped in relation to how digital technology has radically transformed the way we are able to research and comprehend film history. When I first began doctoral research in 2003, technology was already well integrated into academic life; we worked with the Internet and email, virtual hard drives, Project Muse and electronic journals. But online moving image archives did not exist. While a range of classic films were available on video and DVD – the films that I then studied – the majority of less 'canonical' films were only accessible at physical archives or through specialist independent companies who made small runs of videocassettes that were both expensive and difficult to locate. I remember my excitement when a video copy of *Orlacs Hände* finally arrived in my department; produced by Facets Multimedia in Chicago, it had taken months to locate, order, produce and then post across the Atlantic. Similarly, it cost hundreds of pounds for me to travel to and stay in London in order to watch *Körkarlen* at the BFI. Yet now as I finish this book, a few presses of the keyboard take me online to watch hundreds of obscure or otherwise marginal films free of charge on sites such as YouTube and Internet Archive or via pay-by-subscription instant streaming on LoveFilm, Netflix and MUBI. Even the BFI's Screenonline, free to educational institutions, offers a range of instant-streaming clips and full-length films from its archive. The Criterion Collection, established in 1984, pre-exists the shift I am charting here, but remains important for the point I wish to make. Criterion (and since 2004, the UK equivalent, Eureka's Masters of Cinema series) masters high-resolution DVDs and Blu-rays from newly sourced and often combined archival prints, creating versions of the film not previously offered for the home market. Recent years have seen releases of not only *Körkarlen*, the film I had to travel 200 miles to see as a student, but also *Vampyr, The Most Dangerous Game* and *Island of Lost Souls*. Criterion has inevitably gone online, and via the US website Hulu, many of its carefully restored films can now be screened instantly.

It is not only the films that have become more accessible. We now have unprecedented online access to critical materials that are, or can be, related to 1930s cinema. A number of newspapers, such as *New York Times* and *Los Angeles Times,* and film trade papers including *Variety* have produced complete online archives which offer paid-for-access to invaluable critical reviews, promotional activities, gossip, exploitation strategies and film premieres. Their searchable databases of full-page PDF images hugely reduce the time needed to search indexes and locate material, reducing what might once have taken days or weeks of researching into the work of a few minutes: a search term typed, the enter button clicked, the results listed in order of relevance. The Media History Digital Library has been equally valuable in researching this book: it is an open-access initiative that has digitised limited runs of film trade and fan magazines, including *Film Daily*, *Hollywood Reporter,* *Photoplay* and *Harrison's Reports*, while Cinefiles, an online project from the University of California's Berkeley Art Museum and the Pacific Film Archive, contains a searchable database of scanned images of reviews, press kits, festival programme notes, newspaper articles, and other documents. At the time of finishing *After Dracula*, ProQuest was undertaking a partial, initial launch of its new Entertainment Industry Archive. When complete, this will offer access to not only important American publications such as *Variety* and *Box Office*, but also British periodicals *Film Weekly* and *Picturegoer*.

British newspaper archives have become an increasingly important resource throughout this project. The British Newspaper Archive, a project from the British Library, launched in November 2011, contains most of the runs of newspapers published in the UK since 1800. An initial search on *The Man Who Changed His Mind* or *The Black Cat* (under its alternative UK title *House of Doom*) reveals extensive data on where the film was exhibited across the country from Barnstaple in Devon to Hull in the East Ridings, how it was promoted and what kind of language was used to describe the film. While launched too late for the research stage of this project, it will be an invaluable resource for future work in the field as it opens up a new world of information on horror cinema in British regions and provincial towns. The national broadsheets I have consulted may have had a London-centric focus, but they have provided much-needed material on the British distribution, exhibition and reception of 1930s horror films. The *Guardian* and *Observer* digital archives contain reproductions of every page since 1821 and 1791 respectively, while *The Times* digital

archive spans 1785–1985. Without access to these online materials I would not have been able to explore a central element of
Chapter 6 – how the British broadsheet press made sense of
British horror films, how they compared them with American
films, and how the American press responses to British films
diverged from the British responses. Even anecdotal material
reported in the newspapers can be considered important in certain contexts. In Chapter 1's study of *The Mummy* I explained that
a man was accused of murder in Hyde Park; he attempted to avoid
hanging by saying he was incited to murder by a vision of actor
Lon Chaney. Relying on historical newspapers as source material
has its problems, as historian Adrian Bingham has discussed: in
the past there has been 'widespread scepticism about using newspapers because of their doubtful accuracy and their ephemeral
nature...', but he usefully points out that now 'there are few who
deny the value of newspaper content for understanding politics,
culture and society'.[1] Indeed, the material I have found and used
from newspapers bears witness to the impact of American horror
films on British society, and without the recent developments of
detailed online search engines a lot of the more ephemeral information would never have been found.

In writing *After Dracula* I have come a long way from drift-
ing around the bound journals section of the British Library at
Boston Spa. What I am attempting to demarcate here, though,
is not simply a personal intellectual journey, but rather that in
the ten years since I began graduate research, access to moving
image archives has radically transformed. The time required to
undertake extensive analysis of films and their ephemeral materials is no longer only the province of either the (probably London-
based) fully funded graduate student researching their thesis or
(at the other end of the scale) the research professor with time,
inclination and the research budget to burn. Instantaneous access
to such a wide range of resources fundamentally changes the
nature of film history research practices as well as making archival material accessible to a far greater number of would-be film
historians. In the case of horror film studies, and particularly the
study of 1930s horror film (which in the past has been quite theory
driven), such developments do offer vital and exciting new areas

of research. For example, at the time of writing this book, *The Clairvoyant* (released in America as *The Evil Mind*) had not been granted a home viewing release but I was able to discuss it extensively in Chapter 6 because it is available to watch on YouTube and the Internet Archive. There are inevitably a number of problems with this turn of events. While we can now watch films online, they are not necessarily presented in the format, length or screen ratio originally intended. During my doctoral research I would have paid a not-insignificant amount of money to watch Robert Wiene's German silent film *Genuine* (at the time unavailable); now I can view it on YouTube within seconds but it is a truncated, 44-minute version from the notoriously poor-quality Raymond Rohauer collection, accompanied by an electric guitar score. Similarly, *The Ghoul* is available to watch on the Internet Archive as a public domain print, but it is the unrestored Czech version that has been in circulation for decades.

Furthermore, not all aspects of film history are digitally up for grabs. Censorship records remain resolutely offline and no amount of targeted Web searches can replace visits to places such as the BFI Special Collections in London or the Margaret Herrick Library in Los Angeles. I hope my discussions of the censorship records of *The Man Who Changed His Mind* and *Werewolf of London* are testament to the continuing importance of this kind of research. Physical spaces that house archives remain vitally important to scholarship in this field as targeted Web searches remain just that: specific and to the point. This can be a real problem as you don't always know what you are searching for – until you find it. Sometimes it is the smallest things that are the most rewarding (and amusing) to discover. It was only by travelling to the Brotherton Library at the University of Leeds and reading every single issue of British film magazine *Close Up* that I found a marvellous interview with Ernest Thesiger (*The Old Dark House, The Ghoul* and *Bride of Frankenstein*) in which he expounds upon the pleasures of doing crochet while waiting around on set.[2] This kind of 'disordered' research can really only take place in a physical archive with tangible material; my feelings about this chime closely with Jason Jacobs' experiences of researching television history in the BBC Written Archives Centre in Reading. He writes 'there have to be repeated periods of blind searching, rogue searching, or "chancing it" in the hope that something relevant will turn up, or what seemed irrelevant takes on a new significance in the light of additional findings' – and that by doing this one will gradually accumulate 'a sharper grasp of history or even discover a history one had not anticipated'.[3] This is my experience of researching film history: in order to uncover random, wonderful material that *may later* become meaningful, it is crucial to spend time visiting and using physical archives, a process that cannot be replicated by simply typing commands into a search field. In addition, if we rely on the Internet for historical critical reception sources, our choice of material is limited by the decisions made by other people. For example, while the Media History Digital Library has been an absolutely invaluable resource for researching this book, there are still huge gaps in the digitised print runs offered. Being able to read *Photoplay*'s year runs for 1935 and 1936 online is useful but what I really wanted to get hold of – but could not – was the February 1933 issue, which according to Rhona Berenstein ran a fabulous three-page spread on Charles Laughton and *Island of Lost Souls*.[4] This should not be read as a criticism of the great work done by the Internet Archive so far – I would far rather have partial coverage than none at all – but in its current rather ad hoc state it can never offer a complete picture of a publication.

Relatedly, the publications chosen to be scanned and digitised with searchable indexes are the ones embraced by affluent or charitable organisations that can raise the necessary money or provide willing volunteers. A divide is created: those online and those not, which in turn has repercussions on the kinds of study then carried out. With its easy-to-use digital archive, the *New York Times* is likely to remain the de facto choice for historical reception studies of horror films, even as much smaller newspapers or film periodicals fall by the wayside. A complicating factor is that the majority of film-orientated 1930s reception material available online is American: this can only offer one snapshot of film culture during the decade. The British *Kinematograph Weekly*, which under various guises has run from 1907 to 1971, was originally to be included in the Entertainment Industry Archive but failed to make the final selection. And, while the British Newspaper Archive is likely to make significant interventions into digital scholarship, many British film periodicals published during this period remain without an online home. If online access to (selected) American publications remains so easy and if researchers become less inclined to visit physical archives, what will become of British film publications such as *The Bioscope* (1908-32), *The Cinematograph Times* (1928-39) and *The Daily Film Renter* (1927-57)? Similarly, I hope that my chapter on British cinema of the 1930s will inspire further work in this area, but as matters currently stand it is likely to be undertaken only by UK-based scholars who have the financial wherewithal to visit the BFI and British Library archives in order to view the rare films and to locate and read the ephemeral material. Perhaps film history is not so quickly remade after all.

In his article on memory, technology and horror, Peter Hutchings notes that 'we are constantly surrounded by films from different periods, in the cinema, on television, video and DVD', yet histories of film genre 'tend to focus overwhelmingly on the moment of production'.[5] In its efforts to reconsider the 1930s horror film genre through a specific cycle of films, *After Dracula* is probably equally guilty of emphasising the period of production, but what I have focused on here is Hutchings' broader point about how institutions, technologies and history are mediated. While my references to the technologies of the moment will no doubt date horribly, the point I am making remains an important one: this near-enough instant access to (a small portion of) our cinematic and cultural history has a significant effect upon how we study and make sense of film history. In my academic career to date, my primary goal has always remained the same, the desire to celebrate the film itself and to demonstrate to my reader its most intriguing aspects (in essence, waving a DVD around and shouting about how good the film is), but my methods of interpretation and my turn away from exclusively theoretical readings reflect this recent shift in the ease of access to contextual material. The main aim of *After Dracula* was to complicate histories of horror film by illustrating the diversity of filmmaking during this decade, and its tripartite focus – the interplay between Continental, British and American film texts and contexts, the genre's transatlantic evolution and a rethink of the 'important' American horror films of the 1930s – could not have been achieved without the developments in online film access and archival practice. If we return to the assumptions about genre unpicked in the book's introduction, we can see how digital transformations hugely affect our ability to 'do' film history; it brings to mind Christine Gledhill's comment that 'genres are fictional worlds, but they do not stay within fictional boundaries: their conventions cross into cultural and critical discourse, where we – as audiences, scholars, students and critics – make and remake them'.[6] I'm at pains here not to sweepingly suggest that everything is now available for the taking in our brave new online world, but it cannot be denied that the sheer amount of material freely and instantly available to us today fundamentally changes the way we (re)view horror film history. It certainly offers endless opportunities to make and remake our own canons, and it is very much hoped that *After Dracula* will provide food for thought as you create your own.

NOTES

INTRODUCTION

1. *Dracula* and *Frankenstein* release dates taken from Tom Weaver et al., *Universal Horrors: The Studio's Classic Films, 1931–1946*, 2nd edn (Jefferson, NC: McFarland, 2007), pp.21, 38. *Dr Jekyll and Mr Hyde* premiered at the Rivoli Theatre in New York on 31 December 1932 and went on general release on 2 January 1932. 'Production credits on "ten best"', *Film Daily*, 11 January 1933, p.10.
2. Steve Neale, 'Questions of genre', *Screen* 31/1 (1990), p.50.
3. The 1931–6 demarcation appears in Andrew Tudor, *Monsters and Mad Scientists: A Cultural History of the Horror Movie* (Oxford: Wiley Blackwell, 1989), p.24; Rhona J. Berenstein, *Attack of the Leading Ladies: Gender, Sexuality and Spectatorship in Classic Horror Cinema* (New York, NY: Columbia University Press, 1996), p.1 and Robert Spadoni, *Uncanny Bodies: The Coming of Sound Film and the Origins of the Horror Genre* (Berkeley, CA: University of California Press, 2007), p.2. Reynold Humphries includes 1939–41 in the first cycle, arguing that the three years are 'both a renewal and a widening of the concerns manifest in the films produced up until 1936'. *The Hollywood Horror Film, 1931–1941: Madness in a Social Landscape* (Lanham, MD: Scarecrow Press, 2006), p.viii. David J. Skal views the first cycle as lasting 20 years, beginning in Germany in 1919 and ending in America with Universal's *Son of Frankenstein* in 1939. *The Monster Show: A Cultural History of Horror* (London: Plexus, 1993), p.206.
4. Tom Weaver et al. comment on Laemmle's departure that 'the various management teams that succeeded him were a corps of faceless bankers and producers who, unlike the reigning moguls of the other studios, didn't have the innate instinct for picturemaking', *Universal Horrors*, p.4.
5. The text of the 1930 Production Code is reproduced in Thomas Doherty, *Pre-Code Hollywood: Sex, Immorality and Insurrection in American Cinema, 1930–1934* (New York, NY: Columbia University Press, 1999), pp.346–65. The terms of the 1934 enforcement were as follows: 'any member company of the MPPDA (all major studios) and any producer using the distribution facilities of the majors (thus, any respectable independent) would be bound to process its product through the "Production Code Administration" and acquire a stamped "Certificate of Approval". A violation of the rules would incur a fine of $25,000 for "disrupting the

stability of the industry and causing serious damage to all members of the association'". Reproduced in Thomas Doherty, *Hollywood's Censor: Joseph I. Breen and the Production Code Administration* (New York, NY: Columbia University Press, 2007), p.67.

6. Quoted in Melvin E. Matthews, *Fear Itself: Horror on Screen and in Reality during the Depression and World War II* (Jefferson, NC: McFarland, 2009), p.73.

7. Quoted in James C. Robertson, *The Hidden Cinema: British Film Censorship in Action, 1913–1975* (London: Routledge, 1989), p.66.

8. Quoted in Skal, *The Monster Show*, p.199.

9. For the full list of films classified as 'Horrific' or certified 'H' by the BBFC from 1933 to 1940, see Sarah J. Smith, *Children, Cinema and Censorship: From Dracula to the Dead End Kids* (London: I.B.Tauris, 2005), p.186.

10. *The Man Who Lived Again* Synopsis, BBFC Scenario Report #476, 11 October 1935, BFI Special Collections, London.

11. Berenstein, *Attack of the Leading Ladies*, p.15.

12. Peter Hutchings, *The Horror Film* (Harlow: Longman, 2004), pp.15–16.

13. Amanda Ann Klein, *American Film Cycles: Reframing Genres, Screening Social Problems, and Defining Subcultures* (Austin, TX: University of Texas Press, 2011), p.4.

14. Klein, *American Film Cycles*, p.4.

15. Gary D. Rhodes, '*Drakula halála* (1921): The cinema's first Dracula', *Horror Studies* 1/1 (2010), p.25.

16. 'The Beetle', *Variety* 2 January 1920, p.75.

17. 'Lon Chaney in eerie film at State', *Daily Boston Globe,* 10 January 1928, p.22; 'Weirdness rife in Lon Chaney film at Loews', *Atlanta Constitution,* 11 December 1927, p.C4; Mordaunt Hall, 'Mr Chaney's new role', *New York Times,* 19 June 1927, p.19.

18. Hutchings, *The Horror Film*, p.9; Roy Kinnard, *Horror in Silent Films: A Filmography, 1896–1929* (Jefferson, NC: McFarland, 1995), p.1.

19. Lincoln Geraghty and Mark Jancovich, 'Introduction: Generic canons', in Lincoln Geraghty and Mark Jancovich (eds) *The Shifting Definitions of Genre: Essays on Labelling Films, Television Shows and Media* (Jefferson, NC: McFarland, 2008), p.3.

20. Mark Jancovich, "Thrills and chills": Horror, the woman's film and the origins of film noir', *New Review of Film and Television Studies* 7.2 (2009), pp.157–71.

21. Spadoni, *Uncanny Bodies*, p.52.

22. Mordaunt Hall, 'The screen: Bram Stoker's human vampire', *New York Times* 13 February 1931, p.21; 'Vampires are abroad again in odd drama', *Washington Post* 15 February 1931, p.A4; 'Three powerful pictures open local runs today', *Atlanta Constitution* 21 February 1931, p.21; 'Dracula film at RKO-Keith Theater', *Daily Boston Globe* 4 April 1931, p.4.

23. Quoted in Angela M. Smith, *Hideous Progeny: Disability, Eugenics and Classic Horror Cinema* (New York, NY: Columbia University Press, 2011), p.1.

24. Mae Tinee, '*White Zombie*, horror film, opens theatre', *Chicago Daily Tribune* 26 April 1932, p.11; 'Schedules show cycle of "horror" pictures continuing', *Film Daily*, 1 August 1932, p.1.

25. Philip K. Scheuer, 'Next season's films on way', *Los Angeles Times,* 12 June 1932, p.B11.

26. Mollie Merrick, 'Hollywood in person', *Los Angeles Times,* 16 December 1932, p.4.

27. '*Variety* bulletin', *Variety*, 3 February 1933, p.5.

28. Annette Kuhn, 'Children, "horrific" films and censorship in 1930s Britain', *Historical Journal of Film, Radio and Television* 22/2 (2002), p.200.

29. Mark Jancovich, 'Reviews', *Screen* 48/2 (2007), p.262, emphasis original.

30. Jancovich, 'Reviews', p.263.

31. Christine Gledhill, 'Rethinking genre', in Christine Gledhill and Linda Williams (eds), *Reinventing Film Studies* (London: Arnold, 2003), p.221.

32. Gledhill, 'Rethinking genre', p.221.

33. Jamie Sexton, 'US "indie-horror": Critical reception, genre construction and suspect hybridity', *Cinema Journal* 51/2 (2012), pp.67–86; Tim Snelson, '"From grade B thrillers to deluxe chillers": Prestige horror, female audiences, and allegories of spectatorship in *The Spiral Staircase* (1946)', *New Review of Film and Television Studies,* 7/2 (2009), pp.173–88; Kate Egan, *Trash or Treasure: Censorship and the Changing Meanings of the Video Nasties* (Manchester: Manchester University Press, 2007); Daniel Martin, 'Japan's *Blair Witch*: Restraint, maturity and generic canons in the British critical reception of *Ring*', *Cinema Journal* 48/3 (2009), pp.35–51; Russ Hunter, '"Didn't you used to be Dario Argento?": The cult reception of Dario Argento' in William Hope (ed.), *Italian Film Directors in the New Millennium* (Newcastle: Cambridge Scholars Press, 2010), pp.63–74.

34. Tim Bergfelder, Sue Harris and Sarah Street, *Film Architecture and the Transnational Imagination: Set Design in 1930s European Cinema* (Amsterdam: Amsterdam University Press, 2007), p.11.

35. Klein, *American Film Cycles*, p.19.

36. Karen Hollinger, 'The monster as woman: Two generations of *Cat People*', in Barry Keith Grant (ed.), *The Dread of Difference: Gender and the Horror Film* (Austin, TX: University of Texas Press, 1996), pp.296–308; Elizabeth Young, 'Here comes the bride: Wedding gender and race in *Bride of Frankenstein*', *Feminist Studies* 17/3 (1991), 403–37.

37. George E. Turner, 'Jinxed from the start: *The Monkey's Paw*', *American Cinematographer* 66/11 November (1985), pp.35–40.

38. George E. Turner and Michael H. Price, *Forgotten Horrors: Early Talkie Chillers from Poverty Row* (London: Yoseloff, 1979).

39. Gary D. Rhodes, 'Fantasmas del cine Mexico: The 1930s horror film cycle of Mexico', in Steven Jay Schneider (ed.), *Fear Without Frontiers: Horror Cinema Across the Globe* (Godalming: FAB Press, 2003), pp.93–103.

1   REMEMBERING HORROR IN *THE MUMMY*

1. Edgar Allan Poe, 'Some Words with a Mummy', in *The Collected Tales and Poems of Edgar Allan Poe* (Ware: Wordsworth Library Collection, 2009), p.437.

2. Dominic Montserrat, 'Unidentified human remains: Mummies and the erotics of biography', in Dominic Montserrat (ed.), *Changing Bodies, Changing Meanings: Studies on the Human Body in Antiquity* (London: Routledge, 1998), p.182.

3. 'The University College mummy', *The Times,* 27 December 1889, p.4; 'Mrs Glover', *The Times,* 12 June 1850, p.8.

4. 'The unrolling of the mummy. From the *Pall Mall Gazette*', *New York Times,* 12 January 1890, p.13.

5. Nicholas Daly, 'That obscure object of desire: Victorian commodity culture and fictions of the mummy', *NOVEL: A Forum on Fiction* 28/1 (1994), p.25.

6. Jasmine Day, *The Mummy's Curse: Mummymania in the English-Speaking World* (London: Routledge, 2006), p.3; Karen E. Macfarlane, 'Mummy knows best: Knowledge and the unknowable in turn of the century mummy fiction', *Horror Studies* 1/1 (2010), p.9; Bradley Deane, 'Mummy fiction and the occupation of Egypt: Imperial striptease', *English Literature in Translation* 51/4 (1998), pp.384, 387.

7. The curse story was 'expanded by journalists seeking original stories to break from the exclusive excavation coverage granted to *The Times*'. Carter Lupton, '"Mummymania" for the masses - is Egyptology cursed by the mummy's curse?', in Sally McDonald and Michael Rice (eds), *Consuming Ancient Egypt* (London: UCL Press, 2003), pp.31–2.

8. '*The Mummy* with Boris Karloff: Weird, uncanny picture at the Fox', *Atlanta Constitution,* 5 March 1933, p.11A.

9. Arthur Conan Doyle, 'Lot no. 249', in Roger Luckhurst (ed.), *Late Victorian Gothic Tales* (Oxford: Oxford World's Classics, 2005 [1892]), p.115.

10. Pascal Bonitzer, 'Partial vision: Film and the labyrinth', *Wide Angle* 4/4 (1981), p.58.

11. Quoted in Margaret Iversen, 'In the blind field: Hopper and the uncanny', *Art History* 21/3 (1998), p.422.

12. Waly, '*The Mummy*', *Variety,* 10 January 1933, p.15; 'Picture theatres', *Manchester Guardian,* 27 June 1933, p.13.

13. Annette Kuhn, *An Everyday Magic: Cinema and Cultural Memory* (London: I.B. Tauris, 2002), pp.87–92.

14. See Susan D. Cowie and Tom Johnson, *The Mummy in Fact, Fiction and Film* (Jefferson, NC: McFarland, 2002).

15. Macfarlane, 'Mummy knows best', p.6; Deane, 'Mummy fiction', p.384.

16. Roland Barthes, *Camera Lucida: Reflections on Photography* (London: Vintage, 2000), p.9.

17. Susan Sontag, *On Photography* (London: Penguin, 1979), p.15.

18. Bruce Kawin briefly discusses the pool in 'The mummy's pool', in Leo Baudry and Marshall Cohen (eds), *Film Theory and Criticism: Introductory Readings,* 5th edn (Oxford: Oxford University Press, 1998), p.686.

19. Mary Ann Doane, 'The voice in the cinema: The articulation of body and space', *Yale French Studies,* 60 (1980), p.34.

20. A.D.S., 'Life after 3700 years', *New York Times,* 7 January 1933, p.11.

21. The idea of the 'look at the camera' is an area of film studies warranting further detailed investigation. A limited amount of research has been published to date, most recently Tom Brown, *Breaking the Fourth Wall: Direct Address in the Cinema* (Edinburgh: Edinburgh University Press, 2012).

22. 'In the suburbs and the provinces', *Observer* 29 June 1941, p.7.

23. 'Behind the mask', *Film Daily,* 4 February 1932, p.8; 'Night World', *Film Daily,* 14 March 1932, p.5.

24. A.D.S., 'Life after 3700 years', p.11.

25. Sigmund Freud, 'The uncanny', in Albert Dickson (ed.), *Penguin Freud Library 14: Art and Literature* (London: Penguin, 1990 [1919]), p.339.

26. Freud, 'The uncanny', pp.364–66.

27. Quoted in Edith Dietz, 'Horrors ahead! Karloff and Lugosi, masters of terror, prepare new crop of film thrills', *Daily Boston Globe,* 17 March 1935, p.13.

28. Griselda Pollock, 'Freud's Egypt: Mummies and m/others', *Parallax* 13/2 (2007), p.57.

29. Freud, 'The uncanny', pp.363–64.

30. Freud, 'The uncanny', p.340.

31. Maureen Turim, *Flashbacks in Film: Memory and History* (London: Routledge, 1989), p.19.

32. 'Karloff (The Uncanny)', *Variety* 13 December 1932, p.10.

33. The phrase means that the film will make a profit. Waly, '*The Mummy*', p.15.

34. 'Weird romance of reincarnation will go a second week', *Washington Post,* 1 January 1933, p.A1; Tom Johnson, *Censored Screams: The British Ban on Hollywood Horror in the Thirties* (Jefferson, NC: McFarland, 1997), p.80.

35. Phillip J. Riley, *The Mummy* (Galloway, NJ: Universal Filmscripts Series, 1989), p.34; 'Mummy ad stunt wows N.Y. crowds', *Hollywood Reporter,* 7 January 1933, p.2.

36. *Universal Weekly*'s 'Showmanship section' on *The Mummy,* 21 January 1933, pp.28–29. Reproduced in Riley, *The Mummy*, pp.32–33.

37. 'A Sax Rohmer hit comes to life at Palace', *Washington Post,* 13 November 1932, p.A1.

38. 'Karloff reopens Rialto in another creepy role', *Washington Post,* 25 December 1932, p.A1; '*The Mummy* at Fox stars Boris Karloff', *Atlanta Constitution,* 4 March 1933, p.15.

39. 'New Films', *Daily Boston Globe,* 23 January 1933, p.9.
40. Mordaunt Hall, 'Imaginative direction', *New York Times,* 31 October 1926, p.X7; 'Weirdness rife in Lon Chaney Film at Loews', *Atlanta Constitution*, 11 December 1927, p.C4.
41. Rosalind Shaffer, 'Weird talkies come to front in Hollywood', *Chicago Daily Tribune,* 20 December 1932, p.F8.
42. 'Lon Chaney plays role of Paris opera phantom', *New York Times,* 6 September 1925, p.X5.
43. 'Hyde Park murder', *The Times,* 11 January 1929, p.7.
44. 'Hyde Park murder', p.7.
45. Mollie Merrick, 'Hollywood in person', *Atlanta Constitution,* 27 September 1929, p.6.
46. 'Picturing *Dracula*', *New York Times,* 15 February 1931, p.110; 'Death ends career of Lon Chaney at 47', *Washington Post,* 27 August 1930, p.4.
47. Rosalind Shaffer, 'Copies of famous stars find hard sledding in treading path of borrowed glory in Hollywood', *Chicago Daily Tribune,* 19 October 1930, p.G3.
48. Riley McKoy, 'Boris Karloff stars as *The Mummy* at Fox', *Atlanta Constitution,* 6 March 1933, p.3; 'Karloff reopens Rialto', p.A1.
49. This is a play upon the popular Hollywood joke at the time, 'don't step on it, it might be Lon Chaney'. P.L. Mannock, 'On the British sets', *Picturegoer,* 8 April 1933, p.30.
50. 'Projection jottings', *New York Times,* 30 August 1931, p.X5.
51. Katherine Albert, 'Don't envy the stars', *Photoplay* 35/4 March (1929), p.32.
52. Mayne Peak, 'Who will take Lon Chaney's place in filmdom?', *Daily Boston Globe,* 7 September 1930, p.52.
53. Rosalind Shaffer, 'Boris Karloff discards disguise and becomes a gentleman', *Chicago Daily Tribune,* 19 May 1935, p.D4.
54. Stanley Burton, 'Don't call me Lon Chaney', *Photoplay,* 38/2 January (1930), p.78.
55. Bige, '*Werewolf of London*', *Variety,* 15 May 1935, p.9.
56. Nelson B. Bell, 'The new cinema offerings', *Washington Post* 21 November 1931, p.14.
57. 'Movie secret makeup room a chamber of horrors', *Daily Boston Globe* 29 November 1931, p.A58.
58. Mayne Peak, 'Horror man of movie world made first hit without a word spoken', *Daily Boston Globe,* 2 October 1932, p.A51.
59. Peak, 'Horror man of movie world, p.A51.
60. Freud, 'The uncanny', p.357; Robin Wood, 'Return of the repressed', *Film Comment,* 14 July (1978), p.26.
61. 'Calendar of current releases', *Variety,* 13 December 1932, p.27.
62. Riley McKoy, 'Boris Karloff Stars as 'The Mummy' at Fox', *Atlanta Constitution,* 6 March 1933, p.3.

2 'STUBBORN BEAST FLESH': THE PANTHER WOMAN AND *ISLAND OF LOST SOULS*

1. 'Panther woman sought here for lead in big screen role', *Atlanta Constitution,* 19 July 1932, p.16; 'More than two-score girls in "Panther-Woman" contest', *Atlanta Constitution,* 20 July 1932, p.18.

2. 'Maxine Land, daughter of jurist, picked as Atlanta Panther Woman', *Atlanta Constitution,* 27 July 1932, pp.1–2.

3. '25 named for sound film tests in 'Panther Woman' eliminations', *Atlanta Constitution,* 23 July 1932, pp.1, 6; 'Photo standalone 5 - no title', *Atlanta Constitution,* 8 January 1933, p.N5.

4. 'One will be Panther Woman', *Chicago Daily Tribune,* 29 September 1932, p.13; 'Winner', *Chicago Daily Tribune,* 30 September 1932, p.19; Chaplin Hall, 'Pictures and players in Hollywood', *New York Times,* 9 October 1932, p.X5.

5. Robin Wood, 'An introduction to the American horror film', in Bill Nichols (ed.), *Movies and Methods: An Anthology*, vol.2 (Berkeley, CA: University of California Press, 1985), p.201.

6. Barbara Klinger, 'Film history terminable and interminable: Recovering the past in reception studies', *Screen* 38/2 (1997), p.108.

7. Philip K. Scheuer, 'Panther Woman laps up blood? No. Malted milks', *Los Angeles Times,* 20 November 1932, p.B13

8. Scheuer, 'Panther Woman laps up blood?', p.B13.

9. '*Island of Lost Souls*', *Film Daily,* 12 January 1933, p.6; Mordaunt Hall, 'That Koepenick "Captain"', *New York Times,* 22 January 1933, p.X5; Harry M. Benshoff, *Monsters in the Closet: Homosexuality and the Horror Film* (Manchester: Manchester University Press, 1997), p.47.

10. Benshoff points out that in 1930s horror film 'the mad scientist and his sidekick become a major generic convention that is easily read as queer: the secret experiments they conduct together are chronicled in private diaries and kept locked away in closed cupboards and closets', *Monsters in the Closet*, p.48.

11. Rhona J. Berenstein, *Attack of the Leading Ladies: Gender, Sexuality and Spectatorship in Classic Horror Cinema* (New York, NY: Columbia University Press, 1996), p.149.

12. Keith Williams, *H.G. Wells, Modernity and the Movies* (Liverpool: Liverpool University Press, 2007), p.165.

13. 'Recent novels', *The Times,* 17 June 1896, p.17.

14. H.G. Wells, *The Island of Doctor Moreau* (London: Pan Books, 1975 [1896]), p.83.

15. Wells, *The Island of Doctor Moreau*, p.85.

16. Wells, *The Island of Doctor Moreau*, p.85.

17. Wells, *The Island of Doctor Moreau*, p.107.

18. These include '*Island of Lost Souls*', *Film Daily*, p.6 and Philip K. Scheuer, 'Eerie cinema proffered', *Los Angeles Times,* 10 January 1933, p.A7.

19. 'First lady of the movies', *Chicago Daily Tribune,* 27 November 1932, p.D3.
20. 'In black and white', *Chicago Daily Tribune,* 21 November 1932, p.17; 'Tailored pajamas', *Chicago Daily Tribune,* 2 December 1932, p.25.
21. 'Action heroines', *Los Angeles Times,* 20 November 1932, p.12.
22. 'Something NEW hits blasé Broadway', *Variety,* 24 January 1933, p.22.
23. 'Inside stuff - pictures', *Variety* 17 January 1933, p.47.
24. 'Horror cold, animals too', *Variety* 7 February 1933, p.5.
25. 'Screen notes', *New York Times,* 3 January 1933, p.19; 'Pictures for week ending Jan. 27', *New York Times,* 22 January 1933, p.X5. The Paramount-Publix Corporation went into receivership at the end of January 1933 and closed the Criterion Theatre, and on 1 February, gave up control of the Rialto, transferring the film to the Brooklyn Paramount. 'Screen notes', 1 February 1933, p.13; 'Rialto Theatre closes its doors', *New York Times,* 2 February 1933, p.21; 'Screen notes', *New York Times,* 3 February 1933, p.21.
26. Rugh, *'Vampire Bat',* *Variety,* 24 January 1933, p.19.
27. Donald Bogle, *Toms, Coons, Mulattoes, Mammies and Bucks: An Interpretative History of Blacks in American Films,* 3rd edn (Oxford: Roundhouse, 1994), p.13.
28. Steven Jay Schneider, 'Mixed blood couples: Monsters and miscegenation in U.S. horror cinema', in Ruth Bienstock Anolik and Douglas L. Howard (eds), *The Gothic Other: Racial and Social Constructions in the Literary Imagination* (Jefferson, NC: MacFarland, 2004), p.76.
29. Harry M. Benshoff, 'Blaxploitation horror films: Generic reappropriation or reinscription?', *Cinema Journal* 39/2 (2000), p.47.
30. Wells, *The Island of Doctor Moreau,* p.16.
31. Williams, *H.G. Wells, Modernity and the Movies,* p.166.
32. Angela M. Smith, *Hideous Progeny: Disability, Eugenics, and Classic Horror Cinema* (New York, NY: Columbia University Press, 2011), p.215.
33. Cecelia Ager, 'Going places', *Variety,* 24 January 1933, p.19.
34. Mae Tinee, 'Chicago sees "Panther Girl" in first film', *Chicago Daily Tribune,* 29 December 1932, p.9.
35. Wood, 'An introduction to the American horror film', p.203.
36. Scheuer, 'Eerie cinema proffered', p.A7.
37. 'May take censor to court on *Isle of Lost Souls*', *Film Daily,* 9 January 1933, pp.1, 3; 'Passed after slashes', *Film Daily,* 31 January 1933, p.2.
38. David J. Skal, *The Monster Show: A Cultural History of Horror* (London: Plexus, 1993), p.171; Tom Johnson, *Censored Screams: The British Ban on Hollywood Horror in the Thirties* (Jefferson, NC: McFarland, 1997), p.75; James C. Robertson, *The Hidden Cinema: British Film Censorship in Action, 1919–1975* (London: Routledge, 1993), p.52.
39. Peter Hutchings, *The Horror Film* (Harlow: Longman, 2004), p.22. According to surviving BBFC records, the cuts list ran as follows: Reel 3 - Remove 'They're vivisecting a human being - they're cutting a man to pieces'; Reel 4 - Remove the shots of men working a treadmill, and the comment 'Some of my less successful experiments'; Reel 8 - Remove all

shots of beast-men and Moreau after he has been forced back, stand-ing against the outside wall; Remove all shots of Lota struggling with a beast-man after she has first leapt on him. BBFC, *Minutes of Exception,* April (1975), unpaginated. For reviews at the time of its British 'X' clas-sification, see 'A Wellsian film: Horror on Dr. Moreau's island', *The Times* 7 February 1959, p.10; T.B., *'Island of Lost Souls, The'*, *Monthly Film Bulletin,* January 1959, p.3.

40. Elizabeth Thompson, *'Island of Lost Souls*: Sinister, chilling film', *Atlanta Constitution,* 10 January 1933, p.17; Waly, *'Island of Lost Souls'*, p.15.

41. 'Horror film leads Allyn double bill', *The Hartford Courant,* 13 Jan 1933, p.6; *'Island of Lost Souls'*, *Film Daily*, p.6.

42. Scheuer, 'Eerie cinema proffered', p.A7.

43. Tinee, 'Chicago sees "Panther Girl" in first film', p.9

44. Merrick, 'Hollywood in person', 16 December, p.13.

45. Thompson, *'Island of Lost Souls'*, p.17.

46. Phil M. Daly, 'Along the Rialto', *Film Daily,* 4 August 1932, p.4.

47. Jack Alicoate, *'The Sign of the Cross'*, *Film Daily,* 1 December 1932, p.1.

48. Hall, 'The screen', p.19.

49. Mordaunt Hall, 'That Koepenick "Captain"', *New York Times,* 22 Jan 1933, p.X5.

50. Hall, 'That Koepenick "Captain"', p.X5.

51. Thompson, *'Island of Lost Souls'*, p.17; Merrick, 'Hollywood in person', *Los Angeles Times,* 16 December, p.13; Scheuer, 'Eerie cinema proffered', p.A7; Mordaunt Hall, 'The screen', *New York Times,* 13 January 1933; 'Horror film leads Allyn double bill', p.6.

52. Tinee, 'Chicago sees "Panther Girl" in first film', p.9.

53. Rhona J. Berenstein discusses Paramount's targeted focus on female patrons in *Attack of the Leading Ladies*, pp.74–6.

54. Mollie Merrick, 'Hollywood in person', *Los Angeles Times* 29 Dec 1932, p.4; 'Pictures now shooting', *Hollywood Reporter,* 9 January 1933, p.6; A.D.S. 'An imaginative killer', *New York Times,* 3 April 1933, p.13.

55. Scheuer, 'Panther woman laps up blood', p.19.

56. *'Murders in the Zoo* thriller at Georgia', *Atlanta Constitution.* 22 April 1933, p.15; John Scott, *'Murders in Zoo* opens on screen', *Los Angeles Times,* 7 April 1933, p.11.

57. Cecelia Ager, 'Going places', *Variety,* 11 April 1933, p.11.

58. Mrs W., 'The voice of the movie fan', *Chicago Daily Tribune,* 23 July 1933, p.E4.

59. 'Kathleen Burke, movie actress, performed in thrillers of the 30s', *New York Times,* 18 Apr 1980, p.D15.

60. Waly, *'Island of Lost Souls'*, p.15. The reference is probably to the 1929 part-talkie British film, described by the *New York Times* as featuring 'a half-caste woman [who beguiles] the hero, a young Englishman work-ing in the enervating atmosphere of the West Coast of Africa'. Ernest Marshall, 'Film notes from London town', *New York Times,* 1 December 1929, p.143.

61. Klinger, 'Film history terminable and interminable', pp.107–28.

62. Mark Jancovich, 'Female monsters: Horror, the 'femme fatale' and World War II', *European Journal of American Culture* 27 (2008), pp.133–49; Tim Snelson, *Horror on the Home Front: The Female Monster Cycle, World War Two and Historical Reception Studies*, Unpublished PhD Thesis, School of Film and Television Studies, University of East Anglia (2009), p.54.

63. Kim Newman, *Cat People* (London: BFI, 1999), p.11.

3   *WHITE ZOMBIE* AND THE EMERGENCE OF ZOMBIE CINEMA

1. John Edgar Browning, 'Survival horrors, survival spaces: Tracing the modern zombie (cine)myth', *Horror Studies,* 2/1 (2011), p.44.

2. Meghan Sutherland, 'Rigor/mortis: The industrial life of style in American zombie cinema', *Framework: The Journal of Cinema and Media* 48/1 (2007), p.67.

3. Tony Williams, '*White Zombie*: Haitian horror', *Jump Cut* 28 (1981), p.19.

4. A *bokor* is defined as an 'evil priest or sorcerer' in Erika Bourguignon, 'The persistence of folk belief: Some notes on cannibalism and zombis in Haiti', *Journal of American Folklore* 72/283 (1959), p.36.

5. *White Zombie Complete Exhibitors Campaign Book* (New York: United Artists Corp, 1932). Reprinted in Gary D. Rhodes, *White Zombie: Anatomy of a Horror Film* (Jefferson, NC: McFarland, 2001), pp.46–47. Rhodes insists that the film is not racist, but I concur with Jennifer Fay who describes many of the film's publicity stunts as 'designed to promote the film's sensational tale of black magic and white bodies, [trading] on the lurid mixture of xenophobia, exoticism, and sexual slavery'. 'Dead subjectivity: *White Zombie*, black Baghdad', *CR: The New Centennial Review* 8/1 (2008), p.84.

6. Epes W. Sargent, 'Exploitation', *Variety,* 16 August 1932, p.17.

7. 'Zombie for U.A.', *Film Daily,* 13 July 1932, p.3; '*White Zombie* premiere', *Film Daily,* 26 July 1932, p.2.

8. Michael H. Price and George E. Turner, 'The black art of *White Zombie*', in George E. Turner (ed.), *The Cinema of Adventure, Romance and Terror* (Hollywood, CA: The ASC Press, 1989), p.147.

9. Price and Turner, 'The black art of *White Zombie*', p.147.

10. Rhodes, *White Zombie: Anatomy of a Horror Film*, pp.113–15, 141.

11. Rhodes, *White Zombie: Anatomy of a Horror Film*, pp.105, 162.

12. Rhodes, *White Zombie: Anatomy of a Horror Film*, p.103; George E. Turner and Michael H. Price, *Forgotten Horrors: Early Talkie Chillers from Poverty Row* (London: Thomas Yoseloff Ltd., 1979), p.56; Price and Turner, 'The black art of *White Zombie*', pp.147, 154.

13. 'Picturing *Dracula*', *New York Times,* 15 February 1931, p.110.

14. See Edward Lowry and Richard deCordova, 'Enunciation and the production of horror in *White Zombie*', in Barry Keith Grant (ed.), *Planks of Reason: Essays on the Horror Film* (Metuchen, NJ: Scarecrow Press, 1984), pp.349–50.

15. Steven Jay Schneider, 'Mixed blood couples: Monsters and miscegenation in US horror cinema', in Ruth Bienstock Anolik and Douglas L. Howard (eds), *The Gothic Other: Racial and Social Construction in the Literary Imagination* (Jefferson, NC: McFarland, 2004), p.78.

16. Kyle Bishop, *American Zombie Gothic: The Rise and Fall (and Rise) of the Walking Dead in Popular Culture* (Jefferson, NC: McFarland, 2010), pp.12–13.

17. 'Film reviews', *Variety,* 2 August 1932, p.15.

18. Bishop, *American Zombie Gothic*, p.60.

19. William B. Seabrook, *The Magic Island* (London: George G. Harrap & Company Ltd, 1929), pp.93–94.

20. Seabrook, *The Magic Island*, p.94.

21. Seabrook, *The Magic Island*, p.95.

22. Seabrook, *The Magic Island*, p.95.

23. Phil M. Daly, 'Along the Rialto', *Film Daily,* 30 July 1932, p.3.

24. George Eaton Simpson, 'Haitian Peasant Economy', *Journal of Negro History* 25/4 (1940), p.507.

25. Simpson, 'Haitian Peasant Economy', p.507.

26. Laurent Dubois, *Avengers of the New World: The Story of the Haitian Revolution* (Cambridge, MA: The Belknap Press of Harvard University Press, 2004), p.18.

27. Simpson, 'Haitian peasant economy', p.498.

28. Kieran M. Murphy, '*White Zombie*', *Contemporary French and Francophone Studies* 15/1 (2011), pp.47–48.

29. Murphy, '*White Zombie*', p.50.

30. 'Projection jottings', *New York Times,* 17 July 1932, p.X3.

31. L.N., 'The screen: Beyond the pale', *New York Times,* 29 July 1932, p.18.

32. 'New films reviewed', *Daily Boston Globe,* 6 August 1932, p.6; 'Island scene of thrilling voodoo tale', *Washington Post,* 31 July 1932, p.A1.

33. Rhodes, *White Zombie: Anatomy of a Horror Film*, p.162.

34. Lizabeth Paravisini-Gebert, 'Women possessed: Eroticism and exoticism in the representation of woman as zombie', in Margarite Fernández Olmos and Lizabeth Paravisini-Gebert (eds), *Sacred Possessions: Vodou, Santería, Obeah, and the Caribbean* (New Brunswick, NJ: Rutgers University Press, 1997), p.37.

35. Paravisini-Gebert, 'Women possessed', p.39.

36. Rhodes, *White Zombie: Anatomy of a Horror Film*, p.23.

37. Harry M. Benshoff, *Monsters in the Closet: Homosexuality and the Horror Film* (Manchester: Manchester University Press, 1997), p.66.

38. Tanya Krzywinska, *A Skin For Dancing In: Possession, Witchcraft and Voodoo in Film* (Trowbridge: Flicks Books, 2000), p.166.

39. Krzywinska, *A Skin For Dancing In*, p.166.
40. 'Film reviews', *Variety*, p.15.
41. Mae Tinee writes 'you will remember, perhaps, that no Madge Bellamy picture was complete without an undressing scene - the lady having that sort of figure? True to form (no pun intended) *White Zombie* shows her in her bridal veil and teddy'. '*White Zombie*, honor film, opens theater', *Chicago Daily Tribune*, 26 August 1932, p.11.
42. Rhodes, *White Zombie: Anatomy of a Horror Film*, p.52.
43. Rhodes, *White Zombie: Anatomy of a Horror Film*, p.55.
44. '*White Zombie*', *Film Daily* 29 July 1932, p.4.
45. Ellen Draper, 'Zombie women when the gaze is male', *Wide Angle* 10/3 (1988), p.54.
46. Draper, 'Zombie women', p.55.
47. Rhodes also makes a passing reference to the parallels between the two Madelines. *White Zombie: Anatomy of a Horror Film*, p.40.
48. Daly, 'Along the Rialto', p.3; Tinee, '*White Zombie*, horror film, opens theater', p.11.
49. Edgar Allan Poe, 'The fall of the house of Usher', in Helen Trayler (ed.), *The Collected Works of Edgar Allan Poe* (Ware: Wordsworth Library Editions, 2009 [1839]), pp.175–76.
50. Poe, 'The fall of the house of Usher', p.180.
51. Poe, 'The fall of the house of Usher', p.184, original emphasis.
52. Poe, 'The fall of the house of Usher', p.175.
53. E.T.A. Hoffmann, 'Der Sandmann/The sandman', in R.J. Hollingdale (ed.), *Tales of Hoffmann* (Harmondsworth: Penguin, 1982 [1817]), p.99.
54. Hoffmann, 'Der Sandmann', p.116.
55. Tinee, '*White Zombie*, honor film, opens theater', p.11.
56. L.N., 'The screen', p.18.
57. Poe, 'The fall of the house of Usher', p.95.
58. Paravisini-Gebert, 'Women possessed', p.40.
59. Seabrook, *The Magic Island*, p.112.
60. Seabrook, *The Magic Island*, p.112.
61. Robin Wood, 'Foreword: What lies beneath?', in Steven Jay Schneider (ed.), *Horror Film and Psychoanalysis: Freud's Worst Nightmare* (Cambridge: Cambridge University Press, 2004), p.xv, original emphasis.
62. Edna Aizenberg, '*I Walked With a Zombie*: The pleasures and perils of postcolonial hybridity', *World Literature Today* 73/3 (1999), p.462.
63. Seabrook, *The Magic Island*, p.94.

4 *VAMPYR* AND THE EUROPEAN AVANT-GARDE

1. Robin Wood, 'On Carl Dreyer', *Film Comment* 10/2 March–April (1974), p.13.

2. There are many different versions of *Vampyr* in archives and available for home viewing. In turn, academic writing on the film is based on the analysis of a number of different versions of the film. The original version of this chapter was written in 2008 and published in January 2009 in *Studies in European Cinema*; the analysis was based on a Region 1 DVD produced by Image Entertainment released in 1998. The Image Entertainment DVD is an amalgamation of several prints with dialogue dubbed in German and intratextual writing in French and Danish. The Image Entertainment DVD appears to be combined from two main versions, 'an English-titled, German-language version' held by the BFI in 16mm and 35mm prints, and a second English-titled, German-language version, 'distributed by Jorgen S. Jorgensen, Gloria Film'. David Rudkin, *Vampyr* (London: BFI, 2005), p.28. The article was revised for *After Dracula* in 2012, and was based on the Martin Koerber restoration composed of prints from Cineteca del commune di Bologna and Stiftung Deutsche Kinemathek in Berlin, made available on the Eureka Entertainment 'Masters of Cinema' Region 2 DVD released in August 2008.
3. Ginette Vincendeau, 'Issues in European cinema', in John Hill and Pamela Church Gibson (eds), *World Cinema: Critical Approaches* (Oxford: Oxford University Press, 2000), pp.56–64.
4. Joan Hawkins, *Cutting Edge: Art-Horror and the Horrific Avant-Garde* (Minneapolis, MN: University of Minnesota Press), p.27.
5. Vincendeau, 'Issues in European cinema', p.57.
6. 'Censor Objects to *Joan of Arc*', *Film Weekly,* 22 October 1928, unpaginated (courtesy of BFI Special Collections).
7. Ib Monty, 'Carl Th. Dreyer: An Introduction', in Jytte Jensen (ed.), *Carl Th. Dreyer* (New York, NY: Museum of Modern Art, 1988), p.11.
8. Mordaunt Hall, 'Poignant French film', *New York Times,* 31 March 1929, p.107.
9. Jean Drum and Dale D. Drum, *My Only Great Passion: The Life and Films of Carl Th. Dreyer* (Lanham, MD: Scarecrow Press, 2000), p.142.
10. In their unsurpassed study of Dreyer's entire body of work, the Drums write that it was rumoured that Dreyer broke a contract with Société Générale des Films, which he categorically denied, but 'he would not discuss what the problems were. In the fall of 1931 he brought a lawsuit against the company in Paris and this no doubt furthered his reputation among producers of being difficult and not altogether a safe director to employ.' *My Only Great Passion*, pp.145–46.
11. Rudkin, *Vampyr*, pp.18–19.
12. The protagonist is often called 'Alan Gray', 'Allan Gray' or 'David Gray'. Donald Skoller observes that David Gray is the character name, and Alan Gray was used 'in the Aryan version shown in Germany'. *Dreyer in Double Reflection: Translation of Carl Th. Dreyer's Writings About the Film (Om Filmen)* (New York, NY: E.P. Dutton, 1973), p.98. De Gunzberg's name is spelled in a number of different ways. This chapter follows the spelling of

his name in the magazine *Vogue*, where he was Senior Fashion Editor for a number of years. See 'Fashion Department', *Vogue* 161.5 May (1973), p.3.

13. Anon, '*The Strange Adventure of David Gray*', *Close Up* 8/1 March (1931), p.50; Herman G. Weinberg and Gretchen Weinberg, 'An interview with Baron de Gunzburg', *Film Culture*, 32 (1964), pp.57–58.

14. Weinbergs, 'An interview with Baron de Gunzburg', p.57.

15. James C. Robertson, *The British Board of Film Censors: Film Censorship in Britain, 1896–1950* (London: Croom Helm, 1985), p.59; Tom Dewey Matthews, *Censored: The Story of Film Censorship in Britain* (London: Chatto & Windus, 1994), p.79.

16. Casper Tybjerg, 'Waking life', *Sight and Sound* 18/9 (2008), p.33.

17. Tom Weaver et al, *Universal Horrors: The Studio's Classic Films, 1931–1946,* 2nd edn (Jefferson, NC: MacFarland, 2007), pp.21–24.

18. Weinberg, 'An interview with Baron de Gunzburg', p.59.

19. Dreyer discusses his influences in Michael Delahaye, 'Between Heaven and Hell: Interview with Carl Dreyer', *Cahiers du cinéma in English* 4 (1966), p.7. Ten years before *Vampyr*, Dreyer published a rhapsodic essay on Sjöström's *Klostret I Sendomir/The Monastery of Sendomir* (1920), translated by Casper Tybjerg in his 'Dreyer and the National Film in Denmark', *Film History* 13.1 (2001), p. 23.

20. Des O'Rawe, 'The great secret: Silence, cinema and modernism', *Screen* 47/4 (2006), p.399.

21. A Special Correspondent, 'The pictures across the channel', *Observer,* 8 January 1933, p.12. Boerge Trolle makes links between Dreyer, Epstein and the French director René Clair, 'The world of Carl Dreyer', *Sight and Sound* 25/3 Winter (1955–6), p.123.

22. See William Rubin, *Dada, Surrealism and Their Heritage* (New York, NY: Museum of Modern Art, 1968).

23. Malte Hagener, *Moving Forward, Looking Back: The European Avant-Garde and the Invention of Film Culture, 1919–1939* (Amsterdam: Amsterdam University Press, 2007), p.20. For an exploration of avant-garde and experimental film practices in Britain during the interwar period, see Jamie Sexton, *Alternative Film Culture in Inter-War Britain* (Exeter: University of Exeter Press, 2008).

24. Quoted in Drums, *My Only Great Passion*, p.151.

25. Robert Desnos, 'Avant-garde cinema', originally published in *Documents* 7 (1929). Reprinted in Paul Hammond (ed.), *The Shadow and its Shadow: Surrealist Writings on Cinema* (London: BFI, 1978), p.37.

26. The French Surrealist Group, 'Some surrealist advice', originally published in *L'Age du Cinéma*, 4–5, August–November (1951). Reprinted in Paul Hammond (ed.), *The Shadow and its Shadow: Surrealist Writings on Cinema* (London: BFI, 1978), p.25.

27. Ian Christie, 'The avant-gardes and European cinema before 1930', in John Hill and Pamela Church Gibson (eds), *World Cinema: Critical Approaches* (Oxford: Oxford University Press, 2000), p.66.

28. André Breton, *Manifestoes of Surrealism* (Ann Arbor, MI: University of Michigan Press, 1998), p.26.

29. Hagener, *Moving Forward, Looking Back*, p.22.

30. The character of the soldier with the peg leg is not listed in the credits. Rudkin refers to the character as the 'kaporal'. *Vampyr*, p.43. Mark Nash describes him as the 'corporal'. '*Vampyr* and the fantastic', *Screen* 17/3 (1976), p.32.

31. Rudkin, *Vampyr*, p.50.

32. David Bordwell, *The Films of Carl-Theodor Dreyer* (Berkeley, CA: University of California Press, 1981), p.97.

33. Nash, '*Vampyr* and the fantastic', p.53.

34. Wood, 'On Carl Dreyer', p.13. Barbara Creed, *The Monstrous-Feminine: Film, Feminism, Psychoanalysis* (London: Routledge, 1993), p.60

35. Delahaye, 'Between heaven and hell', p.7.

36. Rudkin, *Vampyr*, p.53, emphasis original.

37. Sigmund Freud, *The Interpretation of Dreams* (Hertfordshire: Wordsworth Classics of World Literature, 1997 [1900]), p.20.

38. Freud, *The Interpretation of Dreams*, p.20.

39. Jacques Lacan, 'The dream of Irma's injection', in J.A. Miller (ed.), *The Seminar of Jacques Lacan Vol. 2: The Ego in Freud's Theory and in the Technique of Psychoanalysis 1954–1955* (Cambridge: Cambridge University Press, 1988 [March 1955]), pp.154–55, italics original.

40. Lacan, 'The dream of Irma's injection', p.164.

41. Michael Grant, '"Ultimate formlessness": Cinema, horror, and the limits of meaning', in Steven Jay Schneider (ed.), *Horror Film and Psychoanalysis: Freud's Worst Nightmare* (Cambridge: Cambridge University Press, 2004), pp.177–78.

42. Jonathan Rosenbaum, '*Vampyr: Der Traum des Allan Gray*', *Monthly Film Bulletin* August (1976), p.180.

43. Nash, '*Vampyr* and the fantastic', p.34.

44. Bordwell, *The Films of Carl-Theodor Dreyer*, p.110.

45. Michael Grant makes a similar point in 'Cinema, horror and the abominations of Hell: Carl-Theodor Dreyer's *Vampyr* (1931) and Lucio Fulci's *The Beyond* (1981)', in Andrea Sabbadini (ed.), *The Couch and the Silver Screen: Psychoanalytic Reflections on European Cinema* (Hove: Brunner-Routledge, 2003), p.149.

46. Weinbergs, 'An interview with Baron de Gunzburg', p.58.

47. Delahaye, 'Between heaven and hell', p.16.

48. See Nash's article on *Vampyr*, published in 1976, in which he briefly discusses the provenance of the National Film Archive print. '*Vampyr* and the fantastic' p.30, n.2.

49. Inevitably, there were a number of issues with screening the substandard 68-minute, 16mm print. Howden reveals that the film was 'an un-restored mix of the three original versions with sections in English, German and French. The overall quality was poor in both sound and

vision (the Electric's sound system was not exactly state of the art and the acoustics were those of the silent cinema, which of course it was originally)'. A number of reviews noted the sound and mix of languages; the *Guardian* preview described the print as 'not first-class' with 'distinctly choppy' and 'tacked-on' sound. Personal interview with Peter Howden, email, 11 October 2011; Derek Malcolm, 'Westward, the blend is right', *Guardian*, 17 June 1976, p.10.

50. David Robinson, 'Vengeance and vigilantes', *The Times,* 18 June 1976, p.9.
51. Russell Davies, 'Vengeance in decline', *Observer,* 20 June 1976, p.25; John Coleman, '*Vampyr*', *New Statesman,* 25 June 1976, no page (clipping courtesy of BFI microfiche '*Vampyr*: Clippings and reviews').
52. Richard Comb, '*Vampyr*', *Financial Times,* 18 June 1976; Tom Hutchinson, 'Poetry of terror', *Sunday Telegraph,* 20 June 1976; Dilys Powell, '*Vampyr*', *Sunday Times,* 20 June 1976. No page numbers listed for reviews (all clippings courtesy of BFI microfiche).
53. Brigid Cherry, '*Daughters of Darkness* (aka *Les lèvres rouges*, aka *Blood on the Lips*)', in Steven Jay Schneider (ed.), *100 European Horror Films* (London: BFI, 2007), p.55
54. Ernest Mathijs and Jamie Sexton, *Cult Cinema: An Introduction* (Oxford: Wiley-Blackwell, 2011), p.201.
55. Drums, *My Only Great Passion*, p.159; Herbert L. Matthews, 'Paris views new films and theatres', *New York Times,* 15 January 1933, p.X4.
56. Quoted in Drums, *My Only Great Passion*, p.153.
57. Breton, *Manifestoes of Surrealism*, pp.123–24.
58. Carl Lerner, '"My way of working is in relation to the future": A conversation with Carl Dreyer', *Film Comment* 4/1 Fall (1966), p.65.

5 BAUHAUS OF HORROR: FILM ARCHITECTURE AND *THE BLACK CAT*

1. Several critics have suggested that the character of architect Hjalmar Poelzig can be re-traced as Hans Poelzig, architect and film-set designer, a man considered 'among the great architects of his time'. Noah Isenberg, 'Perennial detour: The cinema of Edgar G. Ulmer and the experience of exile' *Cinema Journal* 43/2 (2004), p.10.
2. Tim Bergfelder, Sue Harris and Sarah Street, *Film Architecture and the Transnational Imagination: Set Design in 1930s European Cinema* (Amsterdam: Amsterdam University Press, 2007), p.15.
3. Steven Jacobs, *The Wrong House: The Architecture of Alfred Hitchcock* (Rotterdam: 010 Publishers, 2007), p.74.
4. Hans Dieter Schaal, 'Spaces of the psyche: German expressionist film', *Architectural Design* 70/1 (2000), p.13.

5. Ian Christie, 'Film as modernist art', in Christopher Wilk (ed.), *Modernism 1914–1939: Designing a New World* (London: V&A Publications, 2006), pp.305–06.

6. Christopher Wilk, 'What was modernism?', in Christopher Wilk (ed.), *Modernism, 1914–1939: Designing a New World* (London: V&A Publications, 2006), p.14.

7. Wilk, 'What was modernism?', p.17.

8. Charlotte Benton and Tim Benton, 'The style and the age', in Charlotte Benton, Tim Benton and Ghislaine Wood (eds), *Art Deco, 1910–1939* (London: V&A Publications, 2003), p.22.

9. Bentons, 'The style and the age', p.21.

10. Gabrielle Esperdy, 'From instruction to consumption: Architecture and design in Hollywood movies of the 1930s', *Journal of American Culture* 30/2 (2007), p.200.

11. Edgar Allan Poe, 'The black cat', in *The Collected Works of Edgar Allan Poe* (Ware: Wordsworth Library Editions, 2009 [1843]), p.65.

12. Paul Mandell, 'Edgar G. Ulmer and *The Black Cat*', *American Cinematographer: The International Journal of Film and Video Production Techniques,* 65/9 October (1984), p.35–36.

13. 'Production finishing today', *Variety,* 17 March 1934, p.3; Mandell, 'Edgar G. Ulmer and *The Black Cat*', p.34.

14. Gregory William Mank, *Bela Lugosi and Boris Karloff: The Expanded Story of a Haunting Collaboration* (Jefferson, NC: McFarland, 2009), p.161.

15. A.D.S., 'Not related to Poe', *New York Times,* 19 May 1934, p.18; 'Scenarists go Poe one better in *The Black Cat*', *Chicago Daily Tribune,* 25 March 1934, p.D6. *New York Daily News* review reprinted in 'New York reviews', *Hollywood Reporter,* 1 June 1934, p.2. Ralph T. Jones of the *Atlanta Constitution* also commented, 'taken from Edgar Allan Poe's story of the same title, it has been modernized and rewritten until there is not much of the original left', 'Reviewing the shows', *Atlanta Constitution,* 12 May 1934, p.10.

16. 'Too much "mugging" in tedious story', *Hollywood Reporter,* 4 May 1934, p.3.

17. Kyle Dawson Edwards, '"Poe, you are avenged!": Edgar Allan Poe and Universal Pictures' *The Raven* (1935)', *Adaptation* 4/2 (2010), p.118.

18. 'Reviews for showmen', *Kine-Weekly,* 22 March 1934, p.26; Lionel Collier, 'On the screens now', *Picturegoer* 4/1674 August 1934, p.24.

19. Eric Schaefer, *"Bold! Daring! Shocking! True!": A History of Exploitation Films, 1919–1959* (Durham, NC: Duke University Press, 1999), p.90.

20. Peter Bogdanovich, *Who the Devil Made It: Conversations with...* (New York, NY: Ballantine Books, 1997), p.576.

21. Bernd Herzogenrath, 'The return of Edgar G. Ulmer', in Bernd Herzogenrath (ed.), *Edgar G. Ulmer: Essays on the King of the B's* (Jefferson, NC: McFarland, 2009), p.4. Isenberg argues that Ulmer's early film career 'has been somewhat embellished by grandiose and

largely specious claims made by the director himself - or, perhaps more accurately, by the émigré director, who no longer intended to return home and continually reinvented himself in America'. 'Perennial detour', p.4.

22. Lotte Eisner, *The Haunted Screen: Expressionism in the German Cinema and the Influence of Max Reinhardt* (Berkeley, CA: University of California Press, 1969), p.352.

23. Isenberg, 'Perennial detour', p.4.

24. The work of Cedric Gibbons, head of MGM's art department, is synonymous with art deco in 1930s Hollywood and epitomised by the *moderne* design of *Grand Hotel* (1932). Ghislaine Wood, 'Art Deco and Hollywood film', in Charlotte Benton, Tim Benton and Ghislaine Wood (eds) *Art Deco, 1910–1939* (London: V&A Publications, 2003), p.329; Christina Wilson, 'Cedric Gibbons: Architect of Hollywood's golden age', in Mark Lamster (ed.), *Architecture and Film* (New York, NY: Princeton Architectural Press, 2000), pp.101–16.

25. Dietrich Neumann, 'Introduction', in Dietrich Neumann (ed.), *Film Architecture: From Metropolis to Blade Runner* (Munich: Prestel-Verlag, 1996), p.8.

26. Quoted in Dietrich Neumann, '*Genuine: Die Tragödie eines seltsamen Hauses*', in Dietrich Neumann (ed.), *Film Architecture: From Metropolis to Blade Runner* (Munich: Prestel-Verlag, 1996), p.58.

27. 'Universal greets the showmen of the M.P.T.O.A. with a timely group of showmen's pictures', *Hollywood Reporter*, 12 April 1934, p.10.

28. In September 1936 an article published in *California Arts and Architecture* recommended that manufacturers of materials such as Bakelite should turn to Hollywood for custom. Esperdy, 'From instruction to consumption', p.209.

29. Donald Albrecht points out that the although the surface of the living room wall 'appears to be formed of a square egg-crate grid of thin fins infilled with frosted glass', it is actually 'a flat assemblage of panels painted with trompe l'oeil fins and shadows'. *Designing Dreams: Modern Architecture in the Movies* (London: Thames and Hudson, 1986), p.101.

30. Keith Memorial, 'New films', *Daily Boston Globe*, 28 May 1934, p.11; 'Rialto', *Washington Post*, 12 May 1934, p.7. *New York Daily News* review reprinted in 'New York reviews', *Hollywood Reporter*, p.2.

31. Edwin Heathcote, 'Modernism as enemy: Film and the portrayal of modern architecture', *Architectural Design* 70/1 (2000), p.2.

32. Joseph Rosa, 'Tearing down the house: Modern homes in the movies', in Mark Lamster (ed.), *Architecture and Film* (New York, NY: Princeton Architectural Press, 2000), p.159.

33. Esperdy, 'From instruction to consumption', p.207; Jacobs, *The Wrong House*, p.307.

34. Rosa, 'Tearing down the house', pp.159–60.

35. Deborah Jermyn, 'You can't keep a dead woman down: The female corpse and textual disruption in contemporary Hollywood', in Elizabeth Klaver (ed.), *Images of the Corpse: From Renaissance to Cyberspace* (Madison, WI: University of Wisconsin Press, 2004), p.154.

36. Clement Meadmore, *The Modern Chair: Classic Designs by Thonet, Breuer, Le Corbusier, Eames and Others* (Mineola, NY: Dover, 1997), p.40; Charlotte and Peter Fiell, *Design of the 20th Century* (London: Taschen, 2001), pp.39–43.

37. Jean-Louis Cohen, *Le Corbusier: The Lyricism of Architecture in the Machine Age* (Köln: Taschen GmbH, 2006), p.26.

38. Review reprinted in 'New York reviews', *Hollywood Reporter*, p.2.

39. R.M.F., '*House of Doom (The)*', *Monthly Film Bulletin* 1/8 September (1934), p.68.

40. 'New films in London', *The Times*, 3 September 1934, p.10.

41. 'U Using 50 Pieces', *Variety*, 13 April 1934, p.6.

42. William H. Rosar, 'Music for the monsters: Universal Picture's horror film scores of the thirties', *Quarterly Journal of the Library of Congress* 40/4 (1983), pp.402–03.

43. Julie Brown, '*Carnival of Souls* and the organs of horror', in Neil Lerner (ed.), *Music in Horror Film: Listening to Fear* (London: Routledge, 2009), p.8.

44. Roy R. Behrens, 'Dessau's Bauhaus', *Leonardo* 39/1 (2006), pp.87–88.

45. Myron Meisel, 'Edgar G. Ulmer: The primacy of the visual', in Todd McCarthy and Charles Flynn (eds), *Kings of the Bs: Working with the Hollywood System* (New York, NY: E.P. Dutton, 1975), pp.148–49.

46. The Ohio, Chicago, Ontario, Quebec and Swedish censor boards cut this scene, and Finland and Italy banned the film. *Variety* reports that Ulmer's native Austria banned the film outright, because 'Austro-Hungarian army and country patriotic and religious feelings are injured by the film'. Gregory William Mank, '*The Black Cat*', in Bernd Herzogenrath (ed.), *Edgar G. Ulmer: Essays on the King of the B's* (Jefferson, NC: McFarland, 2009), p.101; 'A.M. Dailies!', *Variety* 22 August 1935, p.3.

47. Robert J. Landry, '*The Black Cat*', *Variety*, 22 May 1934, p.15.

48. Mank, '*The Black Cat*', p.96.

49. Mank, '*The Black Cat*', p.101.

50. Gary D. Rhodes, '"Tremonstrous" hopes and "Oke" results: The 1934 reception of *The Black Cat*' in Gary D. Rhodes (ed.), *Edgar G. Ulmer: Detour on Poverty Row* (Lanham, MD: Lexington Books, 2008), p.313.

51. Heathcote, 'Modernism as enemy', p.2.

52. Albrecht, *Designing Dreams*, p.xiii.

53. Quoted in Anthony Vidler, 'The explosion of space: Architecture and the filmic imaginary', in Dietrich Neumann (ed.), *Film Architecture: From Metropolis to Blade Runner* (Munich: Prestel-Verlag, 1996), p.14.

6 THE 1930S BRITISH HORROR FILM

1. Ian Conrich, 'Horrific films and 1930s British cinema', in Steve Chibnall and Julian Petley (eds), *British Horror Cinema* (London: Routledge, 2002), p.58.

2. David Pirie shows little enthusiasm for British horror before Hammer and lists only six 1930s films. *A New Heritage of Horror: The English Gothic Cinema* (London: I.B.Tauris, 2008), p.19. Tom Ryall suggests that British censorship and the appropriation of British gothic in American horror films such as *Dracula* are major factors in the absence of a cogent body of films. 'British cinema and genre', *Journal of Popular British Cinema* 1 (1998), p.21.

3. Peter Hutchings, *Hammer and Beyond: The British Horror Film* (Manchester: Manchester University Press, 1993), p.24; James Chapman, 'Celluloid Shockers', in Jeffrey Richards (ed.), *The Unknown 1930s: An Alternative History of British Cinema, 1929–1939* (London: I.B.Tauris, 1998), p.87.

4. At the time of writing this chapter there were 12 British horror films released from 1931 to 1936 (the parameters of *After Dracula*) available either to view at the BFI or to purchase on DVD. This excludes several films that exist as nitrate prints with master preservation status at the BFI - such as *The Scotland Yard Mystery* (1934) - as these are inaccessible to researchers.

5. See Kevin Gough-Yates, 'The British feature film as a European concern: Britain and the émigré film-maker, 1933–45', in Günter Berghaus (ed.), *Theatre and Film in Exile: German Artists in Britain, 1933–1945* (Oxford: Berg, 1989), pp.135–66.

6. John Sedgwick, *Popular Filmgoing in 1930s Britain: A Choice of Pleasures* (Exeter: University of Exeter Press, 2000), p.212.

7. Tim Bergfelder, 'The Production Designer and the *Gesamtkunstwerk*: German Film Technicians in the British Film Industry of the 1930s', in Andrew Higson (ed.), *Dissolving Views: Key Writings on British Cinema* (London: Cassell, 1996), p.24.

8. Allan Eyles, *Gaumont British Cinemas* (London: BFI, 1996), p.13; Geoff Brown, 'Happy ever after? The German adventures of Gaumont-British in 1932', *Journal of British Cinema and Television* 7/3 (2010), p.382; Rachel Low, *The History of British Film, 1918–1929* (London: George Allen & Unwin, 1971), pp.158, 169.

9. 'Inside Stuff - Pictures', *Variety,* 21 March 1933, p.42; 'Pictures', *Variety,* 20 March 1935, p.2.

10. Tom Dewe Matthews, *Censored: The Story of Film Censorship in Britain* (London: Chatto & Windus, 1994), p.50. In the 1930s the senior script examiner was Colonel J.C. Hanna, Vice President of the BBFC, and from 1934 he was assisted by Miss N. Shortt, daughter of Sir Edward Shortt, president of the BBFC from 1929 to 1935. Jeffrey Richards, 'The British Board of Film Censors and content control in the 1930s:

Foreign affairs', *Historical Journal of Film, Radio and Television* 2.1 (1982), p.39.

11. Annette Kuhn, 'Children, "horrific" films, and censorship in 1930s Britain', *Historical Journal of Film, Radio and Television* 22.2 (2002), p.199.

12. Tom Johnson, *Censored Screams: The British Ban on Hollywood Horror in the Thirties* (Jefferson, NC: MacFarland, 1997), p.11.

13. Kuhn, 'Children, "horrific" films, and censorship in 1930s Britain', pp.199–200.

14. James C. Roberston, *The British Board of Film Censors: Film Censorship in Britain, 1896–1950* (London: Croom Helm, 1985), p.58.

15. Johnson, *Censored Screams*, p.88.

16. Robertson, *The British Board of Film Censors*, p.59.

17. *The Ghoul* Synopsis, BBFC Scenario Report #130, 10 February 1933, BFI Special Collections, London.

18. *The Ghoul* Synopsis, BBFC Scenario Report #130.

19. *The Clairvoyant* Synopsis, BBFC Scenario Report #372, 27 December 1934, BFI Special Collections, London.

20. *The Clairvoyant* Synopsis, BBFC Scenario Report #392, 12 Feb 1935, BFI Special Collections, London.

21. *The Clairvoyant* Synopsis, BBFC Scenario Report #392.

22. *The Man Who Lived Again* Synopsis, BBFC Scenario Report #476, 11 October 1935, BFI Special Collections, London.

23. *The Man Who Lived Again* Synopsis, BBFC Scenario Report #476.

24. Following Matthews' account of 1930s BBFC personnel, we can assume 'J.B.W' is Joseph 'Brookie' Wilkinson, the administrative head of the BBFC during this period. *Censored*, p.58.

25. *The Man Who Lived Again* Synopsis, BBFC Scenario Report #476.

26. 'High Court of Justice King's Bench Division, copyright dispute: Alleged infringement by a film, De Maudit v. Gaumont-British Corporation, Limited', *The Times,* 24 November 1939, p.2.

27. Quoted in Tom Weaver, et al, *Universal Horrors: The Studio's Classic Films, 1931–1946,* 2nd edn (Jefferson, NC: McFarland, 2007), p.62.

28. Lee Server, 'Gloria Stuart', *Films in Review,* February (1988), unpaginated.

29. Kim Newman, '*The Ghoul*: A Video Watchdog Round Table Discussion', *Video Watchdog* http://www.videowatchdog.com/home/RoundTable/ghoul.htm [accessed 31 May 2011].

30. 'New films in London', *The Times,* 7 August 1933, p.8.

31. W.A. Whitney, '*The Ghoul*', *Washington Post,* 10 February 1934, p.14.

32. Whitney, '*The Ghoul*', p.14.

33. P.L. Mannock, 'On the British sets', *Picturegoer,* 8 April 1933, p.30.

34. Robert Spadoni has similarly suggested that Karloff's performance as the Monster in *Frankenstein* 'calls to mind the German Expressionist acting style, which to many Veidt in *Caligari* epitomises'. *Uncanny Bodies: The Coming of Sound Film and the Origins of the Horror Genre* (Berkeley, CA: University of California Press, 2007), p.114.

35. Michael Omasta argues that Krampf's contribution to the set design is a 'parody of old German horror films'. 'Famously unknown: Günther Krampf's work as cinematographer in British films', in Tim Bergfelder and Christian Cargnelli (eds) *Destination London: Germany-speaking Emigrés and British Cinema, 1925–1950* (Oxford: Berghahn, 2008), p.79. See also Tobias Hochscherf, *The Continental Connection: German-speaking Émigrés and British Cinema, 1927–45* (Manchester: Manchester University Press, 2011).

36. P.L. Mannock, 'On the British sets', *Picturegoer,* 22 April 1933, p.32.

37. Sarah Street, *British National Cinema*, 2nd edn (London: Routledge, 1997), p.152; Andy Medhurst, 'Music hall and British cinema', in Charles Barr (ed.), *All Our Yesterdays: 90 Years of British Cinema* (London: BFI, 1986), p.170.

38. Relatedly, see Jeffrey Richards, 'Tod Slaughter and the cinema of excess', in Jeffrey Richards (ed.), *The Unknown 1930s: An Alternative History of British Cinema, 1929–1939* (London: I.B.Tauris, 1998), pp.139–59.

39. '*The Clairvoyant* tells vivid story at Little Theatre', *Rochester Journal,* 6 July 1936, p.11.

40. F.S.N., 'At The Roxy', *New York Times,* 8 June 1935, p.12.

41. Philip Larkin, 'Dockery and son', in Anthony Thwaite (ed.), *Collected Poems* (London: Faber and Faber, 1988), p.152.

42. Nelson B. Bell, '*The Clairvoyant* opens tomorrow at the Belasco, with bargain bill tonight', *Washington Post,* 28 September 1935, p.6.

43. B.R. Crisler, 'The monster, incognito', *New York Times,* 9 February 1936, p.X5.

44. 'New films in London', *The Times,* 5 October 1936, p.10.

45. C.A.L., 'British films in America', *Observer,* 12 May 1935, p.11.

46. Ernest Marshall, 'London screen notes', *New York Times,* 18 June 1933, p.X2.

47. Mannock, 'On the British sets', 8 April 1933, p.30.

48. Trade date, Johnson, *Censored Screams*, p.89. UK premiere date, 'Picture theatres', *The Times,* 7 August 1933, p.8. US premiere date, Shan, 'Film reviews', *Variety*, 30 January 1934, p.12.

49. 'New Films in London', *The Times* 7 August, 1933, p.8; 'Films in the suburbs and the provinces', *Observer,* 15 October 1933, p.25.

50. *Frankenstein* was previewed for its London trade show at the Tivoli ('Frankenstein: Film "shocker" that lacks thrills', *Manchester Guardian,* 21 January 1932, p.10) and was reviewed at Manchester's Oxford Theatre (M.C., 'Picture theatres', *Manchester Guardian,* 9 August 1932, p. 11). *The Mummy* was reviewed at Manchester's Theatre Royal (M.C., 'Manchester stage and films', *Manchester Guardian,* 27 June 1933). *Bride of Frankenstein* was reviewed in 'In suburbs and provinces', *Observer,* 29 September 1935, p.16, as was *The Black Cat* under its UK release title *The House of Doom* ('Films in the suburbs and the provinces', 17 March 1935, p.10).

51. Lionel Collier, 'On screens now', *Picturegoer,* 14 October 1933, p.125.

52. 'Display ad 18 - no title', *Chicago Daily Tribune,* 10 May 1934, p.20; 'Karloff in an eerie picture at the Rialto', *Washington Post,* 9 February 1934, p.14.

53. 'Looking' em over', *Motion Picture Daily,* 24 November 1933, p.2.

54. 'New films', *Daily Boston Globe,* 2 April 1934, p.4.

55. A.D.S., 'Back from the grave', *New York Times,* 27 January 1934, p.9.

56. A.D.S., 'Back from the grave', p.9.

57. A.D.S., 'Back from the grave', p.9.

58. C.A.L., 'British films in America', p.11.

59. Lynne Myddleton, 'No screams by request: Fay Wray', *Picturegoer,* 19 January 1935, p.16.

60. 'Fay Wray knocks wood', *New York Times,* 12 May 1935, p.X4.

61. 'Fay Wray knocks wood', p.X4.

62. 'Roxy to get all Gaumont films', *New York Times,* 28 May 1935, p.29.

63. Frank S. Nugent, 'How fared the English visitors last year? Michael Balcon, head of Gaumont-British, reports on film "Invasion"', *New York Times,* 3 March 1935, p.X3.

64. Patrick B. Prescott Jnr, 'Travelers find England being influenced by American-made moving pictures', *Chicago Defender,* 10 November 1934, p.5.

65. Anthony Slide, *Banned in the USA: British Films in the United States and their Censorship, 1933–1960* (London: I.B. Tauris, 1998), p.155.

66. The UK screening date is taken from the first advertisement for the film that I could find. 'Entertainments index', *The Times,* 9 August 1935, p.10.

67. 'New films in London', *The Times,* 12 August 1935, p.8.

68. W.F., '*Clairvoyant (The)*', *Monthly Film Bulletin,* 17 June 1935, p.68.

69. Char, '*The Clairvoyant*', *Variety,* 12 June 1935, p.41.

70. Keith Memorial, '*The Keeper of the Bees, The Clairvoyant*', *Daily Boston Globe,* 20 July 1935, p.12.

71. 'Clairvoyant role for Claude Rains', *Spokane Daily Chronicle,* 6 December 1935, p.12; Anna Nangle, 'Claude Rains is convincing in *The Clairvoyant*', *Chicago Daily Tribune,* 4 September 1935, p.13.

72. Sarah Street, *Transatlantic Crossings: British Feature Films in the United States* (London: Continuum, 2002), p.47.

73. UK trade show date taken from Johnson, *Censored Screams*, p.137; US premiere date taken from Slide, *Banned in the USA*, pp.167–68.

74. '*The Man Who Changed His Mind*', *Kinematograph Weekly*, 17 September 1936, p.25.

75. T.G., '*Man Who Changed His Mind, The*', *Monthly Film Bulletin,* September 1936, p.148; '*The Man Who Changed His Mind*', *Film Weekly,* 10 October 1936, p.32.

76. The *Daily Boston Globe* described the film as 'expertly and imaginatively directed', but was in the minority as a 'straight' review. '*The Man Who Lived Again*; one in a million', *Daily Boston Globe,* 22 February 1937, p.19.

77. Mae Tinee, 'Karloff packs a punch in his newest scare', *Chicago Daily Tribune,* 21 December 1936, p.17.

78. J.T.M., 'At the Rialto', *New York Times,* 16 December 1936, p.35.

79. Street, *Transatlantic Crossings*, p.47.

80. Mark Jancovich's article on how *New York Times* critics responded to horror films in the 1940s is a useful comparison of attitudes. "'Two ways

of looking": The critical reception of 1940s horror', *Cinema Journal* 49/3 (2010), pp.45–66.

81. '*The Ghost Train*', *Film Daily,* 18 February 1933, p.3.
82. Epes W. Sargent, 'Exploitation', *Variety,* 27 March 1934, p.19.
83. Sargent, 'Exploitation', p.19.
84. *The Man Who Lived Again*, Gaumont-British Pictures Corporation Pressbook, 1936, p.8.

7   *WEREWOLF OF LONDON* AND THE ORIGINS OF WEREWOLF CINEMA

1. The narrative similarities have been noted over the years by a number of critics and historians, including Robert Spadoni, 'Old times in *Werewolf of London*', *Journal of Film and Video* 63/4 (2011), p.14; Peter Hutchings, *Historical Dictionary of Horror Cinema* (Lanham, MD: Scarecrow Press, 2008), p.329 and Rick Worland, *The Horror Film: An Introduction* (Oxford: Blackwell, 2007), p.124.
2. Earlier films such as Universal's lost *The Werewolf* (1913) are understood to be about Native American belief and superstition.
3. J. Robert Craig, 'The origin story in werewolf cinema of the 1930s and 1940s', *Studies in Popular Culture,* 27/3 (2005), p.80; Chantal Bourgault Du Coudray, *The Curse of the Werewolf: Fantasy, Horror and the Beast Within* (London: I.B. Tauris, 2006), p.77.
4. Guy Endore, *The Werewolf of Paris* (London: Sphere Books, 1974 [1933]), p.87.
5. See Du Coudray, *The Curse of the Werewolf*, pp.12–43, and Mark Valentine, 'Introduction', in *The Werewolf Pack: An Anthology* (London: Wordsworth Editions, 2008), pp.vii–xii.
6. Endore, *The Werewolf of Paris*, p.118.
7. Endore, *The Werewolf of Paris*, p.191.
8. Endore, *The Werewolf of Paris*, p.236.
9. Robert Bloch, 'Foreword', in Guy Endore, *The Werewolf of Paris* (New York, NY: Citadel Press, 1992), p.2.
10. 'Harris is offered unit post at Universal', *Variety,* 4 April 1935, p.4.
11. Bloch, 'Preface', p.1.
12. Philip K. Scheuer, 'A town called Hollywood', *Los Angeles Times,* 21 July 1935, p.A1.
13. Endore is interviewed about *Mark of the Vampire* in 'Film's dialogue to have the most terrifying words', *Los Angeles Times,* 26 February 1935, p.13.
14. Endore left MGM in October 1935 to write for United Artists, then went on to work for Republic and RKO for the remainder of the decade. 'Pictures', *Variety,* 18 September 1934, p.25; 'Film previews', *Variety,*

27 June 1935, p.3; 'Devil's Island story for Barrymore', *Variety*, 16 September 1935, p.7.

15. Philip K. Scheuer, 'A town called Hollywood', *Los Angeles Times*, 28 October 1934, p.3.

16. Quoted in James Chapman, *Cinemas of the World* (London: Reaktion, 2003), p.100.

17. Chapman, *Cinemas of the World*, p.100.

18. Joseph I. Breen, 'Letter to Mr Harry Zehner', 15 January 1935, Box #778/26851, *Werewolf of London* Production Code Administration File (PCA), Margaret Herrick Library (MHL), Academy of Motion Picture Arts and Sciences (AMPAS), Los Angeles, California.

19. Breen, 'Letter to Mr Harry Zehner', 15 January 1935.

20. Anon, 'Horror story well written and played', *Hollywood Reporter*, 27 April 1935, p.3

21. Dates and costs from Tom Weaver, Michael Brunas and John Brunas, *Universal Hororrs: The Studio's Classic Films, 1931–1946*, 2nd edn (Jefferson, NC: McFarland, 2007), pp.130–36.

22. Joseph I. Breen, 'Letter to Mr Harry Zehner', 23 March 1935, Box #778 / 26851.

23. Theodore Strauss, 'Roll out the barrel: The convivial ghosts of the old Rialto are summoned for an anniversary', *New York Times*, 20 April 1941, p.X5.

24. Tim Snelson and Mark Jancovich, '"No hits, no runs, just terrors": Exhibition, cultural distinctions and cult audiences at the Rialto cinema in the 1930s and 1940s', in Richard Maltby et al. (eds), *Explorations in New Cinema History: Approaches and Case Studies* (Oxford: Wiley-Blackwell, 2011), p.199.

25. Snelson and Jancovich, '"No hits, no runs, just terrors"', p.200.

26. The film then moved to the Criterion Theatre. The Rialto reopened in December of the same year as a much smaller *Art Moderne* building. 'Screen notes', *New York Times*, 16 May 1935, p.20; Snelson and Jancovich, '"No hits, no runs, just terrors"', p.203.

27. Alison Peirse, 'Destroying the male body in British horror cinema', in Santiago Fouz-Hernández (ed.), *Mysterious Skin: Male Bodies in Contemporary Cinema* (London: I.B.Tauris, 2009), p.162.

28. Carol Clover, *Men, Women and Chainsaws: Gender in the Modern Horror Film* (London: BFI, 1992), p.32.

29. See Gina Marchetti, *Romance and the 'Yellow Peril': Race, Sex, and Discursive Strategies in Hollywood Fiction* (Berkeley, CA: University of California Press, 1993). Oland died three years after making *Werewolf of London* and his *New York Times* obituary discusses his association with 'Oriental' roles in Hollywood. 'Warner Oland, 57, screen star, dies', *New York Times*, 7 August 1938, p.32.

30. McCarthy, '*The Werewolf of London*', *Motion Picture Herald*, 4 May 1935, pp.38–39; 'Horror story well written and played', p.3; '*Werewolf of London*', *Motion Picture Daily*, 30 April 1935, p.10.

31. Harry M. Benshoff, *Monsters in the Closet: Homosexuality and the Horror Film* (Manchester: Manchester University Press, 1997), p.59.

32. Oscar Wilde (non de plume 'C.3.3.'), 'The Ballad of Reading Gaol' (New York, NY: Brentanos, 1906), p.3.

33. Quoted in Weaver et al., *Universal Horrors*, p.133.

34. 'Pictures', *Variety*, 27 February 1935, p.3.

35. 'Henry Hull uses weird make-up in film thriller', *Los Angeles Times*, 18 May 1935, p.A7.

36. 'Henry Hull uses weird make-up', p.A7.

37. Joseph I. Breen, 'Letter to Mr Harry Zehner', 28 March 1935, Box #778/26851, *Werewolf of London* PCA, MHL, AMPAS, Los Angeles, California.

38. Robert Harris, 'Letter to Mr Joseph I. Breen', 30 January 1935, Box #778/26851, *Werewolf of London* PCA, MHL, AMPAS, Los Angeles, California.

39. 'Foreign film news', *Variety* 6 September 1932, p.11. *Dr Jekyll and Mr Hyde* was released on 31 December 1931 hence its inclusion in the 1932 *Film Daily* list. '*Grand Hotel* leads ten best list', *Film Daily,* 11 January 1933, p.1.

40. John Mc. H. Stuart, 'Memorandum', 7 February 1935, Box #778/26851, *Werewolf of London* PCA, MHL, AMPAS, Los Angeles, California.

41. Robert Louis Stevenson, *The Strange Case of Dr Jekyll and Mr Hyde* (London: Penguin, 1994 [1886]), p.81.

42. Peter Hutchings, 'Horror London', *Journal of British Cinema and Television* 6/2 (2009), p.190.

43. Linda Williams, 'Film bodies: Gender, genre, and excess', *Film Quarterly* 44/4 (1991), p.4, her emphasis.

44. Breen, 'Letter to Mr Harry Zehner', 15 January 1935.

45. Robert Harris, 'Letter to Mr Joseph I. Breen', 30 January 1935. For further discussion of the correspondence between the Hays office and the film's producers, see Worland, *The Horror Film*, pp.124–25; Skal, *The Monster Show*, p.194; Spadoni, 'Strange botany', p.55 and Reynold Humphries, *The Hollywood Horror Film 1931–1941: Madness in a Social Landscape* (Lanham, MD: Scarecrow Press, 2006), pp.57–58.

46. 'Horror story well written and played', p.3.

47. Endore, *The Werewolf of Paris*, p.148.

48. The quote refers to the final line in the poem 'Two Loves' by Lord Alfred Douglas, which can be interpreted as an ode to homosexual love. It was published in *The Chameleon* in 1894, an issue to which Wilde had also contributed. Wilde was confronted with the poem during his indecency trial. Lisa Hamilton, 'Oscar Wilde, new women and the rhetoric of effeminacy', in Joseph Bristow (ed.), *Wilde Writings: Contextual Conditions* (London: The Regents University of California, 2003), p.242.

49. Wilde, 'The Ballad of Reading Gaol', p.3.

50. '*Werewolf of London*', *Chicago Daily Tribune*, 19 May 1935, p.D7.

51. C.C., '*Werewolf of London* now playing Georgia', *Atlanta Constitution,* 9 July 1935, p.12; J.W.U.T, '*Werewolf of London*', *Monthly Film Bulletin* 2/16

May 1935, p.57; 'Werewolf of London', Harrison's Reports 18 May 1935, p.78; 'Werewolf of London', Motion Picture Daily, p.10.

52. F.S.N., 'At the Rialto', New York Times, 10 May 1935, p.25.

53. Relatedly, Robert Spadoni has argued that the film has an obvious gay subtext, but 'perhaps this overtness is one reason why it is hard to find an extended queer reading of this film; it may seem that there is little work of interpretation to do when so much lies on the surface'. 'Old times in Werewolf of London', p.3.

54. Sigmund Freud, 'Civilisation and its discontents', in Angela Richards (ed.), Penguin Freud Library 12: Civilisation, Society and Religion (London: Penguin, 1991 [1930]), p.302. Translation: 'Man is a wolf to man'.

55. 'Werewolf of London', Harrison's Reports, 18 May 1935, p.78.

56. References to Jekyll and Hyde are in 'The Werewolf of London', Time, 20 May 1935, p.32; Bige, 'Werewolf of London', Variety, 15 May 1935, p.9; F.S.N., 'At the Rialto', p.25; Andrew Sennwald, 'On a swan song', New York Times, 19 May 1935, p.3; 'The shadow stage', Photoplay, July 1935, p.104. References to The Invisible Man in F.S.N., 'At the Rialto', p.25, and Marguerite Tazelaar, 'Werewolf of London - Rialto', New York Herald Tribune, 10 May 1935, no page number given.

57. 'Horror story well written and played', p.3.

58. 'The shadow stage', p.104.

59. 'Werewolf of London', Motion Picture Daily, p.10.

60. Mae Tinee, 'Werewolf of London gives thrills, chills', Chicago Daily Tribune, 19 May 1935, p.D6.

61. Mae Tinee, 'Doctor X: Another movie made to scare you', Chicago Daily Tribune, 12 September 1932, p.15.

62. Philip K. Scheuer, 'New horror film eerie', Los Angeles Times, 19 May 1935, p.25; Sennwald, 'On a swan song', p.X3.

63. Tazelaar, 'Werewolf of London - Rialto', unpaginated.

64. J.W.U.T., 'Werewolf of London', p.57; 'Werewolf of London', Film Daily, 10 May 1935, p.11.

65. Figures from Alberto Manguel, Bride of Frankenstein (London: BFI, 1997), p.14.

66. Manguel, Bride of Frankenstein, p.11.

67. Quoted in Weaver et al., Universal Horrors, pp.138–39.

68. 'New films in London', The Times, 10 June 1935, p.8.

69. 'Picture crosses', Variety, 24 April 1935, p.29.

70. Sennwald, 'On a swan song', p.X3; 'Screen notes', New York Times, 9 May 1935, p.25.

71. 'Werewolf of London', Philadelphia Exhibitor 15 May 1935, unpaginated; Scheuer, 'New horror film eerie', p.25.

72. Bige, 'Werewolf of London', p.9.

73. Kauf, 'Bride of Frankenstein', Variety, 15 May 1935, p.9.

74. 'Screen news here and in Hollywood', New York Times, 26 August 1942, p.22.

75. Kauf, 'Bride of Frankenstein', p.9; Bige, 'Werewolf of London', p.9.

76. 'Screen notes', *New York Times,* 7 May 1935, p.28. *Mister Dynamite* was then reviewed in New York on 2 June. Andre Sennwald, 'Reading the log for May and April', *New York Times,* 2 June 1935, p.X3.

77. *'Werewolf of London', Film Daily* p.11; *'The Werewolf of London', Time,* p.32.

78. Lionel Collier, 'On screens now', *Picturegoer,* 9 November 1935, p.23.

79. William Troy, 'Films: Through the closet door', *The Nation,* 29 May 1935, p.640.

80. Nelson B. Bell, 'Thoughts on horror era, renaissance and Miss Ulric', *Washington Post,* 21 February 1932, p.A1; Philip K. Scheuer, 'Eerie cinema proffered', *Los Angeles Times,* 10 January 1933, p.A7.

81. Eric Schaefer, *"Bold! Daring! Shocking! True!" A History of Exploitation Films, 1919–1959* (Durham, NC: Duke University Press, 1999), p.153.

82. Schaefer, *"Bold! Daring! Shocking! True!",* p.153.

83. Humphries, *The Hollywood Horror Film,* p.viii.

CONCLUSION

1. Adrian Bingham, 'The digitization of newspaper archives: Opportunities and challenges for historians', *Twentieth Century British History* 21/2 (2010), p.225.

2. O.B., 'Comment and review: Actor's viewpoint', *Close Up* 6/5 May (1930), pp.212–13.

3. Jason Jacobs, 'The television archive: Past, present, future', *Critical Studies in Television* 1/1 (2006), p.17.

4. Rhona J. Berenstein, *Attack of the Leading Ladies: Gender, Sexuality and Spectatorship in Classic Horror Cinema* (New York, NY: Columbia University Press, 1996), p.76.

5. Peter Hutchings, 'Monster legacies: Memory, technology and horror history', in Lincoln Geraghty and Mark Jancovich (eds), *The Shifting Definitions of Genre: Essays on Labelling Films, Television Shows and Media* (Jefferson, NC: McFarland, 2008), p.219.

6. Christine Gledhill, 'Rethinking genre', in Christine Gledhill and Linda Williams (eds), *Reinventing Film Studies* (London: Arnold, 2003), p.241.

FILMOGRAPHY

Alias Bulldog Drummond (1935, Walter Forde, Gaumont International, USA)
Alraune (1930, Richard Oswald, Richard-Oswald-Produktion, Germany)
An American Werewolf in London (1981, John Landis, PolyGram Filmed Entertainment/Lycanthrope Films, UK/USA)
At the Villa Rose (1920, Maurice Elvey, Stoll Picture Productions, UK)
At the Villa Rose (1930, Leslie S. Hiscott, Julius Hagen Productions, UK)
Avenging Hand, The (1915, Charles Calvert, Cricks, UK)
Beetle, The (1919, Alexander Butler, Barker, UK)
Behind the Mask (1932, John Francis Dillon, Columbia Pictures Corporation, USA)
Black Cat, The (1934, Edgar G. Ulmer, Universal Pictures, USA)
Black Moon (1934, Roy William Neill, Columbia, USA)
Bride of Frankenstein (1935, James Whale, Universal Pictures, USA)
Brood, The (1979, David Cronenberg, Canadian Film Development Corporation/Elgin International Films Ltd/Mutual Productions Ltd/ Victor Solnicki Productions, Canada)
Cabinet of Dr Caligari, The (1920, Robert Wiene, Decla-Bioscop AG, Germany)
Carrie (1976, Brian De Palma, Red Band Films/United Artists, USA)
Cat and the Canary, The (1927, Paul Leni, Universal Pictures, USA)
Cat People (1942, Jacques Tourneur, RKO Radio Pictures, USA)
Clairvoyant, The (1935, Maurice Elvey, Gaumont-British Picture Corporation, UK)
Condemned to Live (1935, Frank R. Strayer, Invincible Pictures Corp., USA)
Dark Eyes of London, The (1939, Walter Summers, Associated British-Pathé/ John Argyle Productions, UK)
Der Golem (1920, Carl Boese and Paul Wegener, Projektions-AG Union, Germany)
Der Student von Prag (1935, Arthur Robison, Cine-Allianz Tonfilm-produktions GmbH, Germany)
Detour (1945, Edgar G. Ulmer, PRC Pictures, Inc., USA)
Devil and the Deep (1932, Marion Gering, Paramount Pictures, USA)
Devil Doll, The (1936, Tod Browning, Metro-Goldwyn-Mayer, USA)
Doctor X (1932, Michael Curtis, First National Pictures/Warner Bros. Pictures, USA)
Dog Soldiers (2002, Neil Marshall, The Noel Gay Motion Picture Company/Carousel Picture Company, The/The Victor Film Group/ Luxembourg Film Fund, UK/Luxembourg/USA)

Dr Jekyll and Mr Hyde (1931, Rouben Mamoulian, Paramount Publix Corporation, USA)

Dracula (1931, Tod Browning, Universal Pictures, USA)

Dracula's Daughter (1936, Lambert Hillyer, Universal Pictures, USA)

Drakula halála (1921, Károly Lajthay, Lapa Film Studio, Hungary)

Exorcist, The (1973, William Friedkin, Warner Bros. Pictures, USA)

Fall of the House of Usher, The (1928, James Sibley Watson and Melville Webber, USA)

Faust (1926, F.W. Murnau, Universum Film AG, Germany)

Frankenstein (1931, James Whale, Universal Pictures, USA)

Freaks (1932, Tod Browning, Metro-Goldwyn-Mayer, USA)

Genuine: Die Tragödie eines seltsamen Hauses/Genuine: The Tragedy of a Strange House (1920, Robert Wiene, Decla-Bioscop AG, Germany)

Ghost Train, The (1931, Walter Forde, Gainsborough Pictures, UK)

Ghoul, The (1933, T. Hayes Hunter, Gaumont British Picture Corporation, UK)

Golden West, The (1932, David Howard, Fox Film Corporation, USA)

Grand Hotel (1932, Edmund Golding, Metro-Goldwyn-Mayer, USA)

Great Expectations (1934, Stuart Walker, Universal Pictures, USA)

Haunted Curiosity Shop, The (1901, W.R. Booth, Robert W. Paul, UK)

Häxan (1922, Benjamin Christensen, Aljosha Production Company/Svensk Filmindustri (SF), Denmark/Sweden)

Hunchback of Notre Dame, The (1923, Wallace Worsley, Universal Pictures, USA)

I Walked With a Zombie (1943, Jacques Tourneur, RKO Radio Pictures, USA)

I Was a Spy (1933, Victor Saville, Gaumont-British Picture Corporation, UK)

If I Had A Million (1932, Ernst Lubitsch, Paramount Pictures, USA)

Invisible Man, The (1932, James Whale, Universal Pictures, USA)

Invisible Ray, The (1936, Lambert Hillyer, Universal Pictures, USA)

Island of Lost Souls (1932, Erle C. Kenton, Paramount Productions, USA)

Kaibyo nazo no shamisen/The Ghost Cat and the Mysterious Shamisen (1938, Kiyohiko Ushihara, Shinkô Kinema, Japan)

King Kong (1933, Merian C. Cooper and Ernest B. Schoedsack, RKO Radio Pictures, USA)

King of Kings, The (1927, Cecil B. DeMille, DeMille Pictures Corporation, USA)

Klostret I Sendomir/The Monastery of Sendomir (1920, Victor Sjöström, Svenska Biografteatern AB, Sweden)

Körkarlen/The Phantom Carriage (1921, Victor Sjöström, Svensk Film-industri, Sweden)

L'Âge d'Or (1930, Luis Buñuel, Vicomte de Noailles, France)

La chute de la maison Usher/The Fall of the House of Usher (1928, Jean Epstein, Films Jean Epstein, France)

Lady Vanishes, The (1938, Alfred Hitchcock, Gainsborough Pictures, UK)

La passion de Jeanne d'Arc (1928, Carl Theodor Dreyer, Société générale des films, France)

Last Laugh, The (1924, F.W. Murnau, Universum Film AG, Germany)

Le ballet mécanique (1924, Fernand Léger, France)

Les lèvres rouges/Daughters of Darkness (1971, Harry Kümel, Showking Films/Maya Films/Ciné Vog Films/Roxy Film, Belgium/France/West Germany)

Lèvres de sang/Lips of Blood (1975, Jean Rollin, Nordia Films/Off Production/Scorpion V, France)

Lodger, The (1927, Alfred Hitchcock, Gainsborough Pictures, UK)

London after Midnight (1928, Tod Browning, Metro-Goldwyn-Mayer, USA)

Lot in Sodom (1933, James Sibley Watson, USA)

M (1931, Fritz Lang, Nero-Film AG, Germany)

Mad Love (1935, Karl Freund, Metro-Goldwyn-Mayer, USA)

Magician, The (1926, Rex Ingram, Metro-Goldwyn Mayer, USA)

Maniac (1934, Dwain Esper, Hollywood Producers and Distributors, USA)

Man Who Changed His Mind, The (1936, Robert Stevenson, Gainsborough Pictures, UK)

Mark of the Vampire (1935, Tod Browning, Metro-Goldwyn-Mayer, USA)

Mask of Fu Manchu, The (1932, Charles Brabin, Cosmopolitan Productions/Metro-Goldwyn-Mayer, USA)

Medium, The (1934, Vernon Sewell, Test Films, UK)

Metropolis (1927, Fritz Lang, Universum Film AG, Germany)

Miracle Man, The (1919, George Loane Tucker, Paramount Pictures, USA)

Mister Dynamite (1935, Alan Crosland, Universal Pictures, USA)

Monkey's Paw, The (1933, Wesley Ruggles and Ernest B. Schoedsack, RKO Radio Pictures, USA)

Monster Walks, The (1932, Frank R. Strayer, Ralph M. Like Productions, USA)

Most Dangerous Game, The (1932, Irving Pichel and Ernest B. Schoedsack, RKO Radio Pictures, USA)

Mummy, The (1932, Karl Freund, Universal Pictures, USA)

Mummy's Curse, The (1944, Leslie Goodwins, Universal Pictures, USA)

Mummy's Ghost, The (1944, Reginald Le Borg, Universal Pictures, USA)

Mummy's Hand, The (1940, Christy Cabanne, Universal Pictures, USA)

Mummy's Tomb, The (1942, Harold Young, Universal Pictures, USA)

Murders in the Rue Morgue (1932, Robert Florey, Universal Pictures, USA)

Murders in the Zoo (1933, A. Edward Sutherland, Paramount Productions, USA)

Mystery of Edwin Drood, The (1935, Stuart Walker, Universal Pictures, USA)

Mystery of the Wax Museum (1933, Michael Curtis, Warner Bros. Pictures/The Vitaphone Corp., USA)

Night of the Demon (1957, Jacques Tourneur, Sabre Film Production, UK)

Night of the Living Dead (1968, George A. Romero, Image Ten/Laurel Group/Market Square Productions/Off Color Films, USA)

Night World (1932, Hobart Henley, Universal Pictures, USA)

Nosferatu (1922, F.W. Murnau, Jofa-Atelier Berlin-Johannisthal/Prana-Film GmbH, Germany)

Old Dark House, The (1932, James Whale, Universal Pictures, USA)

Orlacs Hände (1924, Robert Wiene, Berolina Film GmbH/Pan Films, Germany/Austria)

Other Person, The (1921, B.E. Doxat-Pratt, Granger-Binger, UK)

Ouanga (1936, George Terwilliger, George Terwilliger Productions, USA)

Payment Deferred (1932, Lothar Mendes, Metro-Goldwyn-Mayer, USA)

Phantom of the Opera, The (1925, Rupert Julian, Universal Pictures, USA)

Private Life of Henry VIII, The (1933, Alexander Korda, London Film Productions, UK)

Raven, The (1935, Lew Landers, Universal Pictures, USA)

Revolt of the Zombies (1936, Victor Halperin, Edward Halperin Productions/Victor Halperin Productions, USA)

Road to Mandalay, The (1926, Tod Browning, Metro-Goldwyn-Mayer, USA)

Scotland Yard Mystery, The (1934, Thomas Bentley, British International Pictures, UK)

Séance on a Wet Afternoon (1964, Bryan Forbes, Beaver Films/Allied Film Makers, UK)

Sign of the Cross, The (1932, Cecil B. DeMille, Paramount Pictures, USA)

Svengali (1931, Archie Mayo, Warner Bros. Pictures, USA)

Tell Tale Heart, The (1934, Brian Desmond Hurst, Clifton-Hurst, UK)

Texas Chainsaw Massacre, The (1974, Tobe Hooper, Vortex, USA)

Un Chien Andalou (1929, Luis Buñuel, France)

Undying Monster, The (1942, John Brahm, Twentieth Century Fox Film Corporation, USA)

Unheimliche Geschichten (1932, Richard Oswald, Roto Film/G.P. Film GmbH, Germany)

Unknown, The (1927, Tod Browning, Metro-Goldwyn-Mayer, USA)

Vampire Bat, The (1933, Frank R. Strayer, Majestic Pictures, USA)

Vampyr: Der Traum des Allan Gray/Vampyr: The Strange Adventure of David Gray (1932, Carl Theodor Dreyer, Tobis Filmkunst, Germany)

Waltz Time (1933, Wilhelm Thiele, Gaumont-British Picture Corporation, UK)

Werewolf, The (1913, Henry MacRae, Universal Pictures, USA)

Werewolf of London (1935, Stuart Walker, Universal Pictures, USA)

When Soul Meets Soul (1913, Norman MacDonald, Essanay Film Manufacturing Company, USA)

White Cargo (1929, J.B. Williams, Neo-Art Productions, UK)

White Zombie (1932, Victor Halperin, Edward Halperin Productions/Victor Halperin Productions, USA)

Wolf Man, The (1941, George Waggner, Universal Pictures, USA)

Ye Ban Ge Sheng/Song at Midnight (1937, Ma-Xu Weibang, Xinhua, China)

SELECTED BIBLIOGRAPHY

Aizenberg, Edna, '*I Walked With a Zombie*: The Pleasures and Perils of Postcolonial Hybridity', *World Literature Today* 73.3 (1999), pp.461–66.

Albrecht, Donald, *Designing Dreams: Modern Architecture in the Movies* (London: Thames and Hudson, 1986).

Barthes, Roland, *Camera Lucida: Reflections on Photography* (London: Vintage, 2000).

Behrens, Roy R., 'Dessau's Bauhaus', *Leonardo* 39.1 (2006), pp.87–88.

Benshoff, Harry M. 'Blaxploitation Horror Films: Generic Reappropriation or Reinscription?', *Cinema Journal* 39/2 (2000), pp.31–50.

——, *Monsters in the Closet: Homosexuality and the Horror Film* (Manchester: Manchester University Press, 1997).

Benton, Charlotte and Tim Benton, 'The style and the age', in Charlotte Benton, Tim Benton and Ghislaine Wood (eds), *Art Deco, 1910–1939* (London: V&A Publications, 2003), pp.12–27.

Berenstein, Rhona J., *Attack of the Leading Ladies: Gender, Sexuality and Spectatorship in Classic Horror Cinema* (New York, NY: Columbia University Press, 1996).

Bergfelder, Tim, 'The production designer and the *gesamtkunstwerk*: German film technicians in the British film industry of the 1930s', in Andrew Higson (ed.), *Dissolving Views: Key Writings on British Cinema* (London: Cassell, 1996), pp.20–37.

Bergfelder, Tim, Sue Harris and Sarah Street, *Film Architecture and the Transnational Imagination: Set Design in 1930s European Cinema* (Amsterdam: Amsterdam University Press, 2007).

Bingham, Adrian, 'The digitization of newspaper archives: Opportunities and challenges for historians', *Twentieth Century British History* 21/2 (2010), pp.225–31.

Bishop, Kyle, *American Zombie Gothic: The Rise and Fall (and Rise) of the Walking Dead in Popular Culture* (Jefferson, NC: McFarland, 2010).

Bloch, Robert, 'Foreword', in Guy Endore, *The Werewolf of Paris* (New York, NY: Citadel Press, 1992), pp.2–5.

Bogdanovich, Peter, *Who the Devil Made It: Conversations with...* (New York, NY: Ballantine Books, 1997).

Bogle, Donald, *Toms, Coons, Mulattoes, Mammies and Bucks: An Interpretative History of Blacks in American Films,* 3rd edn (Oxford: Roundhouse, 1994).

Bonitzer, Pascal, 'Partial vision: Film and the labyrinth', *Wide Angle* 4/4 (1981): pp.56–63.

Bordwell, David, *The Films of Carl-Theodor Dreyer* (Berkeley, CA: University of California Press, 1981).

Bourguignon, Erika, 'The persistence of folk belief: Some notes on canni-balism and zombis in Haiti', *Journal of American Folklore* 72.283 (1959), pp.36–46.

Breton, André, *Manifestoes of Surrealism* (Ann Arbor, MI: University of Michigan Press, 1998).

Brown, Geoff, 'Happy ever after? The German adventures of Gaumont-British in 1932', *Journal of British Cinema and Television* 7/3 (2010), pp.378–400.

Brown, Julie, '*Carnival of Souls* and the organs of horror', in Neil Lerner (ed.), *Music in Horror Film: Listening to Fear* (London: Routledge, 2009), pp.1–20.

Brown, Tom, *Breaking the Fourth Wall: Direct Address in the Cinema* (Edinburgh: Edinburgh University Press, 2012).

Browning, John Edgar, 'Survival horrors, survival spaces: Tracing the modern zombie (cine)myth', *Horror Studies* 2/1 (2011), pp.41–59.

Chapman, James, 'Celluloid shockers', in Jeffrey Richards (ed.), *The Unknown 1930s: An Alternative History of British Cinema, 1929–1939* (London: I.B. Tauris, 1998), pp.75–97.

Christie, Ian, 'Film as a modernist art', in Christopher Wilk (ed.), *Modernism 1914–1939: Designing a New World* (London: V&A Pub-lications, 2006), pp.297–310.

——, 'The avant-gardes and European cinema before 1930', in John Hill and Pamela Church Gibson (eds), *World Cinema: Critical Approaches* (Oxford: Oxford University Press, 2000), pp.65–70.

Clover, Carol, *Men, Women and Chainsaws: Gender in the Modern Horror Film* (London: BFI, 1992).

Cohen, Louis, *Le Corbusier: The Lyricism of Architecture in the Machine Age* (Köln: Taschen GmbH, 2006).

Conan Doyle, Arthur, 'Lot no. 249' in Roger Luckhurst (ed.), *Late Victorian Gothic Tales* (Oxford: Oxford World's Classics, 2005 [1892]), pp.109–40.

Conrich, Ian, 'Horrific films and 1930s British cinema', in Steve Chibnall and Julian Petley (eds), *British Horror Cinema* (London: Routledge, 2002), pp.58–70.

Coudray, Chantal Bourgault Du, *The Curse of the Werewolf: Fantasy, Horror and the Beast Within* (London: I.B. Tauris, 2006).

Cowie, Susan D. and Tom Johnson, *The Mummy in Fact, Fiction and Film* (Jefferson, NC: McFarland, 2002).

Craig, J. Robert, 'The origin story in werewolf cinema of the 1930s and 1940s', *Studies in Popular Culture* 27/3 (2005), pp.75–86.

Daly, Nicholas, 'That obscure object of desire: Victorian commodity culture and fictions of the mummy', *NOVEL: A Forum on Fiction* 28/1 (1994), pp.24–51.

Day, Jasmine, *The Mummys Curse: Mummymania in the English-Speaking World* (London: Routledge, 2006).

Deane, Bradley, 'Mummy fiction and the occupation of Egypt: Imperial striptease', *English Literature in Translation* 51/4 (1998), pp.381–410.

Delahaye, Michael, 'Between heaven and hell: Interview with Carl Dreyer', *Cahiers du cinéma in English* 4 (1966), pp.7–17.

Desnos, Robert, 'Avant-garde cinema', originally published in *Documents* 7 (1929). Reprinted in Paul Hammond (ed.), *The Shadow and its Shadow: Surrealist Writings on Cinema* (London: BFI, 1978), pp.36–38.

Doane, Mary Ann, 'The voice in the cinema: The articulation of body and space', *Yale French Studies* 60 (1980), pp.33–50.

Doherty, Thomas, *Pre-Code Hollywood: Sex, Immorality and Insurrection in American Cinema, 1930–1934* (New York, NY: Columbia University Press, 1999).

——, *Hollywood's Censor: Joseph I. Breen and the Production Code Administration* (New York, NY: Columbia University Press, 2007).

Draper, Ellen, 'Zombie women when the gaze is male', *Wide Angle* 10/3 (1988), pp.52–62.

Drum, Jean and Dale D. Drum, *My Only Great Passion: The Life and Films of Carl Th. Dreyer* (Lanham, MD: Scarecrow Press, 2000).

Dubois, Laurent, *Avengers of the New World: The Story of the Haitian Revolution* (Cambridge, MA: The Belknap Press of Harvard University Press, 2004).

Edwards, Kyle Dawson, '"Poe, you are avenged!": Edgar Allan Poe and Universal Pictures' *The Raven* (1935)', *Adaptation* 4/2 (2010), pp.117–36.

Egan, Kate, *Trash or Treasure: Censorship and the Changing Meanings of the Video Nasties* (Manchester: Manchester University Press, 2007).

Eisner, Lotte, *The Haunted Screen: Expressionism in the German Cinema and the Influence of Max Reinhardt* (Berkeley, CA: University of California Press, 1969).

Endore, Guy, *The Werewolf of Paris* (London: Sphere Books, 1974 [1933]).

Esperdy, Gabrielle, 'From instruction to consumption: Architecture and design in Hollywood movies of the 1930s', *Journal of American Culture* 30/2 (2007), pp.198–211.

Eyles, Allan, *Gaumont British Cinemas* (London: BFI, 1996).

Fay, Jennifer, 'Dead subjectivity: *White Zombie*, Black Baghdad', *CR: The New Centennial Review* 8/1 (2008), pp.81–101.

Fiell, Charlotte and Peter Fiell, *Design of the 20th Century* (London: Taschen, 2001).

French Surrealist Group, The, 'Some surrealist advice', originally published in *L'Age du Cinéma*, 4–5, August-November (1951). Reprinted in

Paul Hammond (ed.), *The Shadow and its Shadow: Surrealist Writings on Cinema* (London: BFI, 1978), pp.25–26.

Freud, Sigmund, 'Civilisation and its discontents', in Angela Richards (ed.), *Penguin Freud Library 12: Civilisation, Society and Religion* (London: Penguin, 1991 [1930]), pp.243–340.

——, *The Interpretation of Dreams* (Hertfordshire: Wordsworth Classics of World Literature, 1997 [1900]).

——, 'The uncanny', in Albert Dickson (ed.), *Penguin Freud Library 14: Art and Literature* (London: Penguin, 1991 [1919]), pp.335–76.

Geraghty, Lincoln and Mark Jancovich, 'Introduction: Generic canons', in Lincoln Geraghty and Mark Jancovich (eds), *The Shifting Definitions of Genre: Essays on Labelling Films, Television Shows and Media* (Jefferson, NC: McFarland, 2008), pp.1–12.

Gledhill, Christine, 'Rethinking genre', in Christine Gledhill and Linda Williams (eds), *Reinventing Film Studies* (London: Arnold, 2003), pp.221–43.

Gough-Yates, Kevin, 'The British feature film as a European concern: Britain and the émigré film-maker, 1933–45', in Günter Berghaus (ed.), *Theatre and Film in Exile: German Artists in Britain, 1933–1945* (Oxford: Berg, 1989), pp.135–66.

Grant, Michael, '"Ultimate formlessness": Cinema, horror, and the limits of meaning', in Steven Jay Schneider (ed.), *Horror Film and Psychoanalysis: Freud's Worst Nightmare*, Cambridge: Cambridge University Press, 2004), pp.177–87.

——, 'Cinema, horror and the abominations of hell: Carl-Theodor Dreyer's *Vampyr* (1931) [*sic*] and Lucio Fulci's *The Beyond* (1981)', in Andrea Sabbadini (ed.), *The Couch and the Silver Screen: Psychoanalytic Reflections on European Cinema* (Hove: Brunner-Routledge, 2003), pp.145–55.

Hagener, Malte, *Moving Forward, Looking Back: The European Avant-Garde and the Invention of Film Culture, 1919–1939* (Amsterdam: Amsterdam University Press, 2007).

Hamilton, Lisa, 'Oscar Wilde, new women and the rhetoric of effeminacy', in Joseph Bristow (ed.), *Wilde Writings: Contextual Conditions* (London: The Regents University of California, 2003), pp.239–41.

Hawkins, Joan, *Cutting Edge: Art-Horror and the Horrific Avant-Garde* (Minneapolis, MN: University of Minnesota Press, 2000).

Heathcote, Edwin, 'Modernism as enemy: Film and the portrayal of modern architecture', *Architectural Design* 70/1 (2000), pp.20–25.

Herzogenrath, Bernd, 'The return of Edgar G. Ulmer', in Bernd Herzogenrath (ed.), *Edgar G. Ulmer: Essays on the King of the B's* (Jefferson, NC: McFarland, 2009), pp.3–21.

Hochscherf, Tobias, *The Continental Connection: German-speaking Émigrés and British Cinema, 1927–45* (Manchester: Manchester University Press, 2011).

Hoffmann, E.T.A., 'Der Sandmann', in R.J. Hollingdale (ed.), *Tales of Hoffmann* (Harmondsworth: Penguin, 1982 [1817]), pp.85–125.

Hollinger, Karen, 'The monster as woman: Two generations of cat people', in Barry Keith Grant (ed.) *The Dread of Difference: Gender and the Horror Film* (Austin, TX: University of Texas Press, 1996), pp.296–308.

Humphries, Reynold, *The Hollywood Horror Film: 1931–1941: Madness in a Social Landscape* (Lanham, MD: Scarecrow Press, 2006).

Hunter, Russ, '"Didn't you used to be Dario Argento?": The cult reception of Dario Argento' in William Hope (ed.), *Italian Film Directors in the New Millennium* (Newcastle: Cambridge Scholars Press, 2010), pp.63–74.

Hutchings, Peter, 'Horror London', *Journal of British Cinema and Television* 6/2 (2009), pp.190–206.

——, 'Monster legacies: Memory, technology and horror history', in Lincoln Geraghty and Mark Jancovich (eds), *The Shifting Definitions of Genre: Essays on Labelling Films, Television Shows and Media* (Jefferson, NC: McFarland, 2008), pp.216–28.

——, *Hammer and Beyond: The British Horror Film* (Manchester: Manchester University Press, 1993).

——, *Historical Dictionary of Horror Cinema* (Lanham, MD: Scarecrow Press, 2008).

——, *The Horror Film* (Harlow: Longman, 2004).

Isenberg, Noah, 'Perennial detour: The cinema of Edgar G. Ulmer and the experience of exile', *Cinema Journal* 43/2 (2004), pp.3–25.

Iversen, Margaret, 'In the blind field: Hopper and the uncanny', *Art History* 21/3 (1998), pp.409–29.

Jacobs, Jason, 'The television archive: Past, present, future', *Critical Studies in Television* 1/1 (2006), pp.13–20.

Jacobs, Steven, *The Wrong House: The Architecture of Alfred Hitchcock* (Rotterdam: 010 Publishers, 2007).

Jancovich, Mark, '"Two ways of looking": The critical reception of 1940s horror', *Cinema Journal* 49/3 (2010), pp.45–66.

——, 'Female monsters: Horror, the "femme fatale" and World War II', *European Journal of American Culture* 27 (2008), pp.133–49.

——, 'Reviews', *Screen* 48/2 (2007), pp.261–66.

——, '"Thrills and chills": Horror, the woman's film and the origins of film noir', *New Review of Film and Television Studies* 7/2 (2009), pp.157–71.

Jermyn, Deborah, 'You can't keep a dead woman down: The female corpse and textual disruption in contemporary Hollywood', in Elizabeth Klaver (ed.), *Images of the Corpse: From Renaissance to Cyberspace* (Madison, WI: University of Wisconsin Press, 2004), pp.153–68.

Johnson, Tom, *Censored Screams: The British Ban on Hollywood Horror in the Thirties* (Jefferson, NC: McFarland, 1997).

Kawin, Bruce, 'The mummy's pool', in Leo Baudry and Marshall Cohen (eds), *Film Theory and Criticism: Introductory Readings*. 5th edn (Oxford: Oxford University Press, 1998), pp.679–91.

Kinnard, Roy, *Horror in Silent Films: A Filmography, 1896–1929* (Jefferson, NC: McFarland, 1995).

Klein, Amanda Ann, *American Film Cycles: Reframing Genres, Screening Social Problems, and Defining Subcultures* (Austin, TX: University of Texas Press, 2011).

Klinger, Barbara, 'Film history terminable and interminable: Recovering the past in reception studies', *Screen* 38/2 (1997), pp.107–28.

Krzywinska, Tanya, *A Skin For Dancing In: Possession, Witchcraft and Voodoo in Film* (Trowbridge: Flicks Books, 2000).

Kuhn, Annette, 'Children, "horrific" films, and censorship in 1930s Britain', *Historical Journal of Film, Radio and Television* 22/2 (2002), pp.197–202.

——, *An Everyday Magic: Cinema and Cultural Memory* (London: I.B.Tauris, 2002).

Lacan, Jacques, 'The dream of Irma's injection', in J.A. Miller (ed.), *The Seminar of Jacques Lacan Vol. 2: The Ego in Freud's Theory and in the Technique of Psychoanalysis 1954–1955* (Cambridge: Cambridge University Press, 1988 [March 1955]), pp.146–71.

Larkin, Philip, 'Dockery and Son', in Anthony Thwaite (ed.) *Collected Poems* (London: Faber and Faber, 1988), pp.152–53.

Lerner, Carl, '"My way of working is in relation to the future": A conversation with Carl Dreyer', *Film Comment* 4/1 Fall (1966), pp.62–67.

Low, Rachel, *The History of British Film, 1918–1929* (London: George Allen & Unwin, 1971).

Lowry, Edward and Richard deCordova, 'Enunciation and the production of horror in *White Zombie*', in Barry Keith Grant (ed.), *Planks of Reason: Essays on the Horror Film* (Metuchen, NJ: Scarecrow Press, 1984), pp.346–89.

Lupton, Carter, '"Mummymania" for the masses – is Egyptology cursed by the mummy's curse?', in Sally McDonald and Michael Rice (eds), *Consuming Ancient Egypt* (London: UCL Press, 2003), pp.23–46.

Macfarlane, Karen E., 'Mummy knows best: Knowledge and the unknowable in turn of the century mummy fiction', *Horror Studies* 1/1 (2010), pp.5–24.

Mandell, Paul, 'Edgar G. Ulmer and *The Black Cat*', *American Cinematographer: The International Journal of Film and Video Production Techniques* 65/9 October (1984), pp.34–47.

Manguel, Alberto, *Bride of Frankenstein* (London: BFI, 1997).

Mank, Gregory William, '*The Black Cat*', in Bernd Herzogenrath (ed.), *Edgar G. Ulmer: Essays on the King of the B's* (Jefferson, NC: McFarland, 2009), pp.89–104.

——, *Bela Lugosi and Boris Karloff: The Expanded Story of a Haunting Collaboration* (Jefferson, NC: McFarland, 2009).

Marchetti, Gina, *Romance and the 'Yellow Peril': Race, Sex, and Discursive Strategies in Hollywood Fiction* (Berkeley, CA: University of California Press, 1993).

Martin, Daniel, 'Japan's *Blair Witch*: Restraint, maturity and generic canons in the British critical reception of *Ring*', *Cinema Journal* 48/3 (2009): pp.35–51.

Mathijs, Ernest and Jamie Sexton, *Cult Cinema: An Introduction* (Oxford: Wiley-Blackwell, 2011).

Matthews, Melvin E., *Fear Itself: Horror on Screen and in Reality during the Depression and World War II* (Jefferson, NC: McFarland, 2009).

Matthews, Tom Dewey, *Censored: The Story of Film Censorship in Britain* (London: Chatto & Windus, 1994).

Meadmore, Clement, *The Modern Chair: Classic Designs by Thonet, Breuer, Le Corbusier, Eames and Others* (Mineola, NY: Dover, 1997).

Medhurst, Andy, 'Music hall and British cinema', in Charles Barr (ed.), *All Our Yesterdays: 90 Years of British Cinema* (London: BFI, 1986), pp.168–88.

Meisel, Myron. 'Edgar G. Ulmer: The primacy of the visual', in Todd McCarthy and Charles Flynn (eds), *Kings of the Bs: Working Within the Hollywood System* (New York: E.P. Dutton, 1975), pp.147–52.

Montserrat, Dominic, 'Unidentified human remains: Mummies and the erotics of biography', in Dominic Montserrat (ed.), *Changing Bodies, Changing Meanings: Studies on the Human Body in Antiquity* (London: Routledge, 1998), pp.162–97.

Monty, Ib, 'Carl Th. Dreyer: An introduction', in Jytte Jensen (ed.), *Carl Th. Dreyer* (New York, NY: Museum of Modern Art, 1988), pp.9–16.

Murphy, Kieran M., '*White Zombie*', *Contemporary French and Francophone Studies* 15/1 (2011), pp.47–55.

Nash, Mark, '*Vampyr* and the Fantastic', *Screen* 17/3 (1976), pp.29–67.

Neale, Steve, 'Questions of Genre', *Screen* 31/1 (1990), pp.45–66.

Neumann, Dietrich, '*Genuine: Die Tragödie eines seltsamen Hauses*', in Dietrich Neumann (ed.), *Film Architecture: Set Design from Metropolis to Blade Runner* (Munich: Prestel-Verlag, 1996), pp.58–61.

——, 'Introduction', in Dietrich Neumann (ed.), *Film Architecture: Set Design from Metropolis to Blade Runner* (Munich: Prestel-Verlag, 1996), pp.7–9.

Newman, Kim, *Cat People* (London: BFI, 1999).

O'Rawe, Des, 'The great secret: Silence, cinema and modernism', *Screen* 47/4 (2006), pp.395–405.

Omasta, Michael, 'Famously unknown: Günther Krampf's work as cinematographer in British films', in Tim Bergfelder and Christian Cargnelli (eds), *Destination London: German-speaking Emigrés and British Cinema, 1925–1950* (Oxford: Berghahn, 2008), pp.78–88.

Paravisini-Gebert, Lizabeth, 'Women possessed: Eroticism and exoticism in the representation of woman as zombie', in Margarite Fernández

Olmos and Lizabeth Paravisini-Gebert (eds), *Sacred Possessions: Vodou, Santería, Obeah, and the Caribbean* (New Brunswick, NJ: Rutgers University Press, 1997), pp.37–58.

Peirse, Alison, 'Destroying the male body in British horror cinema', in Santiago Fouz-Hernandez (ed.), *Mysterious Skin: Male Bodies in Contemporary Cinema* (London: I.B.Tauris, 2009), pp.159–73.

Pirie, David, *A New Heritage of Horror: The English Gothic Cinema* (London: I.B.Tauris, 2008).

Poe, Edgar Allan, 'Some Words with a Mummy', in Helen Trayler (ed.), *The Collected Works of Edgar Allan Poe* (Ware: Wordsworth Library Collection, 2009 [1845]), pp.433–45.

——, 'The Black Cat', in Helen Trayler (ed.), *The Collected Works of Edgar Allan Poe* (Ware: Wordsworth Library Editions, 2009 [1843]), pp.61–68.

——, 'The Fall of the House of Usher', in Helen Trayler (ed.), *The Collected Works of Edgar Allan Poe* (Ware: Wordsworth Library Editions, 2009 [1839]), pp.171–84.

Pollock, Griselda, 'Freud's Egypt: Mummies and M/Others', *Parallax* 13/2 (2007), pp.56–79.

Price, Michael H. and George E. Turner, 'The black art of *White Zombie*', in George E. Turner (ed.), *The Cinema of Adventure, Romance and Terror* (Hollywood, CA: ASC Press, 1989), pp.147–54.

Rhodes, Gary D., '"Tremonstrous" hopes and "oke" results: The 1934 reception of *The Black Cat*', in Gary D. Rhodes (ed.), *Edgar G. Ulmer: Detour on Poverty Row* (Lanham, MD: Lexington Books, 2008), pp.301–23.

——, '*Drakula halála* (1921): The cinema's first Dracula', *Horror Studies* 1/1 (2010), pp.25–47.

——, 'Fantasmas del cine Mexicano: The 1930s horror film cycle of Mexico', in Steven Jay Schneider (ed.), *Fear Without Frontiers: Horror Cinema Across the Globe* (Godalming: FAB Press, 2003), pp.93–103.

——, *White Zombie: Anatomy of a Horror Film* (Jefferson, NC: McFarland, 2001).

Richards, Jeffrey, 'The British Board of Film Censors and content control in the 1930s: Foreign affairs', *Historical Journal of Film, Radio and Television* 2/1 (1982), pp.39–48.

——, 'Tod Slaughter and the cinema of excess', in Jeffrey Richards (ed.), *The Unknown 1930s: An Alternative History of British Cinema, 1929–1939* (London: I.B.Tauris, 1998), pp.139–60.

Riley, Phillip J., *The Mummy* (Galloway, NJ: Universal Filmscripts Series, 1989).

Robertson, James C., *The British Board of Film Censors: Film Censorship in Britain, 1896–1950* (London: Croom Helm, 1985).

——, *The Hidden Cinema: British Film Censorship in Action, 1919–1975* (London: Routledge, 1993).

Rosa, Joseph, 'Tearing down the house: Modern homes in the movies', in Mark Lamster (ed.), *Architecture and Film* (New York, NY: Princeton Architectural Press, 2000), pp.159–67.

Rosar, William H., 'Music for the monsters: Universal Pictures' horror film scores of the thirties', *Quarterly Journal of the Library of Congress* 40.4 (1983), pp.391–421.

Rosenbaum, Jonathan, '*Vampyr: Der Traum des Allan Gray*', *Monthly Film Bulletin,* August (1976), p.180.

Rubin, William, *Dada, Surrealism and Their Heritage* (New York, NY: Museum of Modern Art, 1968).

Rudkin, David, *Vampyr* (London: BFI, 2005).

Ryall, Tom, 'British cinema and genre', *Journal of Popular British Cinema* 1 (1998), pp.18–24.

Schaal, Hans Dieter, 'Spaces of the psyche in German expressionist film', *Architectural Design* 70/1 (2000), pp.12–15.

Schaefer, Eric, *"Bold! Daring! Shocking! True!" A History of Exploitation Films, 1919–1959* (Durham, NC: Duke University Press, 1999).

Schneider, Steven Jay, 'Mixed blood couples: Monsters and miscegenation in U.S. horror cinema', in Ruth Bienstock Anolik and Douglas L. Howard (eds), *The Gothic Other: Racial and Social Constructions in the Literary Imagination* (Jefferson, NC: McFarland, 2004), pp.72–89.

Seabrook, William B., *The Magic Island* (London: George G. Harrap & Company Ltd, 1929).

Sedgwick, John, *Popular Filmgoing in 1930s Britain: A Choice of Pleasures* (Exeter: University of Exeter Press, 2000).

Server, Lee, 'Gloria Stuart', *Films in Review,* February (1988), unpaginated.

Sexton, Jamie, *Alternative Film Culture in Inter-War Britain* (Exeter: University of Exeter Press, 2008).

—— 'US "indie-horror": Critical reception, genre construction and suspect hybridity', *Cinema Journal* 51/2 (2012), pp.67–86.

Skal, David J., *The Monster Show: A Cultural History of Horror* (London: Plexus, 1993).

Skoller, Donald, *Dreyer in Double Reflection: Translation of Carl Th. Dreyer's Writings About the Film (Om Filmen)* (New York, NY: E.P. Dutton, 1973).

Slide, Anthony, *Banned in the USA: British Films in the United States and their Censorship, 1933–1960* (London: I.B.Tauris, 1998).

Smith, Angela M., *Hideous Progeny: Disability, Eugenics, and Classic Horror Cinema* (New York, NY: Columbia University Press, 2011).

Smith, Sarah J., *Children, Cinema and Censorship: From Dracula to the Dead End Kids* (London: I.B.Tauris, 2005).

Snelson, Tim, '"From grade B thrillers to deluxe chillers": Prestige horror, female audiences, and allegories of spectatorship in *The Spiral Staircase* (1946)', *New Review of Film and Television Studies* 7/2 (2009), pp.173–88.

Snelson, Tim and Mark Jancovich, '"No hits, no runs, just terrors": Exhibition, cultural distinctions and cult audiences at the Rialto Cinema in the 1930s and 1940s', in Richard Maltby *et al.* (eds) *Explorations in New Cinema History: Approaches and Case Studies* (Oxford: Wiley-Blackwell, 2011), pp.199–211.

Sontag, Susan, *On Photography* (London: Penguin, 1979).

Spadoni, Robert, 'Old Times in *Werewolf of London*', *Journal of Film and Video* 63/4 (2011), pp.3–20.

——, *Uncanny Bodies: The Coming of Sound Film and the Origins of the Horror Genre* (Berkeley, CA: University of California Press, 2007).

Stevenson, Robert Louis, *The Strange Case of Dr Jekyll and Mr Hyde* (London: Penguin Popular Classics, 1994 [1886]).

Street, Sarah, *British National Cinema*, 2nd edn (London: Routledge, 2009).

——, *Transatlantic Crossings: British Feature Films in the United States* (London: Continuum, 2002).

Sutherland, Meghan, 'Rigor/mortis: The industrial life of style in American zombie cinema', *Framework: The Journal of Cinema and Media* 48/1 (2007), pp.64–78.

Trolle, Boerge, 'The world of Carl Dreyer', *Sight and Sound* 25/3 Winter (1955–6), pp.123–27.

Turim, Maureen, *Flashbacks in Film: Memory and History* (London: Routledge, 1989).

Turner, George E., 'Jinxed from the start: *The Monkey's Paw*', *American Cinematographer* 66/11 November (1985), pp.35–40.

Turner, George E. and Michael H. Price, *Forgotten Horrors: Early Talkie Chillers from Poverty Row* (London: Thomas Yoseloff, 1979).

Tybjerg, Casper, 'Dreyer and the national film in Denmark', *Film History* 13/1 (2001), pp.23–36.

——, 'Waking life', *Sight and Sound* 18/9 (2008), pp.33–36.

Valentine, Mark, 'Introduction', in Mark Valentine (ed.), *The Werewolf Pack: An Anthology* (London: Wordsworth Editions, 2008), pp.vii-xii.

Vidler, Anthony, 'The explosion of space: Architecture and the filmic imaginary', in Dietrich Neumann (ed.), *Film Architecture: From Metropolis to Blade Runner* (Munich: Prestel-Verlag, 1996), pp.13–25.

Vincendeau, Ginette 'Issues in European cinema', in John Hill and Pamela Church Gibson (eds), *World Cinema: Critical Approaches* (Oxford: Oxford University Press, 2000), pp.56–64.

Weaver, Tom, Michael Brunas and John Brunas, *Universal Horrors: The Studio's Classic Films, 1931–1946,* 2nd edn (Jefferson, NC: McFarland, 2007).

Weinberg, Herman G. and Gretchen Weinberg, '*Vampyr* – An interview with Baron de Gunzberg', *Film Culture* 32 (1964), pp.57–59.

Wells, H.G., *The Island of Doctor Moreau* (London: Pan Books, 1975 [1896]).

Wilde, Oscar, *The Ballad of Reading Gaol* (New York, NY: Brentanos, 1906).

Wilk, Christopher, 'What was modernism?', in Christopher Wilk (ed.), *Modernism, 1914–1939: Designing a New World* (London: V&A Publications, 2006), pp.11–22.

Williams, Keith, *H.G. Wells, Modernity and the Movies* (Liverpool: Liverpool University Press, 2007).

Williams, Linda, 'Film bodies: Gender, genre, and excess', *Film Quarterly* 44/4 (1991), pp.2–13.

Williams, Tony, '*White Zombie*: Haitian horror', *Jump Cut* 28 (1981), pp.18–20.

Wilson, Christina, 'Cedric Gibbons: Architect of Hollywood's golden age', in Mark Lamster (ed.), *Architecture and Film* (New York, NY: Princeton Architectural Press, 2000), pp.101–16.

Wood, Ghislaine, 'Art deco and Hollywood film', in Charlotte Benton, Tim Benton and Ghislaine Wood (eds), *Art Deco, 1910–1939* (London: V&A Publications, 2003), pp.324–33.

Wood, Robin, 'An introduction to the American horror film', in Bill Nichols (ed.), *Movies and Methods: An Anthology*, vol.2. (Berkeley, CA: University of California Press, 1985), pp.195–219.

——, 'Foreword: What lies beneath?', in Steven Jay Schneider (ed.), *Horror Film and Psychoanalysis: Freud's Worst Nightmare* (Cambridge: Cambridge University Press, 2004), pp.xiii–xviii.

——, 'On Carl Dreyer', *Film Comment* 10/2 March–April (1974), pp.10–17.

——, 'Return of the repressed', *Film Comment* 14/4 (1978), pp.24–32.

Worland, Rick, *The Horror Film: An Introduction* (Oxford: Blackwell, 2007).

Young, Elizabeth, 'Here comes the bride: Wedding gender and race in *Bride of Frankenstein*', *Feminist Studies* 17/3 (1991), pp.403–37.

INDEX